Financial Armageddon

THE CORRUPTION OF OUR CURRENCY

Financial Armageddon

THE CORRUPTION OF OUR CURRENCY

David Draughon

CFI
Springville, Utah

The opinions and views expressed herein belong solely to the author are not the opinions or views of Cedar Fort, Inc. Permission for the use of sources, graphics, and pictures is also solely the responsibility of the author.

ISBN 13: 978-1-55517-956-4
ISBN 10: 1-55517-956-8

Published by CFI, an imprint of Cedar Fort, Inc., 2373 W. 700 S., Springville, UT, 84663
Distributed by Cedar Fort, Inc. www.cedarfort.com

LIBRARY OF CONGRESS CATALOGING-IN-PUBLICATION DATA

Draughon, David.
  Financial Armageddon / David Draughon.
    p. cm.
  ISBN-13: 978-1-55517-956-4
  1. Money. 2. United States--Economic conditions. 3. Money--Religious aspects--Church of Jesus Christ of Latter-day Saints. I. Title.
  HG221.D683 2007
  332.4--dc22
                        2006033622

Cover design by Nicole Williams
Cover design © 2006 by Lyle Mortimer

Printed in the United States of America

10 9 8 7 6 5 4 3 2 1

Printed on acid-free paper

Dedication

"Happiness comes from what you are, and not from what you have."
These were the words of Leroy B. Smith, my grandfather.
His actions confirmed his beliefs on a daily basis.
It is to him that this book is dedicated.

Table of Contents

Preface

The very word Armageddon has the tendency to strike fear into the hearts of men. The word in and of itself is relatively harmless. It is the perceived meaning of the word, or what it represents, that causes some to fear. The ancient city of Megiddo lies some sixty miles north of Jerusalem. Armageddon comes from the old Hebrew word Megiddo, and from here one can easily over look the vast plains below where numerous destructive battles have been fought. We are also told that this area will be the future site of many great battles before the Lord comes again, specifically where all nations shall gather together to fight against Jerusalem.

When we think of the above-mentioned battles, we visualize scenes of terror, suffering, debauchery, and other forms of evil. One can easily visualize men voraciously fighting against each other, exchanging vicious blows as they fight hand to hand, each man using all of his strength to come off as victor. Each opposing side hopes that with their strength, and by the ability in which they wield their swords, they will be the ones left standing, and thus place their competitors, if still alive, into bondage.

Currently there are no battles of human destruction raging in the plains of Armageddon, there are, however, different battles being waged and won all over the world. These particular battles are not fought for religious freedoms or to resolve territorial disputes, although the sought-after results are similar to that of the warriors who fought in ages past. They too desire to conquer and control people with their newly acquired power.

Unlike wars of total destruction, which have been and will be fought, and unbeknownst to many, there are certain financial battles that are waged daily, year after year and generation after generation. However, they are waged discretely and subtly, and these warriors work as hard at staying under the cover of darkness as they do at trying to orchestrate all monetary-based decisions.

This long standing war has the same potential to destroy families, communities, and nations as cimeters, swords, and guns have in past centuries. The weapon of choice is not a modern invention—it has been around for centuries. It is capable of complete annihilation and can be as effective as any modern day weapon. The general and his commanders who over see this battle for monetary control have a secret weapon. This weapon of choice has been in their arsenal from the very beginning. It is administered with complete lack of discretion and done so indiscriminately. Amazingly, when this weapon of mass financial destruction is rolled out, rather than fleeing for our lives, most of us actually embrace the very weapon that they created to enslave us. We are speaking of that four-letter word called *debt*, and its partner in crime *debt-based money*, which together fuel the fires of inflation.

Of course, the author and commander in chief of this financial mayhem is none other than Satan himself. He has been able to manipulate man's monetary system for thousands of years and through numerous methods. One of the most accurate arrows from his quiver, once embedded, is the complete binding and suffocating feeling that is always present with overindulged debt. He has skewed the intrinsic value of all currencies that are used throughout the world. He has made a mockery of the scripture that refers to using honest weights and measures that we find in the Bible. He is the epitome of something for nothing. The author of all lies has ironically been true to his word when he said he would buy up armies and navies and influence tyrants to rule with horror upon the earth.

We have identified the commander of this battle, which is a good start. Without such knowledge it can be extremely difficult to wage a war—we must know whom we are fighting against. There are many questions that need to be asked as well as answered in the chapters ahead. We will need a game plan if we are to come off victorious in this economic battle that is currently under way. How we are presently being attacked must also be identified. We must first discover and then try to comprehend the what, why, where, and when. If we can begin to answer some of these questions and uncover some of their battle plans in a timely manner, we may be able to anticipate their next move. Armed with this knowledge, we will be the last ones standing on today's financial battlefield.

Many of us are unaware that this economic battle even exists, and it is with that purpose in mind that this book is written. We will take this journey together. In order to know where we have been and where we are going, it is sometimes necessary to travel back into the past. We will discover if men truly do learn from past mistakes or if history sadly repeats itself. Invaluable teachings and advice from past prophets of our church and other church leaders will also give us insight on how we may win this war. We will seek advice from our founding fathers, who, with the Lord's help and inspiration, framed the Constitution of the United States. We will correlate with numerous other seekers of truth that have had vast experience on the economic fronts. We will search through our ancient and modern scriptures to discover any additional information that will help us prepare and come away conquerors of this financial battle.

It has been said that knowledge is power. What we choose to do with that newly found knowledge will determine whether or not we become empowered or overpowered. So let us begin this quest. The sooner we find the information that we are seeking, the quicker we can implement a game plan. Once armed with a game plan, we can begin to take affirmative action. We will then be able to bring the truth from out of the darkness and begin to fortify ourselves and our loved ones from this imminent attack.

Chapter One

DISCOVERIES

Thinking is hard work, which is why so few people do it.
—Henry Ford

I recall a conversation that I had with an individual many years ago when I was a child. It is now a distant memory, but it is one that I have replayed in my mind numerous times throughout the years.

Since this individual was a few years older than myself, I assumed that he must also be infinitely wiser. He seemed to know what he was talking about because he always had enough money to purchase whatever it was that he wanted. I asked him without any tact, "Where do you get all of your money?" He looked at me unbelievingly and said, "I earned it by working for it."

Wow, what a novel idea, I thought. My mind started racing; this was a concept that had never entered my nine-year-old mind.

The floodgates had opened. I started to bombard him with all kinds of questions. What did he mean by work? What could someone his age do to earn money? Did his parents know that he did this? Did they let him spend his money on whatever he wanted? How long had he been making what appeared to me to be serious money? He was full of good news on that memorable day. His younger brother, I was told, was also in on this glorious concept.

I grew up living in a middle-class family surrounded by neighbors that were, for the most part, all on the same financial footing. My dad was raised on the East Coast along with his twelve brothers and sisters. To say that he and his siblings knew a thing or two about hard work would be a gross understatement. They lived on a farm, not because my grandpa loved animals but because it helped them sustain life. From the different stories I've heard from aunts and uncles over the years, I have been led to believe that they just may have coined the term "working our fingers to the bone." I did not grow up on a farm, but you would be wrong if you thought my dad didn't teach us the value of hard work. My dad instilled many good principles in us kids, mainly by example, and a strong work ethic was undoubtedly one of them.

My siblings and I each had our particular chores, not only within our home but also out in the yard. We didn't always do our chores with smiles on our faces, nor did we get paid to do them. I did, however, earn something else—the sense of accomplishment that comes from hard work.

That is what made this newfound idea of getting paid for working so appealing. In my own mind, I was already a hard worker even at that young age. I was not afraid of work. I did not particularly care for any of those outside jobs that my dad gave me, but I figured if I could work for my dad, then why couldn't I work for someone else?

Getting Paid for Work

As it turned out, the two brothers that introduced me to this concept were earning money by delivering newspapers every morning. They told me how they set their alarm clocks each night to ensure that they would wake up in time to have the papers delivered before their customers awoke. They admitted that they sometimes overslept and, as a result, their boss would get phone calls from angry customers who threatened to discontinue their subscription. They explained that their boss kept track of all the unsatisfied customers. If it happened to be raining one morning, then they had to dress appropriately or get wet. They also had to ensure that the papers they delivered were kept dry. He explained further that there was a lot of responsibility that went along with the privilege of working, such as going door-to-door and collecting the money that was due each month.

It didn't take long before I shared this newfound information with my parents. Fortunately they were willing to let me give this a shot and allowed me the chance to prove myself. Times have changed since then; no longer are young boys across the nation navigating their bicycles in neighborhoods before sunrise throwing papers door-to-door. Most newspapers are now delivered by automobile, and you are lucky to have your paper land on the driveway, or even the porch. Now I have a nine-year-old son, and I wish that he had the same opportunities that I did when I was his age.

Even more contrasting than the change in the paper delivery system, however, are the changes in many people's attitudes about work. The term "something for nothing" is a very literal term for many people. My newfound friend responded to my question with "I earn money by working for it," but many people in society find this idea of working hard to earn money as novel as I did. After all, there are many other ways to earn money with little or no work, as many people have concluded.

From that moment forward an entrepreneurial spirit overtook me. Once I began looking around, I was amazed at how many different ways I could earn money. Some of my friends also caught this spirit, and before long we were selling products door-to-door. However, we quickly learned that certain tactics took much more work to earn the same amount of money than others did.

Growing up we lived down the street from a golf course that was a favorite of the winter visitors, or "snowbirds" as we locals called them. There were two ponds on this course that were not forgiving of wayward or errant shots. One of my friends discovered that we could come up with three or four golf balls in each hand for each dive to the bottom. We would take the golf balls home, clean them up, and return the next day to sell our used golf balls to the snowbirds as they walked down the fairways. This proved to be quite profitable until the golf course management ran us off. Ironically, they later hired us back to pull weeds out of their putting greens.

When I was older and able to drive, I like many other teenagers was able to go farther from home in search of work. My friends and I found work at restaurants, in construction, and in numerous retail outlets.

Business and all of its facets continued to interest me. As I got older, I compared different lines of work with their pay scales and discovered that often the most physically demanding work, such as working on a roof in 115° or digging holes with a pick and shovel, actually paid less money than working in an air-conditioned office! It did not take long to figure out that if I were only going to make $6 an hour in that stage of my life, it would be most beneficial to me to find a job that took me out of the blazing Arizona sun!

It also became apparent that highly paid workers were also highly trained. If I wanted to secure a job or occupation that took me indoors, then I would need to acquire certain skills. These skills could only be found at universities. But enrolling in college was not something that got my adrenaline pumping. I reasoned that to enjoy a comfortable lifestyle, I would need an education. However, punching a timecard and working hard for someone else was not high on my priority list either. So, like many who waffle back and forth, I went ahead and enrolled in college on the premise of starting my own business (whatever it may be) as soon as I could.

Over time I pursued my love for business and entrepreneurship. Of course, things didn't go as planned, but in real life things seldom do. Over the years I started a handful of businesses, some from the ground up and some purchased outright. Some never went further than a business plan, others barely treaded water, and a few failed miserably. But in each incident, whether a failure or success, I continued to learn things that I would then apply the next time around. After weighing all the pros and cons, at the end of the day I could truly say that my decision to hang my own shingle had been the right one.

It has been many years now since I sold newspapers. Many memories come back to me as I think of all the things that I tried to do or sell over the years. I remember trying to sell cookies and Christmas cards, Christmas trees, various plants and trees, empty soda cans, gasoline, furniture, cars, houses, wholesale foods, vending machines, financial instruments, and credit repair. There was unfortunately a lot of blood, sweat, and tears lost to many of the above endeavors. Overall though, the financial rewards have outweighed the risks involved. But just as important to me, if not more so, is the freedom that this lifestyle has brought. Many of the financial freedoms that we enjoy, whether as employers or employees, have slowly been taken from us. We will cover these topics later in great detail.

Defining Money

Regardless of how differently we earn it, the bottom line is that we all need money to provide for ourselves and our families. Without money we would still be trading crops, livestock, or both to acquire daily essentials. So, what is money? Why do we need it? Where did money originate? What is debt money? Is true money that paper bill that is in my pocket? How do we preserve it? Who assigns value to money? Can anyone with power create money? Why does it take more money to buy goods today than it did a year ago? And finally, are gold and silver considered real money?

Let's define money. Certainly many definitions and meanings are attached to the word *money*. I would guess that my understanding of the word money would differ substantially from yours. Some of the definitions found in the dictionary are "an official currency, negotiable paper notes, coins, an amount of cash or credit and a commodity," to name only a few.

As we proceed with this book, let us take the approach of a trained detective. Serious crimes have undoubtedly been committed against our monetary system. We will meticulously gather, sort, and catalogue all evidence of these crimes and comb for hidden clues. We will need to document the correlation between testimonies and eyewitnesses. As detectives, we must be alert and use all of our senses so that we will be able to find out the truth and to see clearly through the many smoke screens that the offenders have used to cover their trails. We will have to determine whether or not the perpetrators responsible for these crimes have altered any of our newfound evidence. Like all good detectives, we will first need to ask ourselves, *who stands to benefit the most from this crime?*

After all the evidence is calculated and sifted, we will be able to answer all of the above questions and quite possibly a whole lot more.

Like Shooting Fish in a Barrel

One of the biggest financial surges in our economy came in the late 1990s. The sheer volume of dollars that people were sinking into various stocks fascinated me. In the eighteen months before the stock market reached its peak, greed and speculation were rampant. The question heard most often in conversations from coast to coast was, how much higher can this thing go? Everyone you spoke with seemed to have a family member who had just heard the latest news about a certain stock, and more times than not, the following day the mentioned stock would soar. For a while it was a no-lose situation. You could literally pull any name of a stock from your hat and you were almost guaranteed at least double-digit returns. It seemed true that "all boats rise with a high tide."

It was hard to avoid the mania created from some companies' increases and, in some cases, parabolic gains. I spoke with many "experts" in the financial field and read everything I could get ahold of in the hopes of figuring out how this insanity could, and if it would, continue. Of course, it did not, and it was soon time to pay the piper for many people. It was just as interesting reading the "experts'" opinions on why the market was now experiencing a "correction."

In a nutshell, one of the many things that I discovered from this experience was that nobody wants to get left behind. Greed raised its ugly head. Citizens all over the world saw the inexplicable returns from many stocks and felt that they too could play this game. They would jump in or out of a stock any time a talking head from the television would commence a new rallying cry. We were told that this was a new economy. Things were different this time. The technological advances that these companies were implementing were going to change the way we lived, worked, and, of course, invested. Never mind that many of these companies were so far in debt through the loans they had taken out or the bonds they had issued that it would be nearly impossible to ever climb out of the red and post real profits. It has now been more than five and a half years since this boom went bust, and with the exception of a select few, stocks are nowhere near their old highs.

In the old days when so-called "investors" put their money into large corporations, they did so in hopes of receiving a dividend from the company. This dividend, a small amount of money paid back to the investor, was usually paid once a year. The size or amount of money given back to the investor each year was determined on how successful or how profitable this particular company was during the previous year. It behooved investors to study and seek out sound, already-profitable companies that would be in a position to pay a handsome dividend each year. It was really another way of earning interest on their money, like taking it to the bank and putting it into a savings account. The attraction for the investor was that these dividends were typically much larger than the meager interest that banks pay you on your savings. These investors were buying stock in companies like IBM not in the hopes that the stock they bought at $10 per share would reach $20 per share in a year or two, or even five, but rather they bought shares for the returns that would come to them through dividends each year.

This contrasts starkly with the idea and beliefs of the late nineties and even today. Many people bought into a certain stock (and with money they cannot afford to lose I might add) and hoped that if they held onto it for a year or two then their initial investment would double, if not increase more. Picture this overly simple analogy. If ten men throw $1000 apiece into a bucket and let it sit there for six months, then ten men cannot pull out $2000 apiece. In a perfect world, the best each man will pull back out is his original $1000. But more often than not, one or two men will pull out a total of $8000 between them, and the remaining eight men will haggle over the last $2000. This is the reality of today's stock market.

The Wealth Effect

After the market's crash, there was pain and heartache in abundance. We have all heard different stories from friends who lost considerable amounts of money in the stock market. It was a historic event when the stock market finally popped after becoming overinflated. Together, greed from those playing this shell game who sought something for nothing, along with the misrepresentation coming from corporate officers who actually ran and oversaw these corporations, burst this economic bubble. Unfortunately, many of the people who suffered great losses multiplied their pain by having entered this game of musical chairs with borrowed funds.

Almost overnight, trillions of dollars had just vanished into thin air. Some parts of the country slid into a mild recession as a direct result of the shrunken money supply. As soon as people no longer had expanding stock portfolios, their "wealth effect" also deflated. Wealth effect is a term that describes how people feel financially. As they watched their stocks and option net worth increase, they *felt* rich. However, they were only rich on paper. The value of that portfolio did them absolutely no good unless they completely cashed out and put the proceeds into the bank or under their mattresses. Unfortunately, many of these people who felt rich went out and purchased new toys, widgets, and gizmos. In many cases they borrowed the money to pay for these items, assuming that their portfolio would only increase in value as the months went by. As we know, most portfolios did not go up indefinitely. These portfolios went down and did so considerably! Now their paper profits and their wealth effect had both become nearly extinct. The problem then compounded. They now owned all of these new toys that they would not otherwise have purchased or borrowed money to purchase had it not been for a rising stock portfolio. As a result, many of these people were forced to retrench and curb their spending habits. They cut back on shopping, vacations, and eating out—all of which contributed to the slight recession.

Financial Phenomena

After the stock market lost most of its fizz, I again began seeing things on the economic landscape that I could not comprehend. Europeans were flying to our east coast to do their Christmas shopping. Apparently their dollars had more purchasing power. This was news to me. Why should their dollars (or euros, as they are called) be valued any differently than our dollars?

Prior to the stock market dive, I had just completed building a new gas station and hoped that this new venture would grow wings and take flight. However, my timing was off, and a major paradigm shift was underway in the retail gasoline business. It wasn't long before this particular endeavor of mine went underground and out of business.

Now, just a few years later, gasoline is going for 35 percent more per gallon than when I was selling it. Why? My primary business is doing well, but I'm certainly not making 35 percent more profit from it. Our health insurance is up more than 16 percent. In a matter of thirty months, my home's value more than doubled! Land values are no different. In 1993 one-acre lots in our neighborhood were going for $40,000–$50,000. By late 2003, one-acre lots were commanding almost $500,000! Today they are closer to $750,000—a concept that defies all logic. Thankfully all of my business ventures did not go out of business. However, I was not making ten times the money in 2003 that I was making back in 1993; in fact, few people could say they were. And yet, using land as our example, it had almost a tenfold increase. Being self-employed, I had the ability to increase my yearly income—but certainly nowhere near a ten-fold increase.

I had heard all of the arguments about land and how "they aren't making any more of it," but I wasn't buying that explanation. I knew that not only had traditional jobs but even the professional ones such as doctors, attorneys, and upper management had not increased their take-home pay by 1000 percent over the last ten years. As a matter of fact real wages, when taking inflation into account, have been flat for years. Of course, there are always exceptions to every rule, and there are certainly people, albeit very few, who increased their take-home pay even beyond 1000 percent in ten years. How was this rapid price increase in land going to continue? I did not have the answer. If collectively our income rose in tandem with the price of land, then it could be somewhat sustainable. However, this was not the case. For the large majority of people in this country, our take-home pay did not keep stair-step pace with the price of land and homes.

In response to my many questions about this phenomenon, I was given reflexive answers to this conundrum, such as "goods and services always go up over an extended period of time" or "it's inflation and there's nothing we can do about it." Others erroneously defined inflation and higher prices as one and the same. This is not the case. Price inflation, in this case homes and land, comes as a result of inflation. For every cause there is an effect. The *cause* is inflation, or those things that ignite inflation, and the *effect* is higher prices.

These are some of the financial conditions that I witnessed toward the end of the summer of 2003. I decided to find the answers to these questions and economic mysteries. I began my search by reading all the books I could find. Then I searched the Internet—an invaluable tool. The scriptures were also a priceless source of information that I used to answer some of my questions about both spiritual and temporal means. Recent prophets along with ancient ones helped shed light on my search.

In the Book of Mormon, Nephi exhorts us to liken all scriptures unto ourselves (see 1 Nephi 19:23). When we face questions or troubles, our church leaders have asked us to turn to the scriptures for guidance and counsel. Many of us have even inserted our own names into verses, as though the Lord himself was giving us comfort and counsel pertaining to certain problems in our lives.

After I finished my search for temporal knowledge concerning these economic matters, I found verses in the Doctrine and Covenants that took on additional meaning for me:

> For there are many yet on the earth among all sects, parties, and denominations, who are blinded by the subtle craftiness of men, whereby they lie in wait to deceive, and who are only kept from the truth because they know not where to find it—Therefore, that we should waste and wear out our lives in bringing to light all the hidden things of darkness, wherein we know them; and they are truly manifest from heaven—These should then be attended to with great earnestness. . . . Therefore, dearly beloved brethren, let us cheerfully do all things that lie in our power. (D&C 123:12–15, 17)

This powerful scripture speaks not only of gospel truths but also of all truths in general. Regrettably, as far as our topic is concerned, many of us have been kept in the dark because of the "subtle craftiness of men." These crafty men have been deceiving us for many generations. It has been easy for them to deceive us because we have not only become complacent, but also many of us do not know where to look for truth. In the above verses, we are admonished to bring *all* things of darkness out of the shadows and *into the light* and to do so with *great earnestness*—and to do *everything in our power* to accomplish that goal.

I have alluded to a financial battle. A battle implies a form of aggression, fight, or war. Where there is a war there is certainly an enemy. The dictionary defines "enemy" as a "foe" or one who "opposes another." There can be no greater foe known to mankind than Satan and those who are under his power.

I hope that by the time you have finished reading this book, you will have seen the light concerning the financial principles that have been discovered, and with *great eagerness* you too will want to perpetuate its truth.

Chapter Two

CHIMPS AND PAPER CLIPS

It is to be regretted that the rich and powerful too often bend the acts of government to their selfish purposes.
—Andrew Jackson

With so many different definitions of what money is, it may be difficult to come to any definite conclusions. Few of us would have a hard time explaining what money is used for; that part is easy—we use it to purchase goods and services that we need or want.

Money is used as a medium of exchange; this simply means that two or more parties engaging in a transaction have previously determined how many dollars or how much *money* it will take to complete the sale. If pre-determining the value of a certain object in advance to pay for goods and services is all that is needed, then literally anything can be used as a medium of exchange.

If my neighbor and I are both avid NBA playing card collectors, then we could use these cards as a form of money between us. We would have previously determined the value of these cards by using their condition, availability, and whether or not any of the cards were signed by the players. The two of us, having previously determined their worth, can now use and exchange these cards for goods and services between ourselves. I could then go across the street and wash my neighbor's car with the understanding that I would be paid in a certain number of NBA cards.

This may sound like a crazy idea to many of us. Many other bizarre sounding ideas have been used in the past, such as seashells, bark from a certain tree, beads, diamonds, and paper receipts, just to name a few. As long as all these items had their value predetermined by the group of people using them, the items could be considered money. Ultimately though, all of the above items would eventually cease to be used as money for various reasons. They would not be able to stand the test of time. Seashells, for example, are in great abundance and require no work or toil to produce. Even diamonds have their shortcomings: they are not always pure. It is difficult to judge the quality and clarity of diamonds, thus making it almost impossible to predetermine a set value. They are not divisible either. If someone tried to split off a small portion of the diamond to purchase a lesser amount of goods, he risks ruining the diamond altogether and his medium of exchange becoming almost worthless.

What if the government made the announcement that at the beginning of the next year they would begin implementing paper clips as the new form of currency to be used as the medium of exchange? Would you laugh? Would you roll your eyes and say "whatever"? Would you start to use them if your friends and neighbors did? Maybe you would hold out and claim that it was unconstitutional. Who would put their faith in paper clips? Would you hoard your old paper dollars, stuffing them in your mattress and up in the attic, believing to yourself that they still did or would in the future hold a certain value? What if the government announced later that all paper dollars now belonged to the government and anyone found holding them would receive jail time and/or monetary fines? Left with few choices, do you think you would now begin using the paper clips?

Learning from Chimpanzees

I came across an interesting story some years ago that I will try to relate to the best of my memory. A university was studying various behaviors in animals. This particular study dealt with chimpanzees and their ability to reason. Six chimpanzees were put in a large room with a set of stairs leading to the top. At the top of the stairs was a door. There was also a door on the main floor. The experiment went something like this. One of the professors would open the door at the top of the stairs, slide a bunch of bananas through the open door, and quickly shut it. As you can imagine, the quickest, strongest, or most alert of the chimpanzees barreled up the stairs toward the bananas. As soon as the chimpanzee reached the top of the stairs and grasped the bananas, the professor's assistant would open the door downstairs and spray all of the other chimpanzees with a fire hose. They repeated this process until they could place the bananas at the top of the stairs—out in plain view—and none of them would move a muscle. They had learned rather quickly that partaking of the bananas ensured a quick, cold blast from the hose! Next, the experimenters took one chimpanzee from the room and replaced it with a new one. When the bananas were delivered, this new chimpanzee started going up the stairs. Unfortunately for him, before he could reach the top, he was tackled and dragged down by the rest of the group. This routine was repeated two or three times and after that, when the newest chimpanzee saw the bananas arrive, he too did not move a muscle. This scenario of removing one of the original chimpanzees and putting a new one in its place was repeated until all of the original chimpanzees had been removed. Interestingly, the last chimpanzee to move in to complete the cycle was paralyzed. Soon thereafter, as had been the routine for months, the assistant slid the bananas through the doorway at the top of the stairs, and, of course, nobody moved. The newest member of the group, the paralyzed one, saw the strange scenario play out in front of him. If he could have, he would've scratched his head in wonderment. Although paralyzed, he could still communicate, and he asked the other chimpanzees why none of them were racing up to the bananas. The patriarch of the group then explained that every time one of them entered the room and tried to obtain the bananas, they were beaten up and dragged back down the stairs. This too made the newest chimpanzee want to scratch his head. "Why would you beat each other up?" he asked. To which the patriarch answered, "None of us are really sure, that's just how it's always been done around here."

None of the six replacement chimpanzees ever knew that the original six were sprayed with a cold fire hose. When they had attempted to get the bananas, they just knew what they saw, which was that any time a chimpanzee tried to get up the stairs, he took a good beating. This simplistic story illustrates how easy it can be to follow the crowd. Many of us don't stop and think about the answer to many of life's questions, especially when the given explanation happens to be, "That's the way things have always been done around here." Of course, this is only a story to illustrate a point; we are, after all, much more intelligent than the smartest chimpanzee, right?

A 50-Paper-Clip Gift Certificate

We will assume that for reasons discussed earlier, you decided to fall in line and begin using paper clips. You didn't feel comfortable using them initially and you knew this new form of currency was nothing more than a bent-up piece of wire, holding no intrinsic value. However, you had to buy and sell goods and services to sustain your lifestyle and knowing this caused you to throw in the towel. The years pass; you marry and raise a family. It seems to take more paper clips than it used to in order to buy a week's worth of groceries. All in all though, the paper clips have served their purpose as a medium of exchange. Now your children have had children. You are at a birthday party for one of your grandsons who just turned 16. It is a difficult age to shop for, so you purchased a 50-paper-clip gift certificate at one of the electronics stores for him. As the party winds down, you overhear your grandson talking to his friend about what he is going to buy with his newly acquired gift certificate. His friend then wonders out loud how it came to be that we use a bent piece of wire to purchase things. You lean in a bit just in time to hear your grandson say, "That's just what we've always used."

Preservation of Freedom

Has anyone ever asked you why we use a piece of paper to purchase goods and services? If so, did you have an answer? Did you have the *correct* answer? Did your answer resemble that of the "herd mentality"? Did you tell that person that creating a dollar requires very little work, that indeed it only requires a bit of green ink printed on paper? Did you mention that a paper dollar has no intrinsic value? Was the fact mentioned that a dollar is just like a promissory note, which is a promise to pay the stated value sometime in the future? Many years ago this stated value was to be paid back in gold and silver. Did you mention this? What would you tell your children or grandchildren if they came to you with such questions? You would not say, "that's just what we've always used," would you?

If asked, a few people may try explaining to a child or grandchild how greed can easily run rampant and if left unchecked could result in misery and financial slavery. But an explanation like this would be few and far between. Perhaps even fewer people could explain that losing freedom is a far greater threat than losing purchasing power. The words of Ezra Taft Benson might also help a grandchild see this distinction: "And few tasks, if any, are more important for the preservation of freedom than the preservation of a sound monetary system."[1] This statement alone should prompt more serious questions. Of all the things that we can do to ensure our freedoms, none is more important than fighting for an honest currency! But who is currently fighting, and who among us even realizes that the currency is not honest?

Perhaps fewer still could cite history, going back to when the Coinage Act of 1793 was passed. Keeping our country's monetary system financially sound was so important to our founding fathers that anyone caught manipulating or debasing our money was put to death! For our founding fathers to mandate death as a punishment, they must have considered this crime a source of true evil. Perhaps our founding fathers understood what would ultimately happen if men could easily break this law.

The Lord later made his point clear about those who would throw his counsel to the wind in D&C 98:9 when he said, "Nevertheless, when the wicked rule the people mourn."

The Lord mentions this right after he says that the Constitution, which was instituted for this land, was justifiable before him. Most agree that America is the promised land. Sadly, some mistakenly believe that because this was, and is, a land "choice above all others" as the Book of Mormon states numerous times, that nothing could ever harm or destroy us, that the Lord will stand as our protector regardless of our collective actions. The Lord, however, alludes to the contrary:

> For behold, this is a land which is choice above all other lands; wherefore he that doth possess it shall serve God or shall be swept off; for it is the everlasting decree of God. And it is not until the fulness of iniquity among the children of the land, that they are swept off. (Ether 2:10)

There are people among us who cannot answer the many rhetorical questions that were just presented. In order to know not only the answers to these questions but all of the inner workings and history pertaining to what money really is, we will have to first trace its origins.

NOTES

1. Ezra Taft Benson, *An Enemy Hath Done This,* (Salt Lake City: Bookcraft, 1992) 211.

Chapter Three

HISTORY OF MONEY

Irreverence is the champion of liberty and its only sure defense.
—Mark Twain

Why is understanding and defining the concept of money so mysterious? The nature of money has always been elusive to man. Some of us feel that it is beyond our understanding. As a result, we have a tendency to shy away from monetary topics and discussions. This is a condition that many of us have resigned ourselves to. We assume incorrectly that the majority's definition of money is indeed factual. Remember the adage that knowledge is power. I am certain that as you read these chapters, you will learn about money and how to protect it. Our very lives can be greatly influenced for good or bad, depending on our degree of knowledge. In the Old Testament we read, "My people are destroyed for lack of knowledge" (Hosea 4:6).

Regardless of the battle that we may face or the problems that are currently on our plate, without certain knowledge, we will be ineffective in our fight. Another charge comes from President Benson, who said, "Our greatest need in America today is to be alerted and informed."[1]
Thomas Jefferson, a founding father who I hold in high esteem, was certainly aware of the importance of knowledge. He emphasizes this in a letter to Dupont de Nemours by saying, "Our people must have the facts. There is safety in an informed public."[2]

Having a nonchalant or naïve attitude concerning money and its functions was not always the state of the majority. There was a time in the not so distant past when the average citizen was well-versed in financial matters. In the late 1800s many political opponents based their campaigns on how and what they thought about currency and banking. Somewhere along the way, we had a great paradigm shift. Men of great wealth and influence, along with our own government, have led us to believe that these monetary matters are much too complex, and therefore must be left to professionals.

Different Types of Money

The word *money* itself has many different definitions, which we have already defined: paper notes, cash, and coins to rename a few. The very fact that numerous meanings or definitions are given for the word *money* lends support to those statements we discussed earlier about money being mysterious. The money and policy makers can keep us in a mist of darkness by merely failing to agree to a rock-solid definition of what money really is. Earlier we discussed that money could be anything that is accepted as a medium of exchange. We briefly touched on NBA cards, paper clips, and past currencies of seashells and even diamonds. We could list dozens of things that could be used as a medium of exchange. There are, however, four primary forms of money: commodity, receipt, fiat, and fractional.

All four of these forms of money are defined completely separate from one another. We must be able to differentiate between these four groups in order to fully understand how our money is created, disbursed, handled, and controlled.

There is one other medium of exchange that, although it is not considered money, does have intrinsic value. All throughout history man has traded with one another. The term for this type of transaction is *barter*. I could give a set of golf clubs to my neighbor across the street in exchange for his snow skis. Both of these items have intrinsic value to each holder. We could also trade service or labor, such as washing his car in exchange for him helping me paint my shed. These items of service also have a perceived intrinsic value.

Thousands of years ago, bartering was the main system of exchange. Some items were more frequently used to barter with than others. Typically these items were highly sought-after goods, which were needed to make everyday life easier. Some of the more popular bartering items were grains, such as corn, wheat, and barley. All of these were essential for making food and all were looked upon as valuable. Animals were also frequently used for the same reasons. As groups of people began to prosper, these items used for bartering started to accumulate within their respective households. Items of barter were looked upon differently. They began to represent a store of value or wealth. This is where the transition was made from using primitive bartering techniques such as trading food or animals to using true "commodity money."

The Bronze Age

Somewhere in the early time line of history, man discovered ore. I would speculate that it took many attempts to get the refining process down to a science. This is what history considers the Bronze Age. The various types of grains used earlier could not sit in storage for years without going rancid. Animals could become sick. They had to be cared for and would certainly not live forever. For these reasons, the forms of commodity money mentioned above were eventually replaced by metals. It was not long before traders began using these newly found metals from inside the earth. Some of the metals available at this time were iron, brass, copper, bronze, silver, and gold. From near the beginning of time we have recorded history showing not only man but also the Lord placing an esteemed value on precious metals. The Old Testament specifically speaks of these precious metals. In Exodus 25:2–3, the Lord commands Moses to "speak unto the children of Israel, that they bring me an offering: of every man that giveth it willingly with his heart ye shall take my offering. And this is the offering which ye shall take of them; gold, and silver, and brass." The metals offered by the Israelites were used to adorn the tabernacle and the Ark of the Covenant.

There were certain prerequisites for metals to be used as commodity money. They had to have intrinsic value. As I mentioned earlier, diamonds would be a good storehouse for value except that they are not easily divisible. One would run the risk of losing all the pronounced value in a certain diamond if the attempt was made to divide it into smaller pieces. This is what made metals so appealing to our ancestors—the ability to measure wealth precisely. They could melt down a metal and re-pour it into several smaller molds. Not only did metals have intrinsic value, but their value could be measured—in this case by its weight.

Shepherds and traders alike now had other options in storing their wealth. Unlike their grains that would spoil and animals that could become sick and die, leaving them no wealth at all, metals could be weighed, counted, and stored indefinitely. Of all of the things man has at his disposal to measure and store wealth, he has chosen precious metals. Have you ever held real money in your hand? True money, like gold and silver coins? It feels solid and dense and radiates security and stability. Like diamonds, their physical appearance is quite attractive. When you hold gold and silver coins in your hand you cannot help but feel that you are holding something of value.

Of all of the precious metals at man's disposal, why has man throughout history primarily chosen gold as the metal of choice for storing and measuring wealth? It may be because it is one of the rarest metals found on earth. Gold has several industrial uses, and people have always found it alluring enough to use in jewelry. We will never know for sure why gold was chosen over the other metals, but suffice it to say that gold got the nod.

So far we have discussed why metals were the best form of commodity money. They cannot get sick, spoil, or die. Their purity can be confirmed and their weight can be measured precisely. However, there are those who look for faults in metal, and especially gold, as a form of commodity money. As I mentioned previously, gold is a rare resource. Critics use this to their advantage by claiming that there is not enough gold to go around for everyday transactions. Economist G. Edward Griffin refutes these criticisms:

> The deeper reality, however, is that the supply is not even important. Remember that the primary function of money is to *measure* the value of the items for which it is exchanged. In this sense, it serves as a yardstick or ruler of value. It really makes no difference if we measure the length of our rug in inches, feet, yards, or meters. . . . Our rug does not become larger just because we have increased the quantity of measurement units by painting additional markers onto our rulers.
>
> If the supply of gold in relation to the supply of available goods is so small that a one ounce coin would be too valuable for minor transactions, people simply would use half-ounce coins or tenth-ounce coins. The amount of gold in the world does not affect its ability to serve as money, it only affects the *quantity* that will be used to measure any given transaction.[3]

So the physical supply is irrelevant in terms of how much gold is available in a certain economy.

The Village

Let me illustrate a quick example regarding commodity-based money. Let's assume that I live in a tiny village where the commodity-based money of choice just happens to be golf balls. They are easy to store, they do not spoil or get sick, and they are relatively easy to transport. One morning everyone in the village wakes up and, to their astonishment, they find that they have twice the number of golf balls that they had the night before. The commodity-based money, in this case golf balls, has now just collectively doubled. We now have double the amount of "money" in the village, so now according to the critics of gold-based commodity money, wheels of the economy will spin more smoothly and efficiently. It does not take an economics degree to figure out that increasing supply cannot magically improve the efficiency of an existing economy. Ironically when the money supply is increased or inflated by whatever means, it will typically lead to higher prices for goods and services. How does more money translate to higher priced goods and services? In simplistic terms, good old-fashioned supply and demand. When any kind of money, whether it is gold, golf balls, or dollar bills, expands higher and faster than the amount of goods and services available, higher prices result. Although the villagers now have double the money, they do not have double the goods and can expect to see higher prices immediately. This, of course, is an example of inflation. We discussed earlier that many people define inflation simply as higher prices. Again higher prices are the *effect* and inflation is the *cause*. For every cause there is an effect. So are the villagers in our example any better off financially? Are they able to conduct their transactions more easily? Did it benefit the people to have their money supply increase? One would have to reason that it did not.

In this village the prices of camels have now doubled. Has the "value" of a camel really doubled though? Is it not the same camel that it was before the price increase? The camel is certainly not any faster or stronger now. It is not able to go further distances without drinking any water, yet it is now able to command a much higher price because there is now much more money chasing the same amount of goods. The argument could be made that prices didn't really go up, but rather the purchasing power of the money, or golf balls, went down.

Murray Rothbard, a former professor of economics at the University of Nevada at Las Vegas explained it this way:

We come to the startling truth that *it doesn't matter what the supply of money is.* Any supply will do as well as any other supply. The free market will simply adjust by changing the purchasing power, or effectiveness, of its gold-unit. There is no need whatever for any planned increase in the money supply, for the supply to rise to offset any condition, or to follow any artificial criteria. More money does not supply more capital, is not more productive, does not permit "economic growth."[4]

This straightforward logic should refute any critic who would argue that the physical gold supply in the world is inadequate to meet the needs of a large economy. In the above example it is clear that the disadvantages far outweigh the advantages when the money supply is artificially inflated.

The First Coins

It is believed that the first actual gold coins were manufactured in Asia Minor or modern-day Turkey, around 600 B.C. Up until this time, gold's value was determined by its weight. These coins began to spring up in these ancient countries where curious markings and different images were engraved directly into the coin. Gold was still a commodity, but these new coins were actually certified by the various governments. They were very convenient, but it stopped the process of weighing their "money." Now gold was assigned a value per coin rather than letting the free market dictate how much a certain weight would be worth. Gold had been used for thousands of years previously but now that it was fashioned into a decorative disk, as they were first called, people offered their labor and even sold handmade goods in order to acquire these newly sought-after and highly popular coins.

> All classes of men succumbed to money, and those who had formerly been content to produce only for their needs and the necessities of the household, found themselves going to the marketplace with their handicraft, or the fruits of their toil, to exchange them for the coins they might obtain.[5]

Ideas of "something for nothing" began to swirl through people's minds. It was not long before merchants and traders discovered a way to cheat the system. Their insidious ploy was to shave tiny pieces off the edges of the gold coins, take the collective shavings, and melt them down to form new ones. Thus, without much labor or any capital involved, they were able to increase their holdings in gold. It did not take long before governments followed suit and repeated the same process with all of the coins they collected through taxes. You can guess what happened next. The supply of gold had increased but the value certainly had not. It didn't happen overnight, but over time the citizens began to realize that it was taking more coins to purchase the same amount of goods than it used to, and as a result people were required to raise their prices on all goods and services to compensate for the loss of purchasing power. This is one of the first examples in history where men tried to artificially inflate their existing money supply. Had these coins been valued by weight rather than having an official price imprinted on them, the money supply could not have increased.

Governments and kingdoms used this mechanism in order to defraud their citizens. This method benefited the very few men that happened to be in power. It doesn't take much imagination to think of all the ways that this newfound income could benefit a government. By shaving down coins it could literally create new wealth at will. This meant an additional supply of wealth to purchase, horses, chariots, goods from other parts of the world, soldiers' payrolls, and all other things needing to build a vast empire or sustain a small one. Shaving coins was also alluring to these rulers because they could spend the money on all the outlandish programs and expenses they wanted without increasing taxes, which always had the potential for inciting a revolt from their subjects.

Unfortunately, as gold coins were shaved and the money supply increased, higher prices for goods and services resulted. This unpleasant process at first happens quite slowly. It is much more manageable though than having a tax collector bang on your door and ask for a significant increase to cover a king's or government's indiscriminate spending. The gradual increase in the supply of gold coins is similar to the proverbial frog in boiling water. It has been said that if you drop a frog in boiling water, the frog will hop out right away. If you place a frog into warm water and place it on the stove, slowly increasing the heat, it will never jump out. Remember that inflation is an indirect tax. It is much easier for governments to slowly turn the heat up on us, as opposed to announcing that they are in need of more money and are coming to us, the taxpayers, to obtain it. So they are able to take a large portion of what they need to finance their debts through inflation. Those who have clearly seen through this mechanism have termed it "confiscation through inflation."

We have been talking about one of the four different kinds of money:

commodity money. We have seen that man has chosen gold and silver as the most popular forms of commodity money. As we know, in today's day and age we no longer use commodity money as a medium of exchange. Paper currencies and digital credits are primarily used and are issued and controlled by banks. Although we do not use gold and silver coins as money, there are unfortunately other ways that governments can and do devalue and debase currency.

Confiscation through Inflation

Part of this book will explain in great detail how our present-day government is able to artificially increase our money supply, which in turn causes inflation—which is nothing more than a hidden tax.

Alan Greenspan, the current chairman of the Board of Governors at the Federal Reserve System said, "In the absence of the gold standard, there is no way to protect savings from confiscation through inflation. There is no safe store of value. If there were, the government would have to make its holding illegal, as was done in the case of gold."[6]

Sadly, this comment was not given recently. It was given back in 1966, nearly twenty years before Alan Greenspan became the chairman of the Federal Reserve. He mentions that owning gold was illegal in 1966. As Americans, we could not even own gold here in the promised land.

In 1 Nephi 13:30 we find these words: "Nevertheless, thou beholdest that the Gentiles who have gone forth out of captivity, and have been lifted up by the power of God above all other nations, upon the face of the land which is choice above all other lands." Similar comments in other parts of the Book of Mormon confirm that America is indeed a land choice above all others. Why then was it illegal to own gold? What did Alan Greenspan mean when he said there was "no safe store of value"? How will you protect your savings from confiscation through inflation? One can only speculate how Alan Greenspan feels now about gold and all of its positive attributes pertaining to wealth preservation. Today it is once again legal to own gold in the United States, and Mr. Greenspan is now chairman of the Federal Reserve System. Currently in a position of great power, he no longer campaigns for gold, nor does he go to bat on its behalf. The burning question that should come to everyone's mind is, why not?

For some of us, the above questions are proposed here within these pages for the first time. They are also questions that cannot be answered quickly. We will find the answers to not only these questions but also many others as it pertains to preserving our money and the battle others are presently waging in order to financially enslave us.

Notes

1. Ezra Taft Benson, *An Enemy Hath Done This* (Salt Lake City: Bookcraft, 1992), 90.

2. Thomas Jefferson to M. Dupont de Nemours, April 24, 1816; *Works* 6:592.

3. G. Edward Griffin, *The Creature from Jekyll Island: A Second Look at the Federal Reserve* (Westlake Village, CA: American Media, 1998), 141.

4. Murray Rothbard, *What Has Government Done to Our Money?* (Larkspur, Colorado: Pine Tree Press, 1964), 13.

5. Elgin Groseclose, *Money and Man: A survey of Monetary Experience,* 4th ed. (Oklahoma: University of Oklahoma Press, 1976), 13.

6. Alan Greenspan, "Gold and Economic Freedom," in *Capitalism: The Unknown Ideal,* ed. Ayn Rand (New York: Signet Books, 1967), 101.

Chapter Four

RECEIPT MONEY

If the American people ever allow private banks to control the issue of their money, first by inflation and then by deflation, the banks and corporations that will grow up around them, will deprive the people of their property until their children will wake up homeless on the continent their fathers conquered.

—Thomas Jefferson

In the previous chapter we discussed how men, kingdoms, and governments have been able to devalue and dilute the money supply. We have shown some examples of how this was accomplished in the use of gold. We also talked about the effects of this insidious process that leads to inflation, which is a form of confiscation. In general terms, this paints a dreary picture of mankind throughout the ages. It would be unfair, however, if we were to paint all our ancestors with this same brush. As I mentioned earlier, there are always exceptions to every rule. There were many men throughout history that were full of integrity and character and those that were willing to stand up for freedom. President Benson admonished us to follow their example: "Take that long eternal look. Stand up for freedom, no matter what the cost."[1]

Certain noble men throughout the ages were willing to turn from the temptation of obtaining something for nothing. When unethical circumstances presented themselves, these men and women feared God more than man and heeded his timeless counsel given in Deuteronomy

25:15: "But thou shalt have a perfect and just weight, a perfect and just measure shalt thou have: that thy days may be lengthened in the land which the Lord thy God giveth thee."

An interesting thing happened as these people kept greed from creeping in, although it must have been tempting for them to increase their holdings of gold coins. Think how alluring it would be for us today if we could simply print dollar bills from our home printers. These people obviously took the "eternal look" spoken of by President Benson. They realized that diluting the money supply was, in the long run, a form of confiscation. So what was the interesting thing that happened to these people? It is the same thing that happens to all of God's children. When they decide to live righteously, they experience prosperity. In Alma 9:13 we hear the Lord's promise:

> Behold, do ye not remember the words which he spake unto Lehi, saying that: Inasmuch as ye shall keep my commandments, ye shall prosper in the land? And again it is said that: Inasmuch as ye will not keep my commandments ye shall be cut off from the presence of the Lord.

Let us fall back into history again and see if there are any examples pertinent to the above paragraph. Nearly three hundred years after Christ's ministry, the Roman Empire was literally on death's doorstep. Space does not permit me to go into all of the details as to why the great Roman Empire finally crumbled. Suffice it to say that the Romans were notorious for their wickedness and debauchery and gave new meaning to the way in which money was debased with total abandon.

On a more optimistic note, there were people who prospered and practiced lifestyles of integrity. The Byzantine Empire was centered on modern-day Greece and was a prime example of a people honoring the "just weights and measures" principle. As a result of this sound judgment and the ability to straight-arm the temptation to shave gold coins, this ancient society was able to truly "prosper in the land." Their ruler, Constantine, mandated that new gold and silver pieces be minted. These coins were called Solidus and Miliarense, respectively. In unprecedented fashion, these coins were the commodity-based money of choice for the next eight hundred years. As a matter of fact, these coins became so popular and their reputation deemed so highly that they were traded and exchanged all over the free world. How were these fortunate people able to prosper in the land? How were they able to use and accept the same form of money for nearly a thousand years? Because they did not succumb to the philosophy that in order to have a smooth running or elastic economy, the money supply must be increased. They prospered because they were able to keep more money in their pockets. They prospered because they did not have to worry about having their wealth confiscated through inflation. They did not have to worry about inflation because they took the steps necessary to avoid it from the very beginning. In short, they practiced just weights and just measures and the result was hundreds of years of prosperity.

Receipt Money

If you have ever held gold and silver coins in your hand, you know firsthand how heavy even a few hundred dollars can be. The thought of having enough coins to purchase a flock of sheep or a herd of cows is staggering. As mentioned previously, when civilizations and people as a whole prosper, it is because they do not devalue their money supply. As people heed this timeless truth, their wealth accumulates. Centuries ago, people did not have safe deposit boxes available to them as we do now. History has shown us how people considered gold of great value, but these same people had nowhere to store their gold. They certainly were not going to ask their kings or governments to safeguard their gold coins. Ultimately these citizens sought out what were the only vaults or lockboxes available at the time, both of which were owned by goldsmiths. As the name implies, these men worked with and traded precious metals. This line of work could be very lucrative, but along with their wealth came many perils. Just like today's jewelry stores, these shop owners of the past had to be on the defensive, keeping an ever-watchful eye out for potential thieves. In order to safeguard their precious metals against attempted robberies, these goldsmiths constructed safe storage containers called lockboxes or strongboxes. Today we call them vaults or safes. The goldsmith seldom needed all of the room for his personal use, so as a result he began renting this extra space inside of his lockbox. This was a win-win situation for both parties. Goldsmiths were able to earn a little extra income from renting out storage space inside their vaults, and the citizens of these communities were able to sleep soundly at night knowing that their excess gold and silver coins were locked inside one of the most secure places available.

The process was rather simple. Citizens would bring their extra coins to the goldsmith and he in return would issue a deposit receipt, showing the amount of coins being held in the vault that belonged to that person. Whenever a particular person needed access to their coins, all he or she would need to do is return with the deposit receipt and exchange it for the stated number of coins. The only thing left for this person to do was to pay the storage fee to the goldsmith. It was a simple transaction for both parties involved.

As time passed it became customary to simply endorse this deposit receipt, thereby enabling a third party to go to the goldsmith and stake claim to the stated number of coins. These deposit receipts acted as a precursor to our modern-day checks. Once these deposit receipts were endorsed by the original holder, they began to be used to purchase goods and services just like real money. This new method used to purchase goods and services was a big hit with most of the citizens. Not only did the people have the peace of mind knowing that their money was backed by pure gold, but now they had the ease and convenience of using lightweight foldable paper as a medium of exchange. The above scenario was fine-tuned just a bit in order to perfect the system. Making the deposit receipts interchangeable among citizens, as long as the original holder endorsed them, was one more advantage to using receipt money. Finally, the system progressed to the point where the original receipt holder could take back the deposit receipt to the goldsmith and exchange it for numerous smaller receipts totaling the whole amount of deposit. Thus, if someone had ten gold coins deposited, when the need arose, he could go back and exchange the receipt for 10 one-coin receipts. This is another example of how they tweaked their money system, which consisted of deposit receipts or receipt money, and produced positive results within their economy. Now, rather than trying to find merchants who had the exact price tag that matched their deposit receipts, people could use these new, smaller denominational receipts as money to purchase goods at various prices.

Of course, receipt money is only a piece of paper. It has no intrinsic value. Held alone, it is virtually worthless. What this paper represented is what made it valuable. Citizens accepted this receipt money for goods and services because it represented actual gold and silver that was held securely in a vault. They knew that at any time they could go back to the goldsmith and exchange the receipt money for actual gold coins. Trusting that gold coins were actually in a vault was what made this system so successful. This method of exchange foreshadowed how all banks would eventually work. If man had been able to adhere to the principles just discussed, we would not have the exhaustive monetary problems that we as a society are currently battling against.

We are trying to understand what money really is, how it was created, how it benefited civilizations, and what is required to keep a sound currency. It was briefly discussed in the introduction that we would discover if history or man's past mistakes really do repeat themselves. Regrettably, history has shown us that tampering with and manipulating money has a habit of cropping up in almost every civilization. It has been shown and will be proven throughout this book that those with the power to debase and inflate a monetary system have usually not been able to resist such a temptation. The word *temptation* is defined by the dictionary as "to try to get someone to do wrong by a promise of reward."

Satan certainly understood the following verse found in D&C 121:39, which reads, "We have learned by sad experience that it is the nature and disposition of almost all men, as soon as they get a little authority, as they suppose, they will immediately began to exercise unrighteous dominion." It was Satan who whispered to the hearts of men throughout the ages to be dishonest. It was he who planted the seeds of greed within our hearts. He knew from past experience that men would covet his neighbor's possessions. If he could help place certain men into power, he knew without a doubt that unrighteous dominion would be exercised immediately! The reward, which is the second part to the definition of temptation, was promises of vast wealth and unprecedented power and control. How can someone accumulate large amounts of wealth? There are two main avenues in which to acquire fortune. The first method, which I discovered at the age of nine, is to earn it by working for it. The other approach contrasts sharply with the first: obtaining wealth through deceit and dishonesty. We have many examples throughout history where men have tried to falsely gain power and treasures from others—it goes all the way back to the beginnings of man.

A Dangled Carrot

At this point I think we could safely assume that, for the most part, history does repeat itself. Unfortunately Satan is also aware of this fact and is able to use that information to his advantage. Because of this he does not need a vast arsenal of temptations to dangle in front of us. He merely dangles the same carrot that he has for thousands of years. It is easy and efficient. He too has been a student of history and uses this to his advantage. Why has he tempted men throughout the ages with the power that only money can bring? He knows that the actions of a few will drastically affect the lives of the majority, and they will find it almost impossible to climb out of the financial bondage that he has orchestrated. As we know, Satan is currently in a miserable state. Because of this, he does everything in his power to make us like him so that we too must reside with him in his self-sought misery. We learn this concept in 2 Nephi 2:18: "And because he had fallen from heaven, and had become miserable forever, he sought also the misery of all mankind."

One of Satan's methods of temptation is debt. Financial bondage or slavery to debt is a merciless taskmaster. When someone is unable to pay his debts, feelings of inadequacy and total helplessness begin to surface. These feelings of degradation stroke Satan's ego. Misery is positive feedback to Satan that his cunningly devised plans, laid out years in advance, are starting to bear fruit. Knowing Satan's battle plan is a valuable tool; we can use that information to arm ourselves against his methods, which in turn makes us more effective in our fight for financial freedom.

Let's trace back to that point in time where receipt money had begun to prosper as a medium of exchange. It would not take a historian or an economist to guess what happened to this receipt money. We have discovered, as we have taken a jaunt through history, that by one means or another, inflation will somehow enter this scenario.

To review, this quote from Griffin reminds us what it takes to preserve a sound monetary system, whether commodity or receipt:

> Whenever government sets out to manipulate the money supply, regardless of the Intelligence or good intentions of those who attempt to direct the process, the result is inflation, economic chaos, and political upheaval. By contrast whenever government is limited in its monetary power to only the maintenance of honest weights and measures of precious metals, the result is price stability, economic prosperity, and political tranquility. Therefore, for a nation to enjoy economic prosperity and political tranquility, the monetary power of its politicians must be limited solely to the maintenance of honest weights and measures of precious metals.[2]

The above paragraph can be summarized by saying that the road to hell is paved with good intentions. To paraphrase part of our own Constitution, it states that the government is to regulate the value of money, which is what Griffin implied. Nowhere does it state that the government has the power to manipulate or to ever increase the money supply artificially. Yet that is what governments have always done—with a few rare exceptions. The Byzantine Empire, which held its currency stable for over eight hundred years as we discovered earlier, is one such exception.

The Root of Evil

Unfortunately, even today our government here in the promised land continues to distort, devalue, and manipulate our currency system. President Benson makes a powerful statement when he claims, "The root of all evil is money, some say. *But the root of our money evil is government.*"[3]

Was he really speaking about our government? Maybe he was speaking in general terms. Perhaps he was merely reiterating what we have been learning, that man, when given a little bit of power, usually succumbs to temptation and throws the principle of just weights and measures to the wind. Benson continues by saying, "The very beginning of our troubles can be traced to the day when the federal government overstepped its proper defensive function and began to manipulate the monetary system to accomplish political objectives."[4]

As we can see, he is indeed referring to our government. There's that word again—manipulate. It seems to be a recurring premise throughout this study. Think about the last three words. Could he be referring to the nature and disposition of almost all men and what they do when they receive a little authority? Sadly we have learned mostly through experience that politicians began to exercise unrighteous dominion, in this case, for political favors. As we proceed we will continue to uncover the various ways in which man can exercise unrighteous dominion over his brethren.

Some may argue that this quote from President Benson was given from the perspective of a church leader not "in the know" concerning governmental matters. That he was not a true economist and was unfamiliar with the inner workings of government may lead some to conclude that his comments were only opinions. It is my belief that the above assumptions are complete fallacies. President Benson served in a cabinet position with the Eisenhower administration. He was the Secretary of Agriculture under President Eisenhower for eight years. He has held positions on councils, boards, foundations, and institutes—some on international levels. He had relationships with many high-ranking officials in many countries.

Few rivals could say that they had more hands-on experience with the day-to-day operations of a working government. Certainly President Benson understood the intricate details of how and what our government does behind the scenes. These are noteworthy credentials to say the least, however, let us not forget that he was a modern day servant of God. We are living in the fulness of times and thus must assume that today's prophets hold even more light and knowledge than our founding fathers did.

So to hear him say that there is evil in our money system and that our very own government is manipulating that same system, I for one will not try to refute his statements. In fact, just the opposite, this quote from above concurs with all of the research that I have done and only helps solidify my beliefs that we are currently engaged in a monetary battle.

Safe from Destruction?

Some among us may argue that monetary manipulation by the hands of our very own government, which we the people elected, would never come to pass, especially here in the promised land. Let us reread D&C 98:9 when the Lord said: "Nevertheless, when the wicked rule the people mourn."

As inhabitants of America, are we promised anywhere that this nation will always be immune from all forms of destruction? Have we been assured that this nation, which is "choice above all others," will have the indefinite ability to keep the Lord's wrath at bay? From what I can gather I would have to say no, just the opposite. Nowhere are we promised that regardless of our conduct, we as a people will have continual prosperity. In fact, we read in 3 Nephi 20:15–16 that one possibility, if played out in its entirety, would result in death, sorrow, and destruction:

> And I say unto you, that if the Gentiles do not repent after the blessing which they shall receive, after they have scattered my people—Then shall ye, who are a remnant of the house of Jacob, go forth among them; and ye shall be in the midst of them who shall be many; and ye shall be among them as a lion among the beasts of the forest, and as a young lion among the flocks of sheep, who, if he goeth through both treadeth down and teareth in pieces, and none can deliver.

The Lord also warned the brother of Jared,

> That whoso should possess this land of promise, from that time henceforth and forever, should serve him, the true and only God, or

they should be swept off when the fulness of his wrath should come upon them. (Ether 2:8)

This verse also reiterates that our nation is indeed the land of promise, and because of this we are required to serve God or be destroyed. To drive this point home, Moroni uses the next two verses to reiterate what the Lord said. This same message was repeated three times. Each of the three verses, 8, 9, and 10, delivered the same message and only differed by a handful of words. It is obvious that the Lord holds this land in the highest regard. Of all countries on this earth, we have been told here, and in other scripture that this land is choice above all. Some among us have misconceptions concerning our choice land. We must remember that collectively we stand a very good chance of being swept off. In order to help us escape this fate we are exhorted three times to serve God. The facts about this choice land have been plainly laid out. The pending destruction that awaits is stated outright. A formula has been given not once, not twice, but three consecutive times that will help us bypass certain destruction if we follow it.

So, going back to where we originally started, is it possible that our very own government, which happens to reside and operate within this promised land, has been devaluing and manipulating our monetary system? According to President Benson, and from the research I have done, I would say, yes! They would, have, and are manipulating our monetary system. In the chapters ahead I will not only prove that they *are* doing it, but I will show how they are accomplishing this unrighteous dominion.

History can be an invaluable tool for predicting what might transpire in the future. History has shown us what man has chosen to use as a medium of exchange for acquiring sought-after goods and services. We have discovered that civilizations have bartered for their goods with anything from animals to barley. Of all the precious metals available to man, he has chosen gold and silver as a store of value. Further into time, our ancestors turned their gold and silver into coins. History repeated itself; man succumbed to temptation, embraced the philosophy of something for nothing, and began to shave down his gold coins, thus causing an artificial expansion of the money supply, which of course led to misery that only inflation can bring.

Continuing our journey forward we see that man has created a monetary system that we call receipt money—a system which has many positive attributes all of which we have discussed previously.

Disappointingly, there have always been a few men throughout history that could not rebuke the temptations that were so subtly whispered to them by Satan.

Distorting Receipt Money

This receipt money that we are currently studying seems to be a positive approach on all accounts. Surely by now the reader is anticipating that somehow or by some mechanism even this monetary system will become manipulated and distorted. What could possibly dilute the purchasing power of receipt money? The goldsmiths have not lowered themselves to the level of shaving gold coins, nor have any of the citizens. The gold coins are still safely locked inside the vault, and there have been no attempts to steal from the vault. So the question is, how was it possible to increase their money supply without adding additional gold coins? Let me try to explain this by relating the story of two hypothetical goldsmiths.

Rob and Mike were both in the same line of work. Both of them traded and manufactured different items out of gold and silver. They were two of the many goldsmiths that worked in our fictitious town. One day these two men were in the back corner of a dimly lit tavern. After a few good stories, the conversation turned to business, which was typically the case. "I don't know about you, Rob," Mike said, "but if people don't start coming back in to reclaim their coins, I will have to start turning business away. My strongbox is almost completely full of coins. Who would ever had guessed that our customers would start to use our deposit receipts almost exclusively? I for one always assumed that people would come back to reclaim their coins more frequently than they have." Rob told Mike that he was already a step ahead of him, explaining, "I went over to Springville a couple of weeks ago and had Mr. Clark construct a new strongbox for me. My old one was completely full, and I figured if I was going to make more money, I was going to have to provide more rental space, or like you said, I too would have to turn customers away." Mike had already thought of this idea himself and it certainly made sense, however, he had also been entertaining much more insidious thoughts. Hesitantly, Mike said, "I've been giving this a lot of thought, so hear me out on this Rob. As you know, to our amazement people have seldom ever come back to redeem their receipts for the coins that we hold for them. They have been content to hold on to these receipts as though they were actually money. So my question to you is this, what is to stop me from writing you a receipt for the equivalent of ten gold coins and you doing the same or me? I could then take my receipt from you and purchase that new wagon that I have had my eye on, and you in turn could buy that new chest of drawers that your wife has been pleading with you to buy. Not only could we acquire these goods that we seek, but we could also do so without taking any of our own gold coins out of our lockboxes! Call me crazy, but I am telling you I think this could work!"

Rob's mind began to race. *This is truly ingenious,* he thought. Greed began to grip his heart, and rather than rebuking the whisperings of Satan, he embraced them wholeheartedly. His imagination began to run wild. He envisioned all of the things that his newfound wealth could acquire for him. The power and prestige that would come from an inexhaustible supply of money. He could not believe his good fortune—his good friend Mike had just shared with him an invaluable idea that would surely change his life forever. Ironically, not only would it change his life, but it would change the lives and standard of living for thousands of people. It was indeed a day to remember; it was the day that both of them lost their integrity, honor, and self-respect. Above all, it was the day they chose to cast aside the principle of just weights and measures. After listening to the details about this new plan, the first and only comment from Rob was, "How much should I write your receipt out for, my good friend?"

Like other methods we have studied, this new approach of inflating the money supply was also tweaked and fine-tuned. Unlike gold coins that could only be shaved down so much, there were absolutely no limits to the amount of fake deposit receipts that could be written. As time progressed, people began to come to the goldsmiths to borrow money. If and when approved for a short-term loan, the borrower was given receipt money rather than gold coins. This process contributed to inflation on a larger scale. Rob and Mike were not the only goldsmiths in town, and it did not take long before the others were also dumping fake deposit receipts into the economy. We have talked about the dangerous consequences inflation can bring and have familiarized ourselves with its outcome. Although these men did not have printing presses during this time, you could safely bet the farm that they were writing out those receipts as fast as they could.

Who Hurts Most?

Think for a moment how easy this new mechanism was compared to obtaining and shaving down the edges of gold coins. Think of all the time that must have been saved. Think of all the paper and ink that these few men were going through. Think of this process of inflation and who it really hurt the most. Inflation always hurts the poor and the elderly more than any other group of people. The poor and elderly are typically on fixed incomes. If a senior couple is retired, their savings or nest egg is gaining monthly interest in some form of a financial investment. If they previously agreed to receive 2 percent interest on their investment, such as a CD, yet inflation happens to rise to 4 percent, 6 percent, or even 10 percent, then they have just lost purchasing power. If using prescription drugs as our example, and if they have gone up in price 4 percent, than these retired people will now have to spend more dollars to receive the same amount of pills they did previously. Let us not forget that the 2 percent interest that will be paid back to the investor will be taxed, because, ironically, it is considered a source of income. This enables our government to reach into our pockets twice: once by the hidden tax—inflation—and again on the so-called gains from interest of a whopping 2 percent.

Two different forms of money have now been discussed: commodity and receipt. We have seen how men in powerful positions were able to manipulate these currencies for their own benefit, regardless of how it affected others.

According to Ron Paul, Congressman from the state of Texas, things don't appear to be any better today than they were hundreds of years ago:

> The greatest threat facing America today is the disastrous fiscal policies of our own government, marked by shameless deficit spending and Federal Reserve currency devaluation. It is this one-two punch—Congress spending more than it can tax or borrow, and the Fed printing money to make up the difference—that threatens to impoverish us by further destroying the value of our dollars.[5]

This statement echoes some of the things that President Benson stated earlier. It is interesting that Congressman Paul did not mention standing armies, terrorists, or nuclear warheads as our greatest threat to America. He mentioned things that we have previously discussed, such as destroying the value of our dollars and devaluing our currency. Perhaps if we had more men throughout the ages with beliefs that were similar to Ron Paul, who not only understood how money is supposed to work but also had the integrity and inner strength to resist temptations of greed and power, history would not have been full of corrupted tyrants.

NOTES

1. Ezra Taft Benson, *An Enemy Hath Done This* (Salt Lake City: Bookcraft, 1992), 45.

2. G. Edward Griffin, *The Creature from Jekyll Island: A Second Look at the Federal Reserve* (Westlake Village, CA: American Media, 1998), 152.

3. Benson, *An Enemy Hath Done This*, 213.

4. Ibid., 213–14.

5. Ron Paul, "Borrowing, Spending, Counterfeiting," *Texas Straight Talk* on August 22, 2005.

Chapter Five

JUST AND HOLY PRINCIPLES

Yes, we did produce a near-perfect republic. But will they keep it? Or will they, in the enjoyment of plenty, lose the memory of freedom? Material abundance without character is the path of destruction.
—Thomas Jefferson

Some men doubted that it could even be done. Others secretly wished that it would fail. Unbelievably, there were those that fought in open rebellion against it. The feat that this predestined group of men undertook was a truly magnificent and unprecedented accomplishment among the history of men. These men contributed innumerable hours of service in order to accomplish that task that they had previously set out to complete. Their ages and occupations were varied greatly; there were men in their twenties and men well into their eighties. There were doctors, lawyers, farmers, and businessmen, teachers and inventors, to list only a few. While they sometimes differed in their approaches, they all passionately longed for freedom, prosperity, liberty, and peace. It has now been well over two hundred years since these thirty-nine men stood up for their beliefs, no matter what the price. We owe all of these valiant men our most sincere gratitude for the rights, privileges, and freedoms that they sought in our behalf.

Credit must be given to the courageous men who laid the groundwork eleven years prior to the signing of the Constitution. Our founding fathers laid their own lives on the line when they drafted and signed their names to the Declaration of Independence. When this document of presumed independence was signed, there were still many long years of warfare ahead. And had they not come out victorious in that war for independence, they would have paid the price with their lives for treason against their country.

The overall objective of these men was to perpetuate true principles of freedom and all of the things that it would require to secure such. In their words we read,

> We the people of the United States, in order to form a more perfect union, establish justice, ensure domestic tranquility, provide for the common defense, promote the general welfare, and secure the blessings of liberty to ourselves and our posterity, do ordain and establish this Constitution for the United States of America.[1]

There are few things in my life that I value more than freedom. In my home hangs a copy of the Constitution and the Declaration of Independence. Alongside each framed document is a picture of our founding fathers coming together to sign their names. I view these replicas of history on a daily basis with reverence and gratitude. When I contemplate all of the hardships, trials, and burdens that these men went through, I have to believe that they were only able to do so by the hand of our Creator. The finished Constitution was nothing short of miraculous.

Nothing Short of a Miracle

George Washington wrote to his friend that the completion of the Constitution was practically a miracle:

> It appears to me, then, little short of a miracle, that the delegates from so many different states (which states you know are also different from each other, in their manners, circumstances, and prejudices) should unite in forming a system of national government.[2]

James Madison, the father of the Constitution, agreed with our first president in his letter to Thomas Jefferson expressing that it was, "Impossible to consider the degree of concord which ultimately prevailed as less than a miracle."[3]

The framers of our Constitution were so convinced that by adhering to its principles, men all over the world, after reading it, would embrace it wholeheartedly in order that they too might enjoy liberty, freedom, and prosperity. French writer Alexis de Tocqueville spent two years in America during the 1850s studying and observing firsthand how our new way of government worked. He found that among other things America was:

> Not only the most prosperous, but the most stable of all the nations of the earth. . . . The principles on which the American Constitution rests, those principles of order, while the balance of powers, a true liberty, of deep and sincere respect for right, are indispensable to all republics.

This was a highly paid complement to our founding fathers by this foreigner from across the ocean. His neighbor William Gladstone, who was at one time the prime minister of England, also praised the eternal principles found in the Constitution: "It is the greatest piece of work ever struck off at a given time by the brain and purpose of man."[4]

The first prophet of this dispensation, Joseph Smith, also professed his love and admiration for the principles found in our Constitution. One of the greatest freedoms that we enjoy is freedom of religion. Without the freedoms of religion and speech, the chances of the Book of Mormon ever being printed would be remote. Joseph Smith proclaimed:

> The Constitution of the United States is a glorious standard; it is founded in the wisdom of God. It is a heavenly banner; it is to all those who are privileged with the sweets of liberty, like the cooling shades and refreshing waters of a great rock in a thirsty and weary land. It is like a great tree under whose branches man from every clime can be shielded from the burning rays of the sun.[5]

Although Not Perfect

Consider the words of another past prophet, Ezra Taft Benson, as he refers to the founding fathers:

> Not perfect men, but men raised up by the Perfect Man to perform great work. Foreordained were they, to lay the foundation of this republic. . . . Blessed by the Almighty in their struggle for liberty and independence, the power of heaven rested on these founders as they drafted that great document for governing men, the Constitution of the United States. Like the Ten Commandments, the truths on which the Constitution was based were timeless; and also, as with the Decalogue, the hand of the Lord was in it. They filled their mission well. From them we were endowed with a legacy of liberty, a Constitutional republic.[6]

They were not perfect, as president Benson professed. They were, however, inspired and foreordained by God. We believe that the Ten Commandments were given to Moses, and that the truths, principles, and laws that were handed to him were done so by none other than God himself. President Benson tells us that the truths that we find in the Ten Commandments, as well as those found within the Constitution, are timeless. The Lord's doctrines have never changed. Thus, we can determine that any principle of truth that was instilled in his children thousands of years ago is to be embraced and adhered to in our present day.

All of the above quotes pay tribute and respect to the men who have given selflessly of their hearts, minds, and souls so that we, along with our posterity, can be the recipients of their labor now and in the future. These men had character. They lived lives of virtue and possessed integrity. Because of these virtues, they were receptive to the eternal and truthful principles that the Lord inspired them with.

Who were these valiant and courageous men? Were they really inspired by God? After reading some of the above quotes, many would certainly conclude such. After thousands of years of darkness, where did they look for wisdom and truth? How did they obtain these truthful, eternal principles? Why did these men risk their livelihoods and their very lives in order to obtain freedom? Will we find anything pertinent relating to the subject matter of this book written inside the Constitution, or is this just an interesting chapter in history?

Most of us are familiar of George Washington's role in bringing the British Empire to its knees. This miraculous feat enabled us to finally become a sovereign nation. But it did not happen overnight. And certainly not without tremendous sacrifice, not only by George Washington, but by his ill-clothed, under-fed, and poorly-trained troops. The pages of history paint this dreary picture saying that the soldiers,

> Went hungry because nearby farmers preferred to sell to the British in Philadelphia for hard cash . . . soldiers went half naked because merchants in Boston would not move government clothing off their shelves for anything less than profits ranging from 1000 to 1800 percent. Everywhere in America there was a spirit of profiteering and a habit of graft that made Washington grind his teeth in helpless fury.[7]

Interestingly, the British had hard currency. Apparently it was sought after and deemed quite valuable by the farmers and merchants who tried to acquire it. Why did the paper currency, issued from the thirteen colonies, play second string to the coins used by the British?

Valley Forge

During the winter of 1777, conditions worsened. Washington and his men hunkered down in the infamous hills of Valley Forge. Thousands, from the gnawing pain of hunger, threw in the towel. They crossed the lines to join the British so that they could obtain food. Many of those valiant men that stayed loyal to Washington were afraid to fall asleep at night, fearing that death would overtake them before morning. This scenario unfortunately played out hundreds of times during that infamous winter.

The problem facing Washington, not only that winter in Valley Forge but also all throughout the Revolutionary War, was a recurring one. He was unable to replenish his troops as it became necessary to add to their ranks. His pleading with Congress for reinforcements was met many times with silence, which of course meant to Washington that no additional troops would be reporting any time soon. This frequent lack of response from congress was not to show disrespect toward Washington. Our founding fathers held him and the determination that he possessed with the highest regards. Many of these men knew him personally and were pained knowing he was out there going it alone in many respects. The Constitution was only a dream at that time; many battles were yet to be fought and many sacrifices yet to be offered, all of which would be carried out over the next ten years. The above scenario had our founding fathers in a predicament. There was no law yet to force the thirteen colonies to send the extra men that were desperately needed to Washington's aid.

In my office hangs a picture of George Washington entitled "The Prayer at Valley Forge." He is beside his horse, kneeling in the snow, with his head bowed in solemn reverence. To many people it is a memorable scene, and one that stokes feelings of gratitude. This depiction leaves little doubt that he is indeed praying to our Father in Heaven. Admittedly, there is no way of knowing the thoughts of Washington's heart during that time of great tribulation. At the very least he must have had feelings of helplessness, anxiety, and fear. Gratefully, humility was embedded in his nature. He must have tried countless times to suppress his feelings of self-doubt as he saw death blankly staring back at him, through the eyes of his ragged soldiers. It is a great probability that before he came to seek the Lord in prayer, having contemplated all of the future battles which must be waged and won, he concluded that the calling laid before him was more than he could bear. While these thoughts raged in his heart and mind, Washington excused himself from his men and sought refuge in a private stand of trees. Once there, after assuring that he was alone, he knelt down in the snow and with unwavering faith offered up his petition for divine guidance and intervention in behalf of himself, his men, and his future country. Few men in history would have deserved the title, "Father of our country" more than he. His love of country, God, and fellowmen was proved daily by his words, action and his unselfish manner. How truly blessed and fortunate we are to have men like George Washington and our numerous other founding fathers who laid so much on the line in order that we may enjoy all of the freedoms that we have today.

Thomas Jefferson was another positive contributor in helping our young nation secure its inalienable rights. He had the wisdom and maturity of men twice his age. Merely in his mid-thirties, he not only stood shoulder to shoulder with many of the founding fathers while discussing the ins and outs of the Declaration of Independence, but he was primarily responsible for much of the wording and content of the text. Jefferson was on a committee, as was Benjamin Franklin, to create a first draft of the Declaration. Some of the founding fathers wanted Jefferson to author this draft. He declined, and they tried again to persuade him. Finally he relented and said, "Well, if you are decided, I will do as well as I can."[8]

Moses Receives Counsel

Jefferson had previously spent many years studying to pass the Virginia Bar exam and was also fluent in five different languages. He was a Christian with deep religious beliefs and had vast knowledge pertaining to the old and New Testament. In 1779 his credentials were apparently more than sufficient because he was elected governor of his home state Virginia at the age of thirty-six. Five years later in 1784 he was chosen to be a foreign minister to France. This is where he was while our founding fathers, in the Continental Congress, were debating and framing out our Constitution. This assignment did not stop him from lending continual support and invaluable input concerning the laws, freedoms, and principles he had discovered through studying the Law of Moses. It is apparent that our founding fathers not only recognized the wisdom and value of the Law of Moses, but also of the Old Testament. Concurring with the truths discovered within the Law of Moses, they inscribed the message found in Leviticus 25:10 onto the now-famous Liberty Bell: "Proclaim liberty throughout all the land unto all the inhabitants thereof."

Jefferson recognized the eternal truths that were found in the Law of Moses. Through the help of his father-in-law Jethro, Moses was able to structure a government where appointed men oversaw the general well-being of those under them. This was in sharp contrast to the Hebrew Israelites who were used to living under and taking direct orders from a totalitarian regime. Moses, with all of his talents and faith, was only a man. Knowing this, Jethro stepped in and offered his wise and loving counsel. He listened as Moses explained to him how the people would come with their problems, arguments, and sorrows, and how they expected him to be their judge, jury, and executioner concerning their daily strife. At this point, Moses undoubtedly wore many hats among the millions of Israelites camped in the desert. Moses was over eighty years old and it would not be hard to imagine that as Jethro listened to him and saw the exhaustion in his son-in-law's face, he not only gave him a blessing of comfort and strength, but also some much needed counsel: "The thing that thou doest is not good. Thou wilt surely wear away, both thou, and this people that is with thee: for this thing is too heavy for thee; thou art not able to perform it thyself alone" (Exodus 18:17–18).

Jethro had witnessed firsthand the circumstances surrounding Moses and was warning him that trying to serve all the children of Israel without any help was not a prudent idea—eventually he would wear away if he continued doing it.

Moses was probably elated upon the visit from his father-in-law. He had spent forty years with Jethro, and other members of his extended family, studying the Gospel and learning those things that would help prepare him for his future calling in life. Although Jethro was certainly a spiritual giant in his own right, Moses may have been more grateful for his insight and counsel on how to run a successful government. Once this information was passed from Jethro to Moses, he immediately began to take action. He records his actions in Deuteronomy 1:13: "Take you wise men, and understanding, and known among your tribes, and I will make them rulers over you."

Moses had exhorted his people to seek out the wise among them, and those that they trusted and knew to be men of integrity, in order that they may be governed by them. With this new approach to governing, there were now many men who represented and served the people, as opposed to Moses having all the responsibilities on his shoulders alone. Moses further explained his inspired system of government in Deuteronomy 1:15: "So I took the chief of your tribes, wise men, and known, and made them heads over you, captains over thousands, and captains over hundreds, and captains over fifties, and captains over tens, and officers among your tribes."

This must have been a great relief to Moses now that he had many capable men in which to help him serve. Moses was still their leader, and although he may not have been able to go on a much-needed vacation, he certainly must have been more at peace. This newly-implemented style of government would lift his spirits, thus enabling him to put all of his energy and focus into solving the more immediate and complex problems that arose from such a large group of people. Exodus 18:26 reads, "The hard cases they brought to Moses, but every small matter they judged themselves."

We do not have the room here in this book to review all of the details concerning the different principles and truths that were available to the Israelites through honoring the Law of Moses. Like many of the examples found in sacred scripture, we can track the rise and fall of civilizations according to how they observed and kept the laws given to them by God.

Keeping the Commandments

As Jefferson continued through the pages of the Old Testament he discovered that the Israelites, when they strived to keep the Law of Moses and adhere to its principles, were successful and had the Lord's blessings showered upon them.

Jefferson felt that there was no better reference, currently or in the past, that could rival the blueprint of government, which was found in the history of the Israelites. He understood that truth is an eternal principle and if we could incorporate these truths, we would stand just as good a chance as our ancient ancestors in securing freedom, prosperity, and happiness. As a matter of fact, Thomas Jefferson believed that the principles and truths practiced by the Israelites were "The wisest and most perfect ever yet devised by the wit of man."[9]

Moses and the children of Israel were held in such high esteem that Jefferson, along with Benjamin Franklin, honored their history in an additional way. The two of them decided to depict the Israelites on the front of the official seal of the United States. Obviously these two men feared God more than man. Jefferson's proposal was to have, "The children of Israel in the wilderness, led by a cloud by day, and a pillar of fire by night."[10]

Benjamin Franklin's vision of what the future seal should have on it was similar. He wanted to show:

> Moses standing on the shore, and extending his hand over the sea, thereby causing the same to overwhelm Pharaoh who is sitting in an open chariot, a crown on his head and a sword is his hand. Rays from a pillar of fire in the clouds reaching to Moses, to express that he acts by command of the Deity.[11]

How Far Have We Drifted?

Sadly, neither one of these renderings were ever accepted by Congress. They chose the image that currently graces our seal: an eagle holding arrows in one of its talons and a branch from an olive tree in the other. The irony is that today, in some schools, they no longer say the pledge of allegiance on a daily basis because it mentions God. There are people among us who are using all of the power and influence that they possess to remove public displays of the Ten Commandments. These people and others like them certainly contrast those who tried to put the very image of Moses on a government-sponsored idea.

We have certainly drifted away from many of the eternal truths and inspired principles that our founding fathers had intended. One can only wonder what these men would think if they saw our society today. They would certainly recognize that the role of government has ballooned well beyond its original scope. Government was created by and for the benefit of the people. It is we the people that give our government its power to protect us from foreign enemies and ensure our life and liberty in order to pursue happiness. Government, or the creature that man created, as President Benson calls it, is not our master. It is just the contrary:

> Since God created man with certain inalienable rights, and man, in turn, created government to help secure and safeguard those rights, it follows that man is superior to the creature which he created. *Man is superior to government and should remain master over it,* not the other way around. Even the nonbeliever can appreciate the logic of this relationship.[12]

49

What would the framers of the Constitution say if they were among us now? Would they agree that our present government has indeed stayed within the bounds set forth in the Constitution and our Bill of Rights? Could they say that we have held firm and maintained all of the principles that they had incorporated in order to benefit all future generations? What if they were able to ask every man and woman in the United States whether the government currently feared the people or whether we the people feared our government? How would we answer?

It was Thomas Jefferson who said, "Our legislators are not sufficiently apprised [sic] of the rightful limits of their powers; that their true office is to declare and enforce only our natural rights and duties, and to take none of them from us."[13]

George Washington, who knew better than most in terms of what government is and what it can eventually become said, "Government is not reason, it is not eloquence—it is force! Like fire, it is a dangerous servant and a fearful master!"[14]

How would he and our other founding fathers respond after witnessing the desecration of our government's unchecked abuses and distortion, of its people-given power? Would they agree with President Benson and refer to today's form of government as a creature? If government's only role is to protect life, liberty, and property, then this creature has grown many new tentacles over the years. One cannot help noticing these unwanted advances into every facet of our lives. Unfortunately our founding fathers, if alive today, would see firsthand how this creature has turned against us. After witnessing the moral decay, how could they conclude anything differently? Many of them have expressed similar beliefs, such as Cicero did when he said, "No people can maintain freedom unless their political institutions are founded upon faith in God and belief in the existence of moral law."[15]

John Adams, one must conclude, was also a highly religious and God-fearing man. He said, "Our Constitution was made only for a moral and religious people. It is wholly inadequate to the government of any other."[16]

If our founding fathers were indeed able to visit us now, would they agree that as a people we have put our faith in God? Some of us would tell them yes. However, our actions would shout louder than our words. They would ask us where the Pledge of Allegiance and the prayers that used to be offered in our schools have gone. They would want to know why we were removing the Ten Commandments from our courthouses. Did we not know, they would wonder, that many of the eternal truths that they had worked so painfully to include were taken from the Ten Commandments?

What about the laws of morality? Are we collectively abiding by such? Perhaps most of the people who are reading this book could answer in the affirmative, but what about the rest of our nation? Numerous books have been written on this subject alone and go into great detail how society as a whole has spiraled down into an immoral abyss with the increase in abortion, same-sex relations, and so forth. We won't list all of the sexual debaucheries that run rampant throughout our nation; suffice it to say that if our founding fathers were among us today, as a nation, they would certainly label many of us as immoral if not amoral.

Incorporating Eternal Truths

Thomas Jefferson, along with others, took many of the existing principles and laws found within the Law of Moses and dovetailed them into a government that would benefit and protect the people. He was also blessed with great foresight and knew, perhaps from studying history, that there would be times when governments would try to exercise unrighteous dominion. In the Declaration of Independence, it says: "Whenever any form of government becomes destructive of these ends, it is the right of the people to alter or to abolish it, and to institute new Government."

The only way to abolish certain negative aspects of government is to get the people involved, because it is the people that run the government and not the other way around. If men were perfect, we would have no need for laws. Men would not fear for their freedoms, or wonder if governments would ultimately abuse their powers. As James Madison pointed out, "If men were angels, no government would be necessary. If angels were to govern men, neither external nor internal controls on government would be necessary."[17]

What were some of the principles that our founding fathers, and Thomas Jefferson in particular, wanted to perpetuate into our ruling body of government? For the purposes within this book, we will list only a few of them here. People's rights for individual property were protected in Moses's time, as well as their lives and liberties. Leaders or representatives of various families were, of course, chosen by the people. At trials, the accused party would have to be proven guilty by his peers.

There was one additional principle that caught the attention of our founding fathers. It was one of the truths that was specifically mandated by the Lord. Jefferson realized that abandoning this one specific principle could entirely undermine the country that they were trying to build. The truth he discovered and later helped attach to our Constitution was the importance of having a monetary system that was fair, honest, and impossible to manipulate. He read the Lord's council and warning in Deuteronomy 25:15, "But thou shalt have a perfect and just weight, a perfect and just measure shalt thou have: that thy days may be lengthened in the land which the Lord thy God giveth thee."

The Lord then says that if men are to engage in anything other than what he has outlined above, it would be "an abomination unto the Lord thy God" (see Deuteronomy 25:16).

This verse refers to the Israelites' monetary system. Remember that at that time they were using gold and silver valued by their weight. Disks or coins had not been developed yet. In order to purchase goods or services, it required a certain measure, or *weight*, of gold. The weight had to be perfect according to the Lord, which meant that it could not be tampered with. Taking a piece of copper and plating it with gold is one example of fraud. The Israelites were also commanded to keep their measures, or scales, perfect and just. If someone secretly recalibrated his scale so that he could cheat others, he would ultimately answer to God.

It was made abundantly clear that if the Israelites wanted to live a long and prosperous life, they had better not manipulate the monetary system that was in place. Whether that manipulation occurred through the form of impure or diluted weights or through rigging the scales, it did not matter. The bottom line was that it had better be honest and fair or these offenders would become abominable in the sight of the Lord.

Throughout the scriptures we are given numerous examples of men who have taken advantage of their brethren. We are taught through these various verses that we are to esteem our brothers as ourselves. We are not to take advantage of one another, either by their words, or as the scripture say, by digging a pit for thy neighbor. The Lord could have just as easily told the Israelites to be honest and left it at that. He did command them, by way of the ten commandments, that they should not steal. The Lord, with his inherent omnipotence, knew that if he left this commandment unexplained it would not be enough to discourage the distortion of the monetary system.

Was it important to the Lord that the Israelites use gold and silver as their store of value and as a medium of exchange? If they had chosen to use copper and brass in place of gold and silver, would that also have been acceptable unto the Lord? Would the Lord have been more pleased if they had used coins to obtain goods and services instead of weighing their precious metals as they did?

The answers to the above questions are not available to us, which leaves us only in a position to speculate. It is my belief that the Lord did not care which metal or metals were used by the children of Israel, or whether they weighed their gold or decided to mint it into coins. What was most important to the Lord was that regardless of what metal they chose, he wanted his children to deal justly with one another, and thus he outlined how this was to be done.

As mentioned above, Thomas Jefferson discovered this eternal truth concerning a fair monetary system located within the pages of the Old Testament. Our founding fathers had witnessed a monetary debacle firsthand over the many years previous to the commencement of the Constitution. They had seen the evils and ill effects that a manipulated and distorted currency could bring. In the next chapter we will go into more detail about how this came about and how it personally affected them and the thirteen colonies. John Adams stated:

> All the perplexities, confusions, and distresses in America arise, not from defects in the Constitution or confederation, not from want of honor or virtue, as much as from downright ignorance of the nature of coin.[18]

Decades later another president, Abraham Lincoln, also advocated this principle. He said there was nothing more imperative in government, than "a sound and uniform currency."[19]

After reading the quotes in this chapter, one can readily assume that our founding fathers would do everything in their power to draft a Constitution that would mandate and honor a sound monetary system.

Studying the Constitution

The reasons that I included a chapter on the Constitution in this book are twofold. The first was to show that the framers of this unprecedented document were undertaken by deeply religious and God-fearing men. We are also trying to discover if these founding fathers not only conducted themselves in a Christian-like manner, but also if they were truly inspired by the Lord. To illustrate his love for God, Benjamin Franklin, the patriarch of this noble group of founding fathers, asked if the convention could be opened by offering a prayer. I wanted to quote parts of his proposal but decided to quote it in its entirety; I found his entire address so moving that I did not want to delete any of his testimony. His proposal states:

> In the beginning of the contest with Britain, when we were sensible of danger, we had daily prayers in this room for divine protection. Our prayers, sir, were heard; and they were graciously answered. All of us who were engaged in the struggle must have observed frequent instances of a superintending Providence in our favor. To that kind Providence we owe this happy opportunity of consulting in peace on the means of establishing our future national felicity. And have we now forgotten that powerful Friend? Or do we imagine that we no longer need [His] assistance?
>
> I have lived, sir, a long time; and the longer I live the more convincing proofs I see of this truth—*that God governs in the affairs of men.* And if a sparrow cannot fall to the ground without His notice, is it probable that an Empire can rise without His aid? We have been assured, sir, in the sacred writings, that "except the Lord build the house, they labour in vain that build it" (Psalm 127:1) [sic]. I firmly believe this; and I also believe that without His concurring aid we shall succeed in this political building no better than the builders of Babel; we shall be divided by our little partial, local interests, our projects will be confounded and we ourselves shall become a reproach and a byword down to future ages. And, what is worse, mankind may hereafter, from this unfortunate instance, despair of establishing government by human wisdom and leave it to chance, war, or conquest.
>
> I, therefore, beg leave to move:
>
> That hereafter prayers, imploring the assistance of Heaven and its blessing on our deliberations, be held in this assembly every morning before we proceed to business.[20]

This outward display of his inner convictions and beliefs is truly inspiring. He reminded his colleagues that in years past while fighting against Britain for their very survival, they had offered up daily prayers seeking protection and intervention on their behalf. They had earlier agreed amongst themselves that many of the outcomes and benefits that they had received were the direct results of God's protective hand. He then asked them if the Lord's help was no longer needed at this critical juncture. He knew that building the government of a free nation without divine help was not possible. He then exhorts the founding fathers to ask for heavenly assistance in the deliberations that they will address.

I would encourage the reader to take a few moments and re-read the words from the oldest, and possibly the wisest and most spiritual, founding father. As you read his words again, consider his gratitude and acknowledgment of the past blessings that came from the power of the Lord. Think for a moment how you would respond to anyone claiming that although our founding fathers may have been God-fearing, Christian men, they were certainly not inspired by God or any heavenly power for that matter. Perhaps this quote by Wilford Woodruff in 1898 would strengthen your current beliefs, enabling you to share your convictions with others:

> Every one of those men that signed the Declaration of Independence, with general Washington, called upon me, as an apostle of the Lord Jesus Christ, in the temple at St. George, two consecutive nights, and demanded at my hands that I should go forth and attend to the ordinances of the house of God for them . . . I told these brethren that it was their duty to go into the temple and labor until they had got endowments for all of them. They did it. Would those spirits have called upon me, as an elder in Israel, to perform that work if they had not been noble spirits before God? They would not.[21]

Here is yet another honorable person, our past prophet Wilford Woodruff, stating that these men were indeed noble spirits working under the guidance of heaven. The very fact that these founding fathers appeared in the temple to Wilford Woodruff, asking for their work to be completed, should solidify our assumption that they were truly inspired by God.

Were These Men Inspired?

This is one question that we have tried to answer: whether our Constitution came together by chance or whether it was purposefully drafted by men that were guided and inspired by the powers of heaven.

It is my belief and conviction that these men were unquestionably directed, guided, and inspired by our Father in Heaven. We have taken a small glimpse into the lives of some of the prominent founding fathers. Some of the trials and hardships that these men had to valiantly endure and ultimately overcome are witnesses that the Lord was indeed at the helm. Many of the founding fathers testified of a divine creator in the above quotes. We read the words from three different prophets of this dispensation testifying of the inspired truths found within our Constitution.

Is there anywhere else that we may turn in order to validate our consensus that the Constitution is laden with eternal truths, and that its formation was created by men inspired by the Lord? Gratefully there is one last and final place from which we may obtain validation to our question. This last source of valuable information resides inside the walls of our own homes and is located within the pages of our sacred scriptures. In D&C 98:5–9 the Lord himself proclaims that:

> The law of the land which is constitutional, supporting that principle of freedom in maintaining rights and privileges, belong to all mankind, and is justifiable before me. Therefore, I the Lord, justify you, and your brethren of my church, in befriending that law which is the constitutional law of the land. And as pertaining to law of man, whatsoever is more or less than this, cometh of evil.

There are volumes of passages throughout the scriptures that illustrate certain types of behavior, attitudes, beliefs, acts of rebellion, and so forth that the Lord frowns upon. Particular verses stating that the Lord is indeed pleased with a certain people or outcome, are definitely more rare. We must unanimously agree that there is no higher authoritative figure, now or in all the pages of history, than that of the Lord. When he says that the Constitution is justifiable before me, that should end all argumentative debates as to whether or not it is full of honorable and truthful principles. The Lord however does not give his stamp of approval and move on to other concerns. We are admonished to embrace and *befriend* the Constitution as well. There is also a warning given to us by the Lord, that evil will come as a result of adding, deleting or manipulating its contents.

The Lord Concurs

Turning to the scriptures again we can see how the Lord's own words solidify our assumptions that our founding fathers were indeed inspired men.

> According to the laws and Constitution of the people, which I have suffered to be established, and should be maintained for the rights

and protection of all flesh, according to just and holy principles. Therefore, it is not right that any man should be in bondage one to another.

And for this purpose have I established the Constitution of this land, by the hands of wise men whom I raised up to this very purpose, and redeemed the land by the shedding of blood. (D&C 101:77, 79–80)

After reading the above words of the Lord, I don't think he needs to elaborate any further on the Constitution. Who among us can doubt after reading the above verses that our founding fathers were not full of integrity and *wisdom*? Who would dispute that these men were not *foreordained* to accomplish the Lord's work here in this land choice above all others? What man could argue sensibly that the Lord did not play an epic role in helping our fathers win the Revolutionary War? What man would dare say that our Constitution was not framed after holy principles? What learned man among us would have the audacity to tell the Lord that we could *take away* certain principles from the Constitution, and still have it be *justifiable* before him?

The Lord has removed all doubt, by making it clear to all those that believe in his words, that our Constitution was based on true principles and carried out by men he raised for that very purpose. This is the answer we have been searching for throughout this chapter. We must be agreeable that the Lord indeed oversaw and presided over the actual framing of the Constitution. We need to collectively believe the Lord, when he says that evil will come, once we add or delete from it. Additionally our conclusions will be void if we can't concur that the Lord is truly omnipotent in all things.

If we have a consensus that our Constitution is full of eternal truths, based upon holy principles that we the people have been requested to honor in exactness, we can then move forward. However, there are two remaining questions that must now be addressed. Why and when did we abandon the practice of using gold and silver coins that was mandated in our Constitution, a sacred document that was orchestrated by the Lord and brought to pass by the hands of wise men?

NOTES

1. Preamble of the U.S. Constitution.

2. John C. Fitzpatrick, ed., *The Writings of George Washington* (Washington: United States Government Printing Office, 1931–44), 29:409.

3. Robert A. Rutland, ed., *The Papers of James Madison*, 10:208.

4. Harry Atwood, *Our Republic*, 62.

5. Joseph Smith, *Teachings of the Prophet Joseph Smith,* compiled by Joseph Fielding Smith, (Salt Lake City: Deseret Book, 1938), 147–48.

6. Ezra Taft Benson, *God, Family, Country: Our Three Great Loyalties* (Salt Lake City: Deseret Book., 1974), 332.

7. Robert Leckie, *The Wars of America*, (New York: HarperCollins, 1968), 1:181.

8. Charles Francis Adams, ed., *The Works of John Adams* (Boston: Little, Brown, 1850), 2:51.

9. Albert Ellery Bergh, ed., *The Writings of Thomas Jefferson* (Washington: Thomas Jefferson Memorial Association, 1907), 1:5.

10. William E. Curtis, *The True Thomas Jefferson* (Philadelphia: J.B. lippincott Company, 1901), 123.

11. Richard S. Patterson and Richardson Dougall, *The Eagle and the Shield: A History of the Great Seal of the United States* (Washington: U.S. Department of State, 1976), 16.

12. Ezra Taft Benson, *An Enemy Hath Done This* (Salt Lake City: Bookcraft, 1992), 129.

13. Thomas Jefferson, To Francis W. Gilmer, June 7, 1816.

14. *The Red Carpet*, 142, quoted in *An Enemy Hath Done This,* 133.

15. Quintus Tullius Cicero, available from http://quotes.liberty-tree.ca/quotes_by/quintus+tullius+cicero.

16. John R. Howe, *The Changing Political Thought of John Adams* (Princeton, NJ: Princeton University Press, 1966), 189.

17. James Madison, "The Federalist No. 51," *Independent Journal*, February 6, 1788.

18. John Adams, *The Works of John Adams,* Charles Francis Adams, ed. (Boston: Little, Brown, 1853) 8:447.

19. Abraham Lincoln, December 26, 1839; *Collected Works,* 1:164.

20. *The Writings of Benjamin Franklin*, Albert Henry Smyth (New York: Haskell House, 1970), 9:600–601.

21. Wilford Woodruff, in Conference Report, Apr. 1898, 89.

Chapter Six

HISTORY IN THE MAKING

A nation of well informed men who have been taught to know and prize the rights which God has given them cannot be enslaved. It is in the region of ignorance that tyranny begins.

—Benjamin Franklin

It was mentioned in the introduction that we are facing economic battles, and that we need to obtain certain information in order to fortify ourselves from impending attacks. Thus far we have studied barter systems, gold as a store of wealth, and why gold was chosen by man thousands of years ago. We have also discovered that there are four different types of money. Commodity and receipt money are two types that we have discussed in some detail.

In this book we have dedicated an entire chapter to our founding fathers, who were responsible for bringing together truthful principles and ideas, many of which came from the laws found within the Old Testament. We have unanimously agreed that these men were guided, directed and inspired by the hand of the Lord. All of us will be forever in their debt for the time, commitment, and service that it took to bring us the rights and freedoms that we still enjoy today.

It was mentioned earlier that a chapter on the Constitution was included for two different reasons. We stated one of those reasons already, which was to prove whether or not the Lord's hand was involved in the creation of this document. The information that this assumption was affirmative has been confirmed in the previous chapter.

The additional reason for including information and background on our Constitution was for a temporal basis. In general terms this book is about money. It is not about how to increase your current holdings, but rather how to protect and preserve your current financial position. You will not find information within the pages of this book, explaining how to seek after treasure, which some refer to as gold and silver. As we continue however, the case will be made that gold and silver will properly arm you against financial destitution. That being said, the Constitution needed to be studied so that we might have a solid foundation in which to build upon.

We will use the Constitution as our compass, in order to determine when and how far we have strayed from the true principles found within it. Obviously the principles that interest us the most concerning this book are the ones that address our monetary system and how they will ensure that we honor the mandate given by the Lord to have honest weights and measures.

Nothing in life ever goes as smoothly as we would like. There are always those unseen events in life that cause us irritation. We would be naïve if we thought that the founding fathers were able to frame out the Constitution without heated arguments or many compromises along the way. What did these men conclude as pertaining to our monetary system? Were these men in a consensus as to what would be allowed and what would not? Did they feel comfortable offering the people a form of currency that was backed by nothing other than faith? Did they want to continue with the system that was already in place, which had been practiced throughout the thirteen colonies? Did they consider using commodity money, the one form that we have recently studied? On a side note, the number one form of commodity money amongst the thirteen colonies before the Constitution was ratified happened to be tobacco.

Various Currencies

Since none of us were in attendance within the continental congress during the summer of 1787, we will need to review the pages of history again in order appreciate their position. One of our founding fathers is on record saying that "This is a favorable moment to shut and bar the door against paper money. The mischiefs of the various experiments which had been made were now fresh in the public mind, and had excited the disgust of all the respectable part of America. . . . Paper money can in no case be necessary. The power may do harm, never good."[1]

A number of these men were so unnerved by the fact that some were actually entertaining the idea of issuing anything but gold and silver as forms of money that they were willing to scrap the whole concept of a Constitution. In order to obtain the same perspective as our founding fathers did concerning money and the abuses of such, we should try to view the surrounding circumstances through their eyes. One way we can do this is to study the success and failures of colonial monetary systems. If we can grasp and get a feel for the colonial era, we can then truly appreciate what our founding fathers were up against, and the challenges that they faced trying to implement a sound financial system. It is important to know what kind of snares and obstacles these men were presented with in order to come to our own conclusions, at a later point in time.

Sometime in the sixteenth century, Spanish silver dollars found their way into the colonies through various routes of trade, and were then used by the colonists. This silver coin was referred to as "pieces of eight" because it represented eight "bits" or pieces of gold, which when combined equaled the value of one Spanish dollar. It was chosen as the coin of choice for its ability to maintain consistent value and purchasing power over hundreds of years. The vast supply of all of these Spanish dollars originated from the colonies throughout Latin America that were currently under Spain's control. The Spanish dollar or "pieces of eight" was not only used throughout the British colonies but throughout the world because of the intrinsic value that it held. The word *dollar* actually originated from another country. The word *thaler* is native to the country of Bohemia, which over time was referred to as a dollar in English terms. This Spanish silver dollar was adopted as the official dollar of the United States for many years.

Initiating Paper Money

The first encounter with paper money originated in Massachusetts during the late 1690s. As the story goes, Massachusetts, on a regular basis, embarked in pillaging raids on their neighbors to the North. These northern neighbors were under the rule of France, and had settled a colony in Quebec, similar to those found south of them. Typically these soldiers from the Massachusetts colony would return with items of great worth and other spoils of war. The government would then in turn sell these ill gotten goods, and with part of the proceeds paying their soldiers' wages. For all parties involved, not counting the Frenchman, it was an easy way to supplement income for the government in Massachusetts. In time they began to reap what they had sewn, and took a severe beating from the French. Now the colonial government in Massachusetts faced a problem similar to what governments the world over would face in the future. This predicament was one in which they had no easy answers to. Where would they get the desperately needed money with which to pay their soldiers for their unsuccessful attempts in plundering their neighbors to the north?

Like most governments that are fiscally irresponsible, they first tried to borrow the money. This avenue was instinctively pursued, but their leads fizzled out one by one, and they soon hit a dead end. They were now staring at angry men demanding to be paid for their services. Unfortunately for them, this colonial government had more liabilities than assets. As we will discover, this is a recurring scenario that will regrettably play out numerous times over the next hundreds of years. We are witnessing yet again, that man will listen to the whisperings of the Devil if he thinks he stands to gain financially. These few men who held the reins of power in this small colony, were tempted to create the money out of nothing, in order to satisfy the outstanding debts in which they owed. We must give these men the benefit of the doubt, hoping that they struggled with this dilemma for an extended amount of time before they succumbed to the temptation of creating money out of nothing.

December 1690 will always be a dark spot in the time line of men. This scar in history was inflicted when this government introduced a pure fiat money system. Fiat money as defined in the dictionary is, "Paper currency, authorized by a government but not based on or convertible into gold or silver."

We can only speculate on the details or in the exact conversations that these men assuredly had one with another, but the outcome speaks for itself. Paper money and its aliases, funny money, and fiat money, embarked on a fateful journey that day back in December of 1690 and has continued traveling, with rare exceptions, for over three hundred years.

This colonialist government knew that these proposed shenanigans had the potential to raise alarms amongst the people. This concept was one in which the people had never even considered, the premise for which it stood was at least agreeably, original. The government was counting on the fact that this scheme was so unique, that the people would be at least willing to give it a shot. To calm their anxiety, they promised the people that not only would this be temporary, but also in fact these paper dollars would be exchangeable for hard gold and silver, once tax revenue was accumulated.

Not surprisingly, over the next two years this government reneged on its pledge, and created a fresh new batch of paper currency. It was unable to spend equal to what it brought in, and as a result, the situation mirrored that of a year previous, when their liabilities exceeded their assets. Many of these newly created paper dollars went unclaimed against gold and silver for decades.

This government was artificially adding currency to the existing money supply within this colony. As we discovered in previous chapters, this mechanism always produces the same results, which is inflation. Inflation acts as a hidden tax and is considered confiscation through the scheme of inflation. Many of the merchants were discovering this firsthand, and for the first time. Understandably, they did not take kindly to the fact that their purchasing power was becoming diminished as more and more paper dollars came online. These merchants got fed up to the point that they began refusing the "funny money" and would only accepted gold and silver coin as payment for goods rendered.

Government began to feel the sting of lost purchasing power, and higher prices as well. They had certain goods and services that they too needed, in order to continue functioning and operating, similar to other businesses. Now the government faced another dilemma. If the people continually refused taking the paper currency as a form of money, it would ultimately be devalued to the point of worthlessness. With a currency that held no value in the eyes of the people, how would the government persuade the colonists to continue using such? If they were unable to convince them that this paper money would be exchangeable in the near future for gold and silver, how would the government find the means in which to pay its bills?

Let's return for a moment to our example of using paper clips as the medium of exchange. If these paper clips had been chosen as a form of money, acceptable for purchasing all goods and services, and had done so for thousands of years, most would resist in giving them up, in exchange for new forms of money. Especially if this new medium of exchange found a way to artificially expand itself and cause prices of assets to rise as a result. Many people would begin to hoard their paper clips as they began to discover this charade, in hopes of protecting and securing what they considered true wealth.

Legal Tender

At this point the government introduced new laws mandating that all paper currency must be used to pay all debts public and private. The colonists now had no other choice but to use, or at least accept, this new funny money. The means in which the government forced the people into accepting paper dollars alongside gold and silver is referred to as legal tender laws. Now the words *legal tender* were stamped across each bill. This process would help ensure confidence in paper money, which was the government's pompous belief. But nothing could be further from the truth. These early colonists put their so-called "faith" into this newly implemented paper currency, only because the penalties were imprisonment or fines, if caught not accepting the new bills for any form of payment. Turning to the dictionary we can find the precise definition of legal tender, "Currency that may be offered in payments of a debt and that a creditor must accept."

If you examine closely our paper dollars today, you will see the inscription stating that the dollar you hold in your hand, is indeed legal tender. Sadly, many people think that this term qualifies this paper dollar legal, as opposed to being counterfeit. The irony surrounding this play on words is that in fact, our dollar bills of today have no more intrinsic value than those found in the late 1690s. Yet according to our government, the words legal tender that are found on all of our dollars, means that we too must accept these paper dollars for all debts public or private, or face imprisonment, fines or both. A question some might ask is, if I wanted to pay my bills to private merchants or even my own government with gold or silver, why is the choice not even available to me here in this land choice above all others?

This is the situation that the early colonists were facing in the late 1690s. As legal tender laws commenced flexing their muscle, people began to store away their coins, knowing that it was the only way to preserve their wealth. Eventually all hard money was driven underground because no one was willing to part with it through daily monetary transactions. Predictably, as word slowly got out that Massachusetts had a format for creating instant revenue and a means by which to make the people accept this fiat money, the idea spread like wildfire through out the other colonies. It was a perfect solution for the bodies of government. By no other means could they produce such windfalls of revenue. Of course for the people of these colonies it was a different story. Inflating the money supply ultimately caused untold hardships as they tried to combat continually rising prices. Here is how one government official put the process of acquiring something for nothing, "Do you think, gentlemen, that I will consent to load my constituents with taxes when we can send to our printer and get a wagon load of money?"[2]

This is a great quote; it sheds light on the mentality of those in charge and the outright abuses to the ancient principle of honest weights and measures.

This shameful process of creating fiat money continued unabated for nearly seventy-five years. Finally, Great Britain, showing a rare display of monetary integrity, halted all fabrication of paper money and demanded the existing supply be exchanged for gold and silver. This was the first time in history that a government abandoned all of its counterfeit money and settled honorably with the people. Unfortunately this scenario has not been repeated in over three hundred years. Daniel Webster had also studied history and was deeply afraid that we as a country would once again repeat past mistakes.

> I have already endeavored to warn the country against irredeemable paper; against the paper of banks which do not pay specie for their own notes; against that miserable, abominable, and fraudulent policy, which attempts to give value to any paper, of any bank, one single moment longer than such paper is redeemable on demand in gold and silver. ... We are in danger of being overwhelmed with irredeemable paper, mere paper, representing not gold nor silver; no, Sir, representing nothing but broken promises, bad faith, bankrupt corporations, cheated creditors, and a ruined people.[3]

You can't accuse Mr. Webster of pulling any punches. His is a no-holds-barred personality, of which we will learn more of later. President Benson certainly would not have to tell this Patriot to "stand up and be counted, no matter what the cost."[4]

The results weren't immediate, but after Great Britain stepped in and put a stop to this government inflicted insanity, things slowly started to change for the better. The colonists who had the foresight to take their coins out of the marketplace and stored them away during this inflationary process were now able to once again use these coins to purchase goods and services. The most beneficial aspect of this transition however, was that over the course of time the marketplace readjusted itself without any government intervention, and prices came back down to pre inflationary levels. As a matter of fact, from this point forward all the way to the beginnings of the Revolutionary War, these early colonists experienced unprecedented prosperity. Giving us further proof that when men honor God's laws, and in this particular case, just weights and measures, he will keep his part of the agreement that: "Inasmuch as ye shall keep my commandments ye shall prosper in the land" (2 Nephi 1:20).

Insufficient Funds for the Revolutionary War

We go forward now to the year 1775, a little more then a decade away from creating the Constitution. This was the year in which the Revolutionary War officially commenced. The Continental Congress was facing that same old song and dance, which was how to obtain more money in order to pay their ever-increasing liabilities? One option was taxing the people outright; understandably there have been few citizens through history that have wholeheartedly endorsed that proposal. Nor has it ever been popular with the politicians, raising taxes was the quickest way to be shown the door by their constituents. Congress's next step shouldn't surprise you when we discover that they decided to fire up the printing presses and create funny money out of thin air—or more politically correct, "fiat money."

History is beginning to sound like a broken record playing over and over again. By now we assuredly know what will take place next concerning the colonists' economy and how it affects them individually. Unfortunately these facts bear repeating.

If you were a merchant who sold horse saddles in colonial times, and prices on the goods and services that you needed in order to sustain life were increasing monthly, what would you do? Most merchants had three options. Raise the prices on your saddles for sale, demand that your customers pay you in only gold and silver coins, cut back on all unnecessary expenditures or implement all of the above.

Those colonists that were able to correctly interpret the writing on the wall no longer allowed their own coins to circulate. They stored them in dresser drawers, under mattresses, and so forth, hoping to preserve what they considered to be true money. Any time a form of money is artificially inflated, it diminishes the purchasing power of all previously created money, which over time becomes worth less and less and ultimately, worthless. If you are wondering if the dollar bills we hold in our pockets today are becoming worth less and less, we will soon uncover the information needed to correctly answer that.

These men of government, which held the power and influence to create fiat money, were now faced with another dilemma. If the people were reluctant in accepting this new paper money, for reasons discussed above, how would they obtain the needed funds to fight the war? Raising taxes was out of the question, and unless the people continued to accept this new currency, Congress would have no means in which to purchase military supplies. To make matters worse, a large percentage of the colonists were still loyal to England. Some of these loyalists related to England the mechanism in which the American colonies were creating money out of thin air. The British used this information and began counterfeiting continental dollars, which they shipped over here to purchase supplies for their own soldiers, those same soldiers that Washington's rag tag army was fighting against.

This was another ingredient added to the brew of distorted and manipulated currencies, providing unnecessary fuel to an already accelerating and dizzying pace of inflation. Congress needed to do something in a hurry. Disdain was rising among the colonists, gold and silver coins were disappearing into various private hiding places, and stabilized prices were nowhere on the horizon. During this point in history, the infamous legal tender laws were again set in motion. Now once again, colonists were facing the same mandates that their earlier relatives had to endure, some seventy-five years previous. They no longer had a choice in which form of money they could accept, in private or public. They could continue to use gold and silver but must also accept paper money when it was presented to purchase goods and services. Like decades before, the legal tender laws stipulated that those not honoring this new paper money could be imprisoned or fined. In order to discourage so-called hoarding, the following arrogant announcement was made: "If any person shall hereafter be so lost to all virtue and regard for his country as to refuse to accept its notes, such person shall be deemed an enemy of his country."[5]

Many of these early colonists recognized the evil and destitution that accompany fiat money. By riding themselves of paper money in order to side step financial poverty, these citizens were declared as traitors and looked upon as enemies of their own country!

It is believed that in 1775 the money supply inside the thirteen colonies was close to $12 million. At the end of the war there was over $600 million floating around within the economy, which was an increase of nearly 5000 percent. These numbers illustrate how quickly fiat money can be created when there are no laws in place to stop it. Washington knew all too well, that a manipulated money system would inevitably push the cost of all goods and services higher. He explained, "A wagon-load of money will scarcely purchase a wagon-load of provisions."[6]

These were the circumstances surrounding our founding fathers as they began to hammer out a form of government that had the potential to benefit all mankind. These were dark days to be sure. Newfound freedom didn't taste as good, when one had to wonder how much longer he could stay afloat financially. Many merchants had to close their doors for good. And unless your pockets ran deep, it was difficult to compete, as costs for all goods and services fluctuated on a daily basis. The fact that prices were spiraling out of control, but daily wages were only moving upward at a snail's pace, did not inspire tranquility amongst the colonists. Washington, again commenting about worsening conditions around him, said, "we are fast approaching into anarchy."[7]

Honorable Men Speak Out

George Mason, another honorable man venting his disdain for paper money to George Washington, wrote, "They may pass a law to issue paper money, but twenty laws will not make the people receive it. Paper money is founded upon fraud and knavery."[8]

The insidious scheme of fiat money obviously got Thomas Paine's blood to boil; he thought that, "The punishment of a member who should move for such a law, ought to be death"[9]

These words are the thoughts and feelings from the men who were trying to implement not only an honorable form of government, but also an economy that reflected the principles found in the Bible, particularly those of honest weights and measures.

Alexander Hamilton's disgust for paper money is clearly visible in this next quote. It would be safe to think that he pounded the table with his fist after delivering this lecture,

> To emit an unfunded paper as the sign of value ought not to continue a formal part of the Constitution, nor ever hereafter to be employed, being, in its nature, repugnant with abuses and liable to be made the engine of imposition and fraud![10]

Fortunately, these views were held by most of the delegates that attended this Constitutional convention. They were adamant about withholding power from the states and particularly the highest government of the land, the federal government, to print up fiat money or bills of credit ever again. The founding fathers debated back and forth in order to agree upon the precise language that would be used to describe what powers would and would not be granted concerning our future monetary system.

After all of the dust settled, our founding fathers concurred with each other, not only in their abhorrent distaste for fiat money, but a consensus was also reached concerning the exact language to be perpetuated to all future generations.

Gold and Silver Coin

Found within the Constitution of the United States, in Article I section 8, we can find what that exact language was:

> The congress shall have power . . . to coin money, regulate the value thereof, and of foreign coin, and fix the standard of weights and measures . . . and to provide for the punishment of counterfeiting the securities and current coin of the United States.

We also know what Congress cannot do, because of the binding powers that are set forth in the Constitution: "No state shall coin money, emit bills of credit, make anything but gold and silver coin a tender in payment of debts."

Could these words have been more simplistic? Our government was not given any authority to print money, only to coin it. The process involved in coining, is accomplished by simply taking a piece of gold or silver and stamping these pieces of metal with insignias and predetermined measured values. Creating IOUs or bills of credit would not be tolerated for a moment. The wording could not be more precise, no state shall emit bills of credit. A bill of credit is a promise to repay the holder sometime in the future, and otherwise known as an IOU. When these bills of credit are not backed by precious metals they are considered fiat money. By studying monetary history it becomes easy to discern the animosity that these men held toward currency that was not backed by silver or gold. There was also a clause concerning counterfeiting. Those that were caught doing such would be swiftly punished. Who should be punished today, considering our bills are not backed by gold or silver, which as we know constitutes true fiat money?

The delegates took this issue one step further when they said the states could only accept, gold and silver as payments for debt. This was one more way in which to discourage fiat money from being created. The states were told in no uncertain terms that they could not receive this form of money from the people.

Through studying early American history, it has become unquestionably clear as to the intent of our founding fathers concerning all facets of future monetary creation and valuation. There is no question that these men wanted to destroy the creature of fiat money, and did so by restricting all levels of government from ever resurrecting bills of credit.

It is also interesting to note how Joseph Smith, our first prophet of this dispensation and first presiding prophet since the Constitution was ratified, felt about paper money. He had previously expressed that many of the best banks around were staring at insolvency. Our prophet also mentioned that he had examined the Constitution concerning this subject, which led him to conclude, "I think it much safer to go upon the hard money system altogether."[11]

Obviously when he refers to a hard money system, he is implying that using gold and silver coins do not involve the risks and financial turmoil that using non backed paper currency can bring.

The Coinage Act

Moving through history we come to the year 1792. This date is when Congress passed "The Coinage Act." This act took the value of gold and silver and set them to a ratio of 1 to 15 respectively. At this same time the government extended power to mint gold coins called "Eagles" and set their value at $10. One gold Eagle was now worth the equivalent of fifteen silver coins. We discussed in previous chapters the different ways in which men could manipulate gold and silver coins. The new Coinage Act included a provision stating that if any persons were caught debasing the money, the penalty would be death. In my research I have not been able to discover when this penalty was lifted. Certainly it must have been repealed, otherwise we would have far fewer men living amongst us today.

The Coinage Act also included another benefit for the people: minting coins for their personal use. For a very small fee, citizens could bring in silver and gold in raw form, along with foreign coins that they held, and the government would convert this into coins for them. This was of course one of the powers that was given to Congress through the Constitution, which was "to coin money."

What happened next in our country's early beginnings should come as no surprise. It had only been a handful of years since the Constitution was ratified, and already prosperity was surfacing in all aspects of life. There were few men who witnessed these positive changes who felt more thankfulness in their heart than George Washington. He wrote to one friend that, "Our country, my dear sir, . . . is fast progressing in its political importance and social happiness."[12]

To another acquaintance he wrote, "The United States enjoys a sense of prosperity and tranquility under the new government that could hardly have been hoped for."[13]

It was a tranquil time to be living in the United States. The war with England was over, and our freedom was ensured. The constant threat of disguised taxation through inflation had been abated. The means in which we would preserve both our physical freedom and our financial freedom were set in place. Griffin describes the following,

> The monetary plan laid down by the Founding Fathers was the product of collective genius. Nowhere in history can one find so many men in one legislative body who understood the fraud inherent in fiat money and the hidden-taxation nature of inflation. There was never such an assembly of scholars and statesmen determined to set a safe course for the nation of their own creation. Literally, they handed us a *treasure map*. All we had to do was follow it to economic security and national prosperity.[14]

The people in general were adhering to all of those truthful principles found in and guaranteed by the Constitution. As a result they were experiencing true prosperity and happiness for the first time within their new country. Regrettably, monetary history quite often parallels many of those lessons found within the Book of Mormon, which is, prosperity is typically followed by disparity.

The First Central Bank

It has been established that according to the Constitution, in no way, shape, or form, is the government to create bills of credit. Unbelievably there were some in Congress who tried to sidestep this mandate. They realized that the government's hands were tied in performing this task, therefore they created an entity that did not have to adhere to the laws set forth in the Constitution.

This preposterous idea was spearheaded by Alexander Hamilton, whose position within the government happened to be Secretary of

Treasury. The ploy was presented to Congress in 1790. Over a year later, and after numerous heated discussions, the unprecedented proposal was passed. What was this insidious proposal? Why was the Congress divided, resulting in a time frame of over a year, in order to resolve and or dispute all concerns? It was the disgraceful approval of resurrecting the creature, the sinister creature of fiat money. These men, led by Hamilton, knew that Congress could not create this paper money, but a private bank could. The Congress could delegate the power and grant a charter to the bank, which in turn could begin printing money. This enabled the government to look directly into the eyes of the people, and claim that they as a government were still abiding by the laws found within the Constitution. And so the first central bank in our history was created, which was appropriately named the First Bank of the United States or FBUS. Fortunately our founding fathers were able to clasp some restraints upon this newly born beast. It was stipulated that this charter would expire after twenty years, thus forcing another vote by congress to renew it. As heated as the debates must have been, this measure ultimately passed for only one reason, to provide a mechanism in which Congress could obtain something for nothing.

By allowing this charter to form a central bank, it was presumed that it would turn around and lend this money, which would not be backed by 100 percent gold or silver, back to the government. This fact was the only motivator to those members of Congress that voted for this proposal. If they were not going to tax the citizens, this was the only alternative. Sadly, Thomas Jefferson and those other honorable men who fought valiantly against all forms of dishonest money, regardless if initiated by government or private institutions, were overruled. Now it was the bankers and those men who held shares in this central bank who dishonored the principle of just weights and measures, although they were not involved in the actual printing of the paper money, Congress was undoubtedly just as guilty, albeit indirectly. Man has been counseled for thousands of years to avoid the very "appearance of evil" (1 Thessalonians 5:22).

Earlier we established the fact that doubling the supply of golf balls overnight in a community, does not translate into a smoother or more efficiently run economy. If Hamilton could have grabbed a hold of this principle, and not have been influenced by his powerful banker friends who assuredly understood that this was a great money making opportunity for them, we may have never commenced this slippery downhill journey, that still continues to this day.

Jefferson and his camp were adamantly against having a central bank. He stated that central banks could deprive the people of their liberty, more so than standing armies. "A private central bank issuing the public currency is a greater menace to the liberties to the people than a standing army."[15]

This of course contrasts with the cheerleaders in Hamilton's corner, which claimed a little debt would not hurt anyone. "A national debt, if it is not excessive, will be to us a national blessing."[16]

How anyone could rationalize that a small dose of debt could be beneficial was certainly a mystery to Jefferson's followers. This quote from Hamilton is similar to that of a first-time drug user trying to convince himself that his first hit will be small and manageable, vigorously denying that it will ever become habit-forming or out of control. Nephi was able to envision this decadent attitude and prophesied:

> And there shall also be many which shall say: Eat, drink, and be merry; nevertheless, fear God—he will justify in committing a little sin; yea, lie a little, take the advantage of one because of his words, dig a pit for thy neighbor; there is no harm in this; and do all these things, for tomorrow we die; and if it so be that we are guilty, God will beat us with a few stripes, and at last we shall be saved in the kingdom of God. (2 Nephi 28:8)

This of course is the modus operandi of a central bank: to lie a little, to take advantage of one by changing the name of the bank, which it does in the future, and in the midterm, commits more than a little sin.

The repetitiveness of history comes full circle once again. Just as assuredly as the stars come out at night, inflation will roll into town after its currency has been artificially inflated. Unfortunately there is no exception to the rule, for every cause there is an effect. The effects as we know were higher prices across the board. Bitterness and resentment are always in abundance when one's purchasing power has become diminished. This was certainly the case, nearly two decades after the twenty-year charter was given for a central bank. Unbelievably, after the outcry from the people and with inflation roaring, there were again spirited and heated debates within Congress concerning the renewal of the charter. One would think that from all of the chaos that resulted from this central bank, it would have gone down in flames when up for renewal. Fortunately, the renewal was defeated by both the house and the senate by a small margin. In fact the victory was attained by only one vote. As we know from personal experience from the last two presidential elections, when one party wins by such a narrow margin, it can cultivate a breeding ground for dissension.

Such was the case concerning the losers of this battle. They, similar to the Lamanites after taking a beating from their rivals the Nephites, went back to their camps, acknowledged that they had lost the battle, but were convinced they could win the war. These bankers and their friends in power now found that their hopes for a renewal were dead, but only in function, for their idea was just as alive as ever. They were just waiting for the precise moment to mount an attack, and it wouldn't be long.

N O T E S

1. James Madison, *The Papers of James Madison*, H. D. Gilpin, ed., 3 vols. (1840), 413–14.

2. See William M. Gouge, *A Short History of Paper Money and Banking in the United States*, Part II (Philadelphia: T.W. Ustick, 1833), 27.

3. Daniel Webster, February 22, 1834; *Works*, 3:541–2.

4. Ezra Taft Benson, *An Enemy Hath Done This* (Salt Lake City: Bookcraft, 1992), 45.

5. F. Tupper Saussy, *The Miracle on Mainstreet* (Sewanee, TN: Spencer Judd, 1980), 12. Also see Anthony Sutton, *The War on Gold*, (Seal Beach, CA: '76 Press, 1977) 47, 48.

6. George Washington, quoted by Albert Bolles, *A Financial History of the United States*, vol. 1, 132.

7. George Washington, quoted by Harry Atwood, *The Constitution Explained*, 4.

8. George Mason, quoted by George Bancroft, *A Plea for the Constitution*, 30.

9. Thomas Paine, Ibid., 43–44.

10. Alexander Hamilton, Ibid., 43–44.

11. Joseph Smith, *Teachings of the Prophet Joseph Smith*, compiled by Joseph Fielding Smith, (Salt Lake City: Deseret Book, 1938), 287.

12. George Washington to LaFayette, former General in the Continental Army. These letters were written in 1790 and 1791, quoted by Atwood, 5–6.

13. George Washington, quoted by Atwood, *The Constitution Explained,* 5–6.

14. G. Edward Griffin, *The Creature from Jekyll Island: A Second Look at the Federal Reserve* (Westlake Village, CA: American Media, 1998), 324.

15. Thomas Jefferson, online, available from http://publiccentralbank. com.

16. Alexander Hamilton, quoted by John H. Makin, *The Global Debt Crisis,* 246.

Chapter Seven

BOOMS, BUSTS, AND BANKS

It is apparent from the whole context of the Constitution as well as a history of the times which gave birth to it, that it was the purpose of the convention to establish a currency consisting of the precious metals. These were adopted by a permanent rule excluding the use of a perishable medium of exchange, such as a certain agricultural commodities recognized by the statutes of some states as tender for debts, or the still more pernicious expedient of paper currency.

—Andrew Jackson

After twenty long years, this mechanism in which the government was able to acquire something for nothing had finally come to a halt. It was a means to an end, some of the delegates reasoned. Where was the harm? They had not taxed the people for the desperately needed funds. Therein laid the fallacy, inflation is always a hidden taxation. What had transpired during those twenty years was unquestionably morally wrong, and the adherence to the honest weights and measures principle was relinquished. President Benson concurs. He mentions that the government fraudulently increases our money supply,

> By spending more than is in the treasury and then merely printing extra money to make up the difference. Technically this is called "deficit spending." *Ethically, it is counterfeiting. Morally it is wrong.*[1]

Fortunately those men who held the power and presided over the counterfeiting scheme were able to label this insidious plot as deficit spending. Otherwise, as we know according to the Coinage Act of 1792, these men would have been put to death!

The first central bank of the United States had become extinct, however there were still plenty of banks throughout the country. These private and state sanctioned banks had learned from a great master the deceitful tricks of fractional banking. They held a fraction of gold and silver in their respective vaults compared to the amount of dollars that they had loaned out, hence the term fractional banking.

Jefferson Retires

Like Mosiah in the Book of Mormon, Thomas Jefferson in his lifetime had "warred a good warfare" (Alma 1:1). After a lifetime of fighting, he finally succumbed to defeat against the battle for honest money. Jefferson states,

> I have ever been the enemy of banks. . . . My zeal against those institutions was so warm and open at the establishment of the bank of the U.S. that I was rated as a Maniac by the tribe of bank-mongers, who were seeking to filch from the public their swindling and barren gains. . . . Shall we build an altar to the old paper money of the revolution, which ruined individuals but saved the republic, and burn on that all the bank charters present and future, and their notes with them? For these are to ruin both republic and individuals. This cannot be done. The Mania is too strong. It has seized by its delusions and corruptions all the members of our governments, general, special, and individual.[2]

These were times of immense melancholy for Jefferson. He was now over seventy years old and would now be retiring to what would later become one of the most famous residences within the United States: Monticello. By his own admission he was referred to as a maniac, and this is the price he paid for standing up and being counted, no matter what the cost. Here was a man of great nobility holding personal integrity and God's blueprint for prosperity, in higher regard than worldly praise and honor of men. Thomas Jefferson knew the difference between right and wrong, black and white, and would not compromise his morals by trying to satisfy his opposition by allowing them to commit just a little sin. He stuck to his guns and was called names because of such. This quote by President Benson certainly did not pertain to men like Jefferson.

Unfortunately, there are to many men like these described below.

> One of our most serious problems is the inferiority complex which people feel when they are not informed and organized. They dare not make a decision on these vital issues. They let other people think for them. They stumble around in the middle of the road to avoid being "controversial" and get hit by traffic going both ways.[3]

Jefferson had done an outstanding job of bringing some of the ancient principles to the awareness of our founding fathers so that they could implement them into our Constitution. He spent decades upholding and fighting those men whose only objective was to make a mockery of those eternal truths. He was a man of superior intellect. With this trait he undoubtedly was able to foresee the approaching train wreck. For within two years of resigning himself to his home at Monticello, the creature was resurrected, and the Second Bank of the United States was granted a twenty-year charter.

The argument to reestablish a central bank within the United States was that a puppet master was needed, in order to orchestrate the ebb and flow of the numerous state and private banks that had manipulated their own currencies during and after the War of 1812. A central bank would restore the confidence among the people and reassure them that all of those smaller banks operating with wild abandon would be reigned in, and forced to comply within an established set of guidelines. This was the argument that those in favor of a new central bank gave to Congress. The very proposal dripped with hypocrisy. It was like the pot calling the kettle black, or having a pack of coyotes run the security detail at a hen house.

Second Bank of the United States

In 1816 the SBUS, or the Second Bank of the United States, was opened for business and given a license to steal, or "charter," for twenty years. The government had come to the rescue yet again; it did not allow free enterprise to work through its natural course. Many of these banks, up until this time, were struggling to stay open. Some actually closed their doors, all as a result of not heeding the principle of just weights and measures.

These banks should have been allowed to sink or swim without the government stepping in and throwing them a buoy, such as a central bank. Obviously those banks that would have ultimately sunk would have done so from the lack of gold needed to back all of their funny money that

81

they had issued. The surviving banks would have known the value and definition of the words honor and integrity, thus never issuing more paper money than what they held in gold. As word would eventually get out, that such and such banks actually redeemed gold on demand for paper currency, people would naturally bank at these financial institutions. Those whose reputations were to the contrary would be out of business, due to the lack of customers. This is what free enterprise is all about. Nowhere in the Constitution does it give congress the power to form central or private banks. Most of the people were discouraged, angry, and confused. They warned, threatened, and pleaded for Congress to step in and do something.

If one had the need to go to their bank and withdraw money for any number of reasons, only to be turned away by an out of business sign, this situation would certainly light the fuse, causing passions to explode. Well, the taxpayer got his wish when the government stepped in and "cleaned house" by granting a charter to the SBUS. Ironically and unbeknownst to the majority of these naïve people, their hidden taxes were once again about to go higher, through the mechanism of inflation.

The war of 1812 had ended victoriously. England had erroneously assumed that by warring against us again and burning down our own White House, that we would once more become their loyal subjects. It was just a couple of years after this that our economy began to boom. It was of course enabled by the participation of the central bank and the loose monetary policies that it, and all of the banks under its direction, had initiated.

The Nations First Real Boom and Bust

It is important to understand why the central bank and all of their pawns wanted the power to create paper money. When the second Bank of the United States, like its predecessor before it, opened its doors for business, it was required to back all of its newly created dollars in gold or silver. This mandate was placed upon it by Congress when the charter was granted.

From the very beginning, the bank began to violate this stipulation. It was ignored for one epic reason: to loan out more money than they actually had sitting in their vaults. They did not loan out money as a hobby or for the better good of the people; they lent it out to make money, lots of money, in the form of interest. Talk about your investment opportunities of a lifetime! Imagine a couple of your buddies getting together and investing a small percentage of your total net worth to open a new business, and assume that all concurred to open a new car dealership. Now picture the windfall of profits that would surely come your way if you were able to fill your lot full of new cars, by merely snapping your fingers. If you did not have to pay for these cars, every single one of them, minus a little bit of overhead, would be pure profit!

And so it was with these bankers. To assume that printing paper money was completely free of charge would be false, however the ink and paper needed to accomplish such were certainly counted as minimum expenses. This was the mechanism in which they used to capture incalculable returns on their investment. It behooved the banks to be liberal in their lending practices, for the more they were able to loan out to people or businesses, the more they were able to collect in interest on their respective loans.

The central bank wasted no time flooding the economy with paper money thru the means of lending. With the war over, things began to heat up. Speculation was running at a hardy pace and many entrepreneurs were headed west in search of adventure and fortune. Economist Murray Rothbard states, "The huge expansion of money and credit impelled a full-scale inflationary boom throughout the country."[4]

Galbraith agreed with this. He said, "In 1816, the postwar boom was full on; there was especially active speculation in western lands. The new Bank joyously participated."[5]

Of course they participated joyously, they were making money hand over fist. It takes two to tango, and the bank could offer financing all day long, but without any borrowers, paper money would just stack up inside the vaults, turning the bankers joy to sorrow.

The financial landscape was beginning to germinate previously sewn seeds, which would harvest America's first "boom-bust" cycle. The boom predictably came about through vast amounts of money chasing too few goods, which is one of the definitions of inflation. The banks were lending money to almost anyone with a pulse. When loaning requirements and credentials were loosened or when loan officers looked the other way, rather than confront an applicants poor, prior credit performance, the nation's money supply would rapidly increase as a result. Thus the old adage of what goes straight up must ultimately come down, was financially beginning to follow suit.

So how does the central bank "cool" down the economy? In what way are they able to attack inflation and begin driving it back downward? Why do they care if inflation begins to spiral out of control? The bank began to raise interest rates on all newly issued loans. They also began to reject those applicants whose past credit performance was not up to snuff. As prices start to escalate out of control, many consumers became locked out of the buying pool. Prices on such things as automobiles or housing become increasingly out of reach, regardless of how much money they are able to borrow from a bank. Ultimately they must be able to repay these loans, and when their appetites for possessions become larger than their paychecks, they miss payments and are foreclosed upon. Banks do not like to foreclose; their residual income in the form of interest disappears every time they do. If the breaks are not applied to inflation, sooner or later the large majority of consumers would be tapped out and unable to supply the banks their coveted interest payments. As a result they began the process of cooling down the economy and applying the "brakes."

> The bank suddenly began to tighten its requirements for new loans and to call in as many of the old loans as possible. This contraction of the money supply was justified to the public then exactly as it is justified today. It was necessary, they said, *to put the brakes on inflation*. The fact that this was the same inflation the Bank had helped to create in the first place, seems to have gone unnoticed.[6]

Another description of what followed from Murray Rothbard, pertaining to the credit tightening,

> The result of the contraction was a massive rash of defaults, bankruptcies of businesses and manufacturers, and liquidation of unsound investments during the boom. There was a vast drop in real estate values and rents and in the prices of freight rates and slaves. Public land sales dropped greatly as a result of the contraction.[7]

This process of flooding the economy by offering easy terms and credit, with money that was not backed by 100 percent gold and silver coins, initiated our country's first "Boom and Bust" cycle. The Bust in any economy unfortunately consists of all the things that were mentioned above, and contrasts sharply with the joyous feelings associated with the Boom.

Andrew Jackson vs. The Creature
The seventh president of the United States was another man known

for his honor and integrity. This advocate for truth was Andrew Jackson. He is the only president in our history that was able to pay off in full the national debt, and he did so in the year 1835. He is also recorded as a hero in history for another reason. Jackson led a successful charge in destroying the Second Bank of the United States. His personal aide, Nicholas Trist, is on record stating that this accomplishment was to be considered, "The crowning glory of [Jackson's] life and the most important service he has ever rendered his country."[8]

The central bank had four years left on its original twenty-year charter. The President of the bank was a man by the name of Nicholas Biddle. He was a staunch enemy of President Jackson, for it was Jackson who made it known to all that he would do everything in his power to snuff out the insidious central bank, which had caused so much grief and thievery among the people. This strong quote from President Jackson should prove his complete disdain for the bank, "You are a den of vipers. I intend to rout you out, and by the Eternal God I will rout you out."[9]

Jackson's first term as president was almost over, and he felt confidant that if he were to run for a second term the people would sustain him again. Biddle felt that if Jackson were to secure a second term as President, his chances of renewing the twenty-year charter for the bank would be slim to none. It was for this reason that Biddle and his associates petitioned Congress to renew the charter four years early. The Bill was petitioned, considered, and then ultimately passed by both the House and the Senate. Biddle considered this a clever move on his part, he felt confident that President Jackson would not veto such a controversial bill such as this during an election year. He was, however, sadly mistaken.

President Jackson did not only veto this bill showing his contempt for the bank, he also put his reelection chances on the line and made abolishing the bank his major platform during his campaign. He told the people all throughout his campaign trail that the people could have, "Bank and no Jackson, or no bank and Jackson!"[10]

Jackson literally gave the people their choice, telling them that if they wanted him as their President, there would be no Bank. His personal conviction of upholding an honest currency outweighed his personal desire to retain the Presidency. This was truly an example of one who stood up and was counted no matter what the cost. Through the eyes of many, what he stood to gain or lose was quite considerable.

He hit the campaign trail full of enthusiasm, his was a message that needed to be delivered to the people. The central bank and all of its deceitfulness needed to be laid out, in laymen's terms so that the people could base their decisions and vote, based on the facts. Jackson feared the unrighteous dominion that was being practiced by the central bank, even more than foreign armies. "Controlling our currency, receiving our public monies, and holding thousands of our citizens in dependence, it would be more formidable and dangerous than a naval and military power of the enemy."[11]

The battle lines were drawn, and Biddle used all of his resources and friends within Congress to paint Jackson as the true enemy. Biddle thought for sure that in the end, his influence was far-reaching enough, that ultimately he could persuade Congress to overrule Jackson's veto. John Randolph from Virginia explained how it appeared to many that the deck of cards was shuffled in Biddle's favor:

> Every man you meet in this House or out of it, with some rare exceptions, which only served to prove the rule, is either a stockholder, president, cashier, clerk or doorkeeper, runner, engraver, paper maker, or mechanic in some other way to a bank.[12]

The election was finally over, and the people had voiced their opinion regarding the bank by reelecting President Jackson. It was a marvelous victory for the president, he was able to capture eighty percent of the vote in the election college. With the people's support behind him, President Jackson was now able to go full speed ahead in his quest to crush, in his own words, "the hydra headed monster."[13]

The president had vetoed the renewal of the Banks charter, but it still legally had four years left in which to manipulate and debase the monetary system. During this battle against the Bank, Jackson attacked by withdrawing all Federal funds from within its grasp. Boldly, the President exclaimed, "I have it chained, I am ready with the screws to draw every tooth and then the stumps."[14]

Clearly he was referring to the monster that represented the central bank and was going to treat it as such, according to his vivid description.

Jackson's nemesis Biddle had just been seriously wounded. He was a man of brilliance who was also blessed with the instincts of a street fighter. Like Jackson, he too was not afraid to make a stand. Biddle of course stood with Satan and all those willing to make a mockery of "just weights and measures." Jackson as we know stood for the eternal truths that are found in our Constitution.

This blow put Biddle down but certainly not out, he was ready to launch a counter attack. His plan was to turn his golden goose in the opposite direction and begin constricting the previous free-flowing spigot of easy terms and credit. This would certainly bring about the same effects and consequences as it did thirteen years prior, when America witnessed its first "boom and bust" cycle. It was Biddle's plan to make Jackson appear as though he was responsible for the upcoming mayhem in the economy. It was after all the President that ordered all of the federal funds to be withdrawn from the central bank. This is the excuse Biddle would give to the media when asked to explain why the sudden turmoil within the banking system. Remini explains:

> Biddle counterattacked. He initiated a general curtailment of loans throughout the entire banking system. . . . It marked the beginning of a bone-crushing struggle between a powerful financier and a determined and equally powerful politician. Biddle understood what he was about. He knew that if he brought enough pressure and agony to the money market, only then could he force the President to restore the deposits.[15]

And in Biddle's own arrogant words we read,

> Nothing but widespread suffering will produce any effect on Congress. . . . Our only safety is in pursuing a steady course of firm restriction—and I have no doubt that such a course will ultimately lead to restoration of the currency and the recharter of the Bank.[16]

These words from Biddle himself, are as equally bold as those remarks from President Jackson concerning what he planned to do against the Monster of paper money. Pompous and bold, Biddle was clearly representing the dark side of man. He was hoping his fellow citizens would become blinded by the subtle craftiness of men. Contrasting harshly were those words and beliefs of President Jackson who was doing all things that were within his power, to bring to light all the hidden things of darkness.

When God-fearing men stand up for that which is right, regardless of which principle they are fighting for, there will unfortunately be some men who will secretly despise and plot against them. Laman and Lemuel are one of many examples that quickly come to mind. Perhaps it was a coincidence when, for the first time in America's history, an assassination was attempted on one of our Presidents. Those who feel that the Constitution was not assembled by men, guided by the Lord himself, may also think it a coincidence that both guns of the assassin misfired, when aimed at President Jackson. It is my belief that it was by the hand of the Lord, that this man of integrity was spared.

The widespread suffering which Biddle proposed to implement, had indeed done just as he had predicted. Fortunately, President Jackson explained to the people the true source from which their financial misery originated. In 1836 the charter finally expired and was put out of business once and for all. Appropriately, Biddle spent the rest of his life defending himself against fraudulent charges committed by the Bank.

Financial Conditions Leading up to the Civil War

The SBUS had been put out of business and the sinister powers which a central bank can dispense became a moot point. This is not to say that those kinds of banking practices did not continue over the next several decades. There were many smaller, private bankers who thought that the philosophies and techniques implemented by the central bank were down right ingenious. As a result, there were several smaller pockets of this type of deception all across the nation. For the most part though, the citizens of our country did not experience the moral and financial devastation that out of control inflation inflicts upon those that are unprepared.

The Civil War was now only a few years away. Financial turmoil once again began to brew within our country, although this time the source of heat was not completely provided by the banks. The underlying motive for the union to succeed was undoubtedly financially driven, consisting of many facets. For example, the South was notoriously known for their ability to grow numerable crops; cotton was their biggest staple and provided untold revenue for the various plantation owners.

The North was home to modern industry and large-scale manufacturing. For decades the two made compatible neighbors: the South would sell agricultural crops to the North, while the North would offer their southern neighbors an array of manufactured goods. Over time, the North apparently began to take an abundance of pride in their workmanship and thought that they deserved higher prices for their products. Within the realms of free enterprise this philosophy is allowable and even encouraged. If the market can bear higher prices, these companies will ultimately pocket more profit. Apparently the South could no longer bear the higher prices for the North's manufactured goods. They began to purchase these items of necessity from other countries, notably England. Even after paying the extra amount required for shipping across the ocean, these acquired goods were still cheaper than purchasing from their northern neighbors.

The owners of these northern manufacturing companies and the bankers that financed them became irritated that the South would have the audacity to shop around for more competitive pricing. They set about to lobby Congress in order that they would impose import duties on all incoming merchandise from other countries. This in turn would make these imported goods far more expensive for the South to purchase, thereby forcing them to purchase goods from the North. Some argued that all the South needed to do to offset the ever-increasing prices for goods from the North, would be to raise their own prices on cotton. Unfortunately for them, all of the railroads that were used to ship their products northward, happened to be owned by corporations that were based up there. Consequently rail fees were continually increased as well.

To make matters worse, England began slowing its orders for cotton in retaliation for having their own goods taxed in the form of a duty. This acted as another kick to the shins for the South, for it was they, not their northern neighbors, that sold cotton.

Some may claim that the above reasons are definitely not the main catalysts involved in bringing about the Civil War. Some would argue that the sole purpose of the war itself was to abolish slavery. This practice of placing one's fellow man into physical bondage was definitely unacceptable through the eyes of God-fearing men, and was morally and ethically wrong as well. However, slavery was not initially the main motivating factor driving the South to break away, nor was it the cause behind the North fighting to maintain a united body.

President Lincoln in his first inaugural address seems to suggest that in the beginning, the separation was not about slavery:

> Apprehension seems to exist among the people of the Southern States that by the ascension of a Republican administration their property and their peace and personal security are to be endangered. . . . I have no purpose, directly or indirectly, to interfere with the institution of slavery in the states where it now exists. I believe I have no lawful right to do so, and I have no inclination to do so.[17]

A few months later the Civil War officially commenced. The year was

1861; President Lincoln again reaffirms his position,

> My paramount object in this struggle is to save the Union, and it is
> *not* either to save or destroy slavery. If I could save the Union without
> freeing any slave, I would do it; and I could save it by freeing *all* the
> slaves, I would do it; and if I could do it by freeing some and leaving
> others alone, I would also do that.[18]

One should not conclude that President Lincoln saw no evil in
slavery, far from it. He is also on record proclaiming his disdain for the
practice of slavery, and personally felt that no man should be subjected by
another through compulsion. Presidents Lincoln was merely letting the
South know that he had no inclination to go to war under the pretense
of slavery.

Greenbacks

It didn't take long before the Civil War was running in high gear. One
mustn't look far, including today's war with Iraq, to appreciate the vast
amounts of money that it takes to wage a war. At this time there were no
amendments to the Constitution that provided a mechanism in which to
tax the people outright. But as we have learned through past and present
history, wars cannot be waged and continued for long without money. If
Congress was unable to secure the funds necessary to continue this battle,
they would be forced to raise the white flag of surrender. However in the
back of many congressmen's minds was the possibility of reuniting once
again, with their old friend fiat money.

Griffin explains the situation facing Congress concerning their
options,

> Previously, the traditional source of funding in time of war had been
> the banks which simply created money under the pretense of loaning
> it. But that method had been severely hampered by the demise of
> the Bank of the United States. The state banks were anxious to step
> into that role; but, by this time, most of them had already defaulted
> in their promise to pay in specie [gold] and were in no position to
> manufacture further money, at least not money which the public
> would be willing to accept.[19]

There are numerous reasons that we have discussed concerning the
motivating factors for fighting the war. Debating which contributing factor
held more weight within Congress and among the people is irrelevant.

The United States was at war with itself, and the power of Congress and that political force resided within the North. In keeping to the theme throughout this book, we are more interested in the financial aspects, and what we may learn from such. Without argument the government needed massive amounts of currency in order to stay afloat financially. When the war first broke out, federal expenditures were close to $66 million per year. Four years later the cash flow needed to pay liabilities was roughly 1.3 billion, a staggering increase to say the least.

After how much debate on whether to print up paper money is unclear, but hopefully there were men within Congress who fought against the distortion and debasing of the currency. Regardless of the number of men who may have stood up and defended the principle of sound money it was not enough, for Congress approved the bill to begin printing. Like their forefathers some two hundred years before, they decided to issue money not backed by gold or silver, true fiat money. They promised, as did those men of power governing Massachusetts years ago, that this would be a one-time deal. It was an *emergency*, otherwise as they proclaimed, they would never contemplate implementing such a horrendous act. Rothbard describes in his book,

> In creating greenbacks in February, Congress resolved that this would be the first and last emergency issue. But printing money is a heady wine, and a second $150 million issue was authorized in July, and still a third $150 million in early 1863. Greenbacks outstanding reached a peak in 1864 of $415.1 million.[20]

These dollars or greenbacks as they were called were printed not by the banks but the U.S. Treasury, and for the first time in our country's history were printed with green ink, hence the nickname, greenbacks.

Not surprisingly, history has repeated itself again. The government gets in a bind financially, so they print their own money. The government promises that this is a one-time only occurrence and is being done under the guise of a full on emergency. The government realizes that in order to make the people accept and use this funny money, laws must be passed dictating such. Going to war without any money obviously does not work, nor does creating fiat money without having the muscle of legal tender laws, making these two unique mechanisms partners in the same crime.

Now the tables had been turned. Instead of the bankers controlling and printing their own paper money, it was the government itself that was doing the creating. These newly issued greenbacks were an irritating thorn in the sides of the banks. How were these smaller, state sanctioned banks going to reap windfalls of profits? Their sacred cash cow, which had produced covetous interest payments, was now being led to a new pasture. This beast of burden to the people was not sent off into retirement, it was unfortunately just grazing in a different environment.

National Banking Act

The bankers were furious; they had to come up with a way in which they could again secure that never-ending stream of recurring interest. In the past when the government needed to borrow funds from private or central banks, they accomplished this by selling them bonds. These bonds were of course considered an IOU and would be paid back at a future date. As we know these banks would create more paper dollars than what their vaults represented in actual gold and silver coins. It was with this funny money that the bonds were purchased from the government by these various banks. Not only did these banks purchase the bonds with newly created money, they also had the nerve to charge our government interest on the loans they provided to them. Now that our government was creating their own money outright, by printing Greenbacks, these banks were hard-pressed to purchase an unlimited amount of bonds as they had become accustom to doing. When a government can print its own money it has no need to borrow from others and as a result can stop selling bonds, thus leaving the bankers in the cold.

A behind-the-scenes-look at the lobbying for new legislation in order to bring about changes favorable to the banks is not necessary. However, in the end, the jousting done on behalf of the banks was successful. The National Banking Act was passed in February 1863. The banks were once again joyous, for the powers granted in this new act were very similar to those given to the old Bank of the United States. There was one major difference this time around. Now there would be numerous national banks, as opposed to one all-powerful central bank.

As the war progressed, the amount of greenbacks that were printed by the U.S. treasury was insufficient to cover all of the growing liabilities. A major part of the national banking act was to begin aggressively selling bonds in order to secure additional financing. Similar to purchasing bonds today, the citizens during the Civil War era were also permitted to purchase government bonds. Many of the investment banking houses acted as underwriters for these bonds and did everything within their power to drum up public support for such. The tactics of one zealous investment banker named Jay Cooke is described by historian Kirkland.

> With characteristic optimism, he [Cooke] flung himself into a bond crusade. He recruited a small army of 2500 subagents among bankers, insurance men, and community leaders and kept them inspired and informed by mail and telegraph. He taught the American people to buy bonds, using lavish advertising in newspapers, broadsides, and posters. God, destiny, duty, courage, patriotism, all were summoned, farmers, mechanics, and capitalists to invest in loans.[21]

We have been discussing financial conditions during the Civil War era and how it affected the northern states and their economy. Little has been mentioned concerning the monetary atmosphere of those that were fighting and lived in the Southern states. As shown above, financial conditions were manipulated and distorted, cultivating a breeding ground for unchecked inflation. Circumstances were even more distraught for the people living in the South. They were not a close-knit, cohesive country with intricate infrastructure and politically organized bodies of government as their neighbors to the North were. Theirs was a sporadic group of states trying to succeed from the whole, their similarities with the North were that neither of them had enough money to fight a war.

Confederate Notes

They had no choice but to succumb to the temptation of creating the most abominable form of money, fiat money. While the North implemented this practice to a degree, but they also issued mass amounts of fractional money, that which is backed by only a fraction of gold or silver. The South did not even possess a fraction of gold; therefore they relied upon 100 percent fiat money. They labeled their newly printed dollars Confederate Notes. When fiat money is used exclusively, there is no better fuel available in which to ignite inflation, causing prices to blast upward at an accelerating pace. After the war had ended, prices in general had increased close to 9000 percent. Like many of the mediums of exchange studied in previous chapters, the Confederate Notes became worth less and less during those years, until ultimately they were completely worthless.

This is a sobering thought to think that one's currency could ultimately be worth nothing more than the paper it is printed upon. How would a 9000 percent price increase affect our daily life? In the past if we could have gone to our favorite restaurant and walked out spending about $40 for a party of two, we would now expect to spend well over $3000 for that same meal using 9000 percent inflation as our guide. Needless to say our desire for dining out would certainly diminish if forced to pay these kinds of prices. Unfortunately, incomes never appreciate as rapidly; inflation is a discriminate taskmaster and prices of goods and services are always the first to be catapulted upward. The South experienced grater price inflation than even their Northern opponents. The citizens of these lower states became financially destitute as the war came to an end. Those that were able to preserve any of their wealth were the ones who had accumulated gold and silver coins before the outbreak of the war.

They had understood as did our founding fathers, and all of the other honorable men that we have quoted, the importance of basing a monetary system strictly on gold and silver. Regrettably there were thousands of people not only in the South, but also in the North, that were virtually left with pennies for every dollar they may have had in savings at the start of the war.

Gold and silver has for thousands of years been a safe and consistent store of value. Let's assume before the Civil War one silver dollar could purchase five gallons of milk. As inflation began to increase, causing the price of milk to triple in terms of paper dollars, the same five gallons of milk would now command three dollars in funny money. However, one could still take this same one-dollar silver coin and purchase the same five gallons of milk. This is accomplished by the fact that real money "silver and gold," as defined in our Constitution, has a greater purchasing power compared to fake, manipulated paper money. So those citizens who had stored their savings mainly in gold and silver were able to maintain their wealth, or another way to look at it is that gold and silver were able to keep pace with inflation. In our example of milk, the price tripled, but it did not take three times the amount of silver to purchase five gallons of milk, it only took three times the amount of paper dollars to acquire it. This is because as more and more funny money was printed, the purchasing power of these dollars declined. If you did not have any gold or silver to use as your medium of exchange, you now had to worry about earning three times your normal income in order to afford goods and services that had risen three fold. Remember the legal tender laws were in place, but they only mandated that by law, you must accept paper money; you could also accept gold and silver coin, which was preferred. The biggest conflict was that you could not refuse paper money for debts, public or private, without risking imprisonment, fines, or both.

Think for a moment about all of your friends and family, and the money that they collectively hold. Think of where most of this wealth is stored—savings accounts, retirement plans, checkbooks, U.S. Bonds, stock market and other financial instruments, all denominated in the form of paper dollars. Now think about this same group of friends and family and the dire circumstances they would find themselves in, if their money became worth less and less over the next four years until it became worthless. This above scenario was certainly not anticipated by any of the citizens during the Civil War, especially those Southerners that ultimately were the bearers of worthless Confederate Notes. This group of people experienced the unimaginable, which was coming to the realization that all of their wealth, which they held in Confederate Notes, would now not even purchase a loaf of bread.

In our trek through history, we are only halfway through the 1800s, and already the boom and bust cycles have become quite repetitive. Is devastating too strong a word to describe the effects of runaway inflation? When you thought of your friends and family while reading the above paragraph, what words came to your mind as you visualized all of their "wealth" gradually becoming worthless over a four year period? Now how would these loved ones purchase new cars? How would they pay to go on vacation? How would they make their mortgage payments? Would they even be able to provide a continual supply of food for their families?

Do you believe that this scenario could repeat itself in today's financial world? Has our paper dollar, which is technically a Federal Reserve Note, lost most of its purchasing power since its inception? I wonder if those citizens that accepted and saw no potential harm in using Confederate Notes thought to themselves, "nothing devastating will fall upon our heads, for we live in a land, choice above all others."

NOTES

1. Ezra Taft Benson, *An Enemy Hath Done This* (Salt Lake City: Bookcraft, 1992), 210.

2. Lester J. Cappon, ed., *The Adams-Jefferson Letters*, Vol. II (New York: Simon and Schuster, 1971), 424.

3. Benson, *An Enemy Hath Done This*, 45.

4. Murray N. Rothbard, *A History of Money and Banking in the United States: The Colonial Era to World War II* (Auburn, AL: Ludwig von Mises Institute, 2002), 88.

5. John Galbraith, *Money: Whence It Came, Where It Went* (Boston: Houghton Mifflin, 1975), *77*

6. G. Edward Griffin, *The Creature from Jekyll Island: A Second Look at the Federal Reserve* (Westlake Village, CA: American Media, 1998), 344.

7. Rothbard, *A History of Money and Banking in the United States,* 89.

8. Nicholas P. Trist in *Final Warning: A History of the New World Order* by David Allen Rivera, available from http://silverbearcafe.com/private/NWO/nwo2.html.

9. Andrew Jackson, quoted by Herman J. Viola, *Andrew Jackson* 1986, 86.

10. Robert Remini, *Andrew Jackson and the Course of American Freedom* (New York: Harper and Row, 1981), 373.

11. Herman E. Krooss, *Documentary History of Banking and Currency in the United States,* 1983, 26–27.

12. *Annals of Congress,* 14 Cong., 1st sess., pp. 1066, 1110ff.

13. Andrew Jackson, online, *Liberty-tree.ca.*

14. Andrew Jackson, quoted by Viola, *Andrew Jackson,* 88.

15. Robert V. Remini, *The Life of Andrew Jackson,* 1984, 265.

16. Robert V. Remini, *Andrew Jackson and the Course of American Democracy,* 1988, 111.

17. Don E. Fehrenbacher, ed., *Abraham Lincoln: Speeches and Writings* (New York: Library of America, 1989), 215.

18. Quoted by Robert L. Polley, ed., *Lincoln: His Words and His World* (Waukesha, WI: Country Beautiful Foundation, 1965), 54.

19. Griffin, *The Creature from Jekyll Island,* 382.

20. Rothbard, *A History of Money and Banking in the United States,* 124.

21. Edward C. Kirkland, *Industry Comes of Age: Business, Labor and Public Policy* (New York: Holt, Rinehart and Winston, 1961), 20.

Chapter Eight

THE GREAT DUCK HUNT

History records that the money changers have used every form of abuse, intrigue, deceit, and violent means possible to maintain their control over governments by controlling the money and its issuance.
                                                                    —James Madison

As we have traversed through history, many concepts, philosophies, and ideas pertaining to money have been presented. Man's various forms of manipulating monetary systems have also been discussed and reviewed. Over the course of just a few chapters we have absorbed a small amount of information on financial history. There are without question volumes of books that have been written and published pertaining to the financial conditions that existed in pre-colonial, Revolutionary War and Civil War times. It is not the intent of this book to document every financial hiccup within certain periods of time, nor to assume that the chronological order in which we have studied could not have been dovetailed with additional facts. It would be nearly impossible and also very lengthy if we dedicated space in this book in order that we might try to apply meaning and extract valuable information from every facet that contributed to financial history. This book is not so much about history, but rather what we can learn from it, and how to prepare ourselves against what the title of this book refers to as the "financial Armageddon."

This quote from President Lincoln accurately describes our quest: "If we could first know *where* we are, and *whither* we are tending, we could

97

then better judge *what* to do, and *how* to do it."[1]

We are striving to expose the craftiness of men in order that we might arm ourselves appropriately against weapons of mass financial destruction. Studying past financial history has shown us the many pros and cons of a sound monetary system. We have seen how various forms of money have become manipulated and how it affects the people within an economy after it has done such. By securing this information into our arsenal, we are now in a position to better judge what to do, and how to do it.

Hopefully some questions have began to surface as we have discovered the Lord's attitude concerning mediums of exchange, and how we have drifted off course from that eternal principle. Our trip into the past has brought us to the end of the Civil War and toward the close of the nineteenth century. Sadly, it has become quite clear that those men throughout history with influence and power, with few exceptions, have debased the monetary systems that the people had entrusted them to preserve. There is another stop in history that must be taken in order to fully understand the consequences that we face concerning today's financial turmoil.

The Federal Reserve

We have previously quoted President Benson where he said, "The root of all evil is money, some say. *But the root of our money evil is government.*"[2]

Let's now pick up the next few sentences that directly follow this last one:

> The very beginning of our troubles can be traced to the day when the federal government overstepped its proper defensive function and began to manipulate the monetary system to accomplish political objectives. The creation of the Federal Reserve Board made it possible for the first time in America for men to arbitrarily change the value of our money.[3]

Why does he say that our monetary system, which has become corrupt or "evil," is the fault of our government? What does it mean that our federal government has overstepped its proper defensive function? What are they supposed to be defending? What is the true definition of the word function? Who is the Federal Reserve System and more importantly what do they do? How is this system able to arbitrarily change the value of our money? We have stumbled upon the word "manipulate" yet again, the words *money*, and *manipulate* are seemingly two peas in the same pod, is it even possible to have the former in an honest form without the latter? Absolutely, all a society would have to do is honor the principle of just weights and measures.

One of the very few powers that was actually granted to our government, found within the Constitution, was not just to coin money but also to "regulate the value thereof . . . and fix the standard of weights and measures, to provide for the punishment of counterfeiting the securities and current coin of the United States."

It appears that President Benson felt that the government was not doing their job in this respect. They were failing to oversee and regulate our monetary system and ensure that it maintained a constant value.

Pulling Back the Curtain

What secretive power is behind the financial curtain of our economy? Who is pushing and pulling the cogs and levers behind the scenes? What entity is secretly hoping that the people never expose, as Dorothy's dog Toto did, their insidious ploy by dragging back the curtains? Knowledge is power, and thus as soon as the curtains were tugged back, Dorothy's knowledge was instantly increased once she discovered who the legendary "Great Oz" actually was. This provided her the power to stand up to the Wizard behind the curtain and tell him that he should be ashamed of himself. If given the chance to face today's wizards, I personally could conjure up a sentence or two that would describe my disdain for the monetary manipulation that has been occurring, and it would be a tad harsher than Dorothy's. Famous automobile manufacturer Henry Ford felt that if the American people discovered how the cogs and levers behind the curtain really worked, they would not be content with derogatory words alone. He said, "It is well that the people of the nation do not understand our banking and monetary system, for if they did, I believe there would be a revolution before tomorrow morning."[4]

His powerful statement reflects the seriousness of today's monetary distortions. He seems to believe that our current monetary debacle, and those bankers creating fiat money behind the curtain, are only looking out for their own best interest, which is acquiring something for nothing at the expense of the taxpayer.

What is the Federal Reserve System and how and where does it derive its absolute power? When asked, many people respond by saying that the Federal Reserve System and our federal government are one and the same.

Others conclude that it is a branch of government similar to the FBI or IRS. Is it true or false that the Federal Reserve controls and oversees our country's monetary system as long as it receives our government's blessing to do such? Do the bankers on the Federal Reserve board sit with their hands tied if the government does not agree or endorse a certain proposal? Can these bankers even propose an idea? Or do any and all proposals first come from the federal government? Interestingly, there are a number of people who claim that the Federal Reserve is no more of a federal entity than the nationwide mail carrier, Federal Express.

We will go into greater detail as we continue, but it is important to understand that the Federal Reserve System is nothing more than a central bank by every imaginable definition. Some naively argue that this is inaccurate from the plain fact that the word "bank" is nowhere embedded in the name.

Our country has had three central banks throughout history. The first rose up in 1782 through the help of Robert Morris; it was called the Bank of North America. In 1791 the second attempt at a central bank developed from the prodding of Alexander Hamilton and was called the First Bank of the United States. Yet again, in 1817 the Second Bank of the United States was formed, though the charter's renewal was denied by the notoriously God-fearing Andrew Jackson. We are aware of the consequences that an inflated and completely fiat-based monetary system can bring to society, and we are also familiar with the arguments that come from those who support implementing central bank policies and ideas.

So the question now is this, do we really need another central bank? The answer is absolutely not; however, it is too late. The Federal Reserve System is the fourth central bank in our country's history. What are the chances that the outcome of inflating our currency will be any different than the three previous attempts at central banking? By the time we finish exploring the Federal Reserve, many will conclude that the three previous central banks were created as a form of tasty appetizers, before serving up the main dish. The Federal Reserve System has now been operating as a central bank longer than all three previous central banks combined. We can use this fact to our advantage because there are close to a hundred years of history and data that we can sift through to acquire information that will help us know what to do and how to do it according to President Lincoln.

Like many of the previous subjects we have studied, there are volumes of books written about the Federal Reserve System. Some books cover only a certain time span or focus on detailed policies that were implemented under various governing boards. The Federal Reserve itself is a source of information for us to use in fortifying ourselves against future financial turmoil. It is not possible to absorb all of the information and infinite details concerning the inner workings of the Federal Reserve within these limited pages. We will, however, discover all of the pertinent facts that will arm us with the knowledge that these bankers have deceitfully and purposely veiled.

Bank Runs

In the early twentieth century, banks with variously different backgrounds, ethics, and protocols were springing up on every available corner. A large portion of these new banks were following the entrepreneurial spirit of men seeking their fortunes in the southern and western states of our country. During this time, there were many private banks scattered throughout the country, but the majority were made up primarily of National banks. These banks had the permission of the federal government to issue their own form of bank notes. They were required to keep a small amount of gold and silver to back these notes, but keeping a one-to-one ratio was not required. As long as the majority of the citizens were comfortable holding these banknotes and did not want to cash out all at once, the banks would prosper. Unfortunately, this scenario did not always play out in favor of the banks. Those bankers who held looser morals then their neighboring banks would start to stretch their reserve ratios between gold held in their vaults and bank notes that they continually lent out in the form of consumer loans. This unscrupulous behavior ultimately led to what is known as a bank run. When word got around that a particular bank may or may not have enough gold to back its issued currency, people literally ran to the bank to exchange paper for gold.

These bank runs and the increasing number of banks popping up all over the southern and in the western states did not please the powerful Wall Street banks. As the country grew and more banks were formed, the American people had many more institutions in which they could bank. This took away potential profits from the long-established and territory-sensitive eastern banks. When banks throughout the country ultimately failed due to their own unethical behavior, a negative shadow was cast on all banks, regardless of whether they were honest or dishonest. If enough banks were to go under due to their own unscrupulous practices, the people might scream for an overhaul in the banking industry, possibly eliminating the covetous stream of interest revenue for all other banks.

This outcry for reform was the last thing these colossal banks wanted to happen. The long-established and powerful banks of the East wanted complete control over every bank in the United States so that they could rein in the loose cannons among their competitors. Their overall goal was to have all banks in the country toe the same line and inch the same distance toward the fire. If all banks worked under the same set of rules and guidelines and had a central bank in which they could turn to in case of disastrous events such as bank runs, they would be fail proof, or close to it. This was their insane reasoning. If the banks did go bankrupt, or close to such, they could then try to blame the economy in general or the government as opposed to pointing fingers at individual banks. What these bankers needed and desperately wanted was to once again establish a central bank within the United States. They did however have something that was just as important: a plan. This plan, if implemented, would usher in their own long sought-after Holy Grail.

This group of men that were primarily responsible for initiating the plan for a central bank was in some ways similar to that group of men who hammered out our Constitution more than 125 years ago. They were intuitive, resourceful, brilliant, and knew the subject at hand thoroughly. Many of these men were born leaders; they were presidents of banks and corporations and men of great political power and influence. What these men proposed would undoubtedly change the lives of thousands of people, just as the plan assembled by their forefathers had done many years before. Of course, these two different groups of men contrasted sharply in at least one way. The first group was led by the hand of the Lord and strived to implement eternal truths into their plan. The latter group was founded on the principles of Satan with no intentions of planning a system that honored the principle of just weights and measures.

Identifying the Players

We have skimmed the surface as to why these bankers were again collaborating in search of a central bank. Let's quickly look at how this plan commenced and discover some of the key details that they wanted to include within this new bank.

Who were some of these men? Were these men responsible for

spearheading the rebirth of the central bank that became the Federal Reserve System through the subtle craftiness of men? If we can discover what they were able to accomplish and under what premise the plan was fashioned, we will be able to confidently conclude that this group of men did indeed try to blind the people.

The list of men is impressive; there were certainly no two-bit politicians hoping to make a name for themselves by riding on the coattails of a few powerful and prominent men. These men were already successful; however, greed tempted this group of activists along with countless others into thinking that they could become larger than life if they could hold the creating and issuing power of the nation's currency. This committee held the famous senator from Rhode Island, Nelson Aldrich, who was one of the most influential men in Washington. He was the Republican whip inside of the Senate and Chairman of the National Monetary commission. Not surprisingly, his son-in-law, John D. Rockefeller Jr., came from one of the richest families in our country's history. Some years later this senator's grandson, Nelson Aldrich Rockefeller, became the Vice President of the United States. Frank Vanderlip was president of the National City Bank of New York, which at that time was one of the largest banks in the country. Paul Warburg, a transplant from Germany, was the brother of Max Warburg, who was the kingpin of the Warburg banking dynasty in Germany. Paul Warburg was the architect of the formal plan that led to the Federal Reserve System; he was well versed pertaining to the intricate details of central banking from his hands-on experience while in Germany. Henry Davidson was a partner of the JP Morgan companies. Abraham Andrew was then the assistant secretary of the U.S. Treasury. There were no slouches on this roster of heavy hitters. These were the five marquee players of the original seven who secretly sought to implement a plan in which to reestablish a central bank.

It would be a fallacy to assume that this elite group of men did not possess infinite knowledge concerning banking and the workings of inner government. These bankers and representatives of banking families were in cahoots with each other to eliminate competition and wanted to create a system wherein they could scratch one another's backs. Interestingly, there was also a government official, Abraham Andrew, in attendance. Why would his presence be necessary if this scheme involved only the banking industry? These men of prestige and influence needed a place where they could collaborate amongst themselves and at the same time be out of public view so as not to raise public alarm over these captains of industry meeting together. Nearly twenty years after this meeting was assembled, *The New York Times* printed on May 3, 1931 that those men representing only the Morgan banking firms were beyond wealthy, that in fact, "One-sixth of the total wealth of the world was represented by members of the Jekyll Island club."[5]

This reference did not include the vast wealth from the Rockefeller Empire or any of the European interests that were also represented at this meeting. It would be safe to assume that combining the net wealth represented directly or indirectly could easily amount to one fourth of the entire wealth in the world. Not a small sum to be spread across only seven dynasties, hence the importance of securing a secluded meeting place in which to resurrect the creature of fiat money.

Jekyll Island or Bust

Their chosen spot of refuge was just off the coast of Georgia. Jekyll Island was a small private resort that was primarily used for the wealthy elite as a place to escape the bitter cold of the Northeast and offered excellent duck and deer hunting as part of the routine recreation. J.P. Morgan was a part owner in this private resort island and, although not in attendance, graciously offered these posh accommodations as a place to hide away and finalize a plan agreeable to everyone that was present.

It was under this guise of hunting that these men took their trip to Jekyll Island. Just in case someone recognized the key members of this group, one of these men boarded the train that would take them to their secret rendezvous with an empty gun case (used to accessorize his hunting motif). In 1910 these men boarded the private railroad car owned by Senator Aldrich that began slowly heading south on a November night, escorted, under the cover of darkness.

> The purpose of this meeting on Jekyll Island was not to hunt ducks. Simply stated, it was to come to an agreement on the structure and operation of a banking cartel. The goal of the cartel, as is true with all of them, was to maximize profits by minimizing competition between members, to make it difficult for new competitors to enter the field, and to utilize the police power of government to enforce the cartel agreement. In more specific terms, the purpose and, indeed, the actual outcome of this meeting was to create the blueprint for the Federal Reserve System.[6]

This group of men not only collaborated with each other in hopes of creating a central bank, but they did it out of public view and behind closed doors. You might be wondering if this is anything more than a conspiracy theory or some form of early twentieth century folklore. We know that the Federal Reserve System currently exists and so there had to be some form of a rough draft hammered out before Congress would approve this Act; but why the secrecy? Maybe there were no secrets; maybe the cloud of haze surrounding these bankers and their meeting is nothing more than a farce. If, however, this meeting did take place off the record, it would reiterate to us the disdain that people held toward large banks at that time that forced this planning session underground. Perhaps if we were to read some documented quotes from those who discovered some of the details of this collaborated plan, then we could decide if this initial meeting was truly fact or fiction.

Secrecy

The founder of *Forbes* magazine, B.C. Forbes, wrote an article in *Leslie's Weekly* a few years after this meeting between the bankers on Jekyll Island:

> Picture a party of the nation's greatest bankers stealing out of New York on a private railroad car under cover of darkness, stealthily heading hundreds of miles South, embarking on a mysterious launch, sneaking on to an island deserted by all but a few servants, living there a full week under such rigid secrecy that the names of not one of them was once mentioned lest the servants learn the identity and disclose to the world this strangest, most secret expedition in the history of American finance.[7]

One would tend to believe that Mr. Forbes, considering the business he was in, financially and editorially, would not exaggerate the circumstances in order to become more popular within certain groups of his peers. Years later in an official biography of Senator Aldrich, completed by Stephen Stephenson, we read:

> In the autumn of 1910, six men [in addition to Aldrich] went out to shoot ducks. That is to say, they told the world that was their purpose. Mr. Warburg, who was of the number, gives an amusing account of his feelings when he boarded a private car in Jersey City, bringing with him all the accoutrements of a duck shooter. The joke was in the

fact that he had never shot a duck in his life and had no intention of shooting any.[8]

These next words are from the architect of this plan, Paul Warburg himself. Nearly twenty years have passed since Warburg attended this meeting, and still it is obvious that this was to be kept secret.

> The results of the conference were entirely confidential. Even the fact there had been a meeting was not permitted to become public. . . . I do not feel free to give a description of this most interesting conference concerning which Senator Aldrich pledged all participants to secrecy.[9]

Sadly this last quote reminded me of a specific verse found in the Book of Mormon where another group of men were bound to secrecy and practiced insidious ploys: "It was the object of all those who belonged to his band to murder, and to rob, and to gain power, and this was their secret plan, and their combination" (Helaman 2:8).

There should be no doubt at this point that the meeting between these men was to be kept secret at all costs. Their very actions before, during, and after their conference define the very word "secret," which is, "to be kept hidden from knowledge or view," according to the dictionary. Their motives were unquestionably to rob, although indirectly, and to gain power. There is no hard evidence to be found anywhere that would suggest that these bankers or those that eventually took their place were ever directly responsible for murder. However, there has not been a single war fought since our country was founded, that did not stem from the root of all evil, which is the love of money. If their plan were executed successfully, these men would be in a position to "Grant unto those who belonged to [their] band that they should be placed in power and authority among the people" (Helaman 2:5).

Could those men who were responsible for bringing about the Federal Reserve System, and those who have overseen and run this central bank ever since, be considered a modern-day chapter of the Gadianton Robbers? These ancient robbers had a "secret plan," as did this group of elite men. Gadianton's men took a secret oath, and Senator Aldrich "pledged all participants to secrecy."[10] These thieves from the Book of Mormon stole directly from the people by the use of force and violence. Modern day bankers are much more refined and sophisticated—picking our pockets indirectly by creating inflation, which is a tax all are compelled to pay.

Sadly, too few of us recognize that a theft has even occurred.

To solidify all that we have discovered and to prove that this meeting not only existed but did so under the cover of darkness, let's read a few words from another one of the men who actually attended that resort as one of the conspirators. Although lengthy, this next quote gives an excellent account of the charade. It was given by Frank Vanderlip, who was the president of the National City Bank of New York. Printed in the *Saturday Evening Post*, dated February 9, 1935, nearly twenty-five years after this meeting occurred, he felt it somewhat safe to discuss it in part:

> Despite my views about the value to society of greater publicity for the affairs of corporations, there was an occasion, near the close of 1910, when I was as secretive—indeed, as furtive—as any conspirator. . . . I do not feel it is any exaggeration to speak of our secret expedition to Jekyll Island as the occasion of the actual conception of what eventually became the Federal Reserve System.
>
> We were told to leave our last names behind us. We were told, further, that we should avoid dining together on the night of our departure. We were instructed to come one at a time and as unobtrusively as possible to the railroad terminal on the New Jersey littoral of the Hudson, where Senator Aldrich's Private car would be in readiness, attached to the rear end of a train. . . .
>
> The servants and train crew may have known the identities of one or two of us, but they did not know all, and it was the names of all printed together, that would have made our mysterious journey significant in Washington, in Wall Street, even in London. Discovery, we knew, simply must not happen, or else all our time and effort would be wasted. If it were to be exposed publicly that our particular group had got together and written a banking bill, that bill would have no chance whatsoever of passage by Congress.[11]

And one more quote from Vanderlip, which states that this outing was intended to be a secret and what it was they were trying to keep in the dark, as explained in his own autobiography, *From Farm Boy to Financier*:

> Our secret expedition to Jekyll Island was the occasion of the actual conception of what eventually became The Federal Reserve System. The essential points of the Aldrich plan were all contained in the Federal Reserve Act as it was passed.[12]

All of these individual quotes pertaining to the details and circumstances surrounding the beginnings of the Federal Reserve System are eye-opening. The men that personally attended this meeting, or those who were given firsthand information years later, have been quoted giving substantial information concerning the proceedings which were carried out on that now infamous island. These men and their overall objectives were no different than those that President Jackson fought against so valiantly and fortunately defeated. Their goal was no different than hundreds of men before them, which was to obtain something for nothing. Regrettably, there was no man with personal courage similar to Jackson's, promising that with the help of God, he would rout these men out. The citizens in general were adamantly against a central bank and everything that it represented. They were fully aware of how a monopoly functioned, and many of them had experienced firsthand the feelings of disbelief and destitution that come after discovering that their local bank has gone out of business. Surely if the banking industry began to lobby Congress, in order that they might blow the breath of life back into a central bank, citizens would become fired up and demand that the government step in and reform the banking industry altogether, delivering just the opposite scenario in which these bankers had originally hoped for.

Creating a Banking Bill

We have studied accounts in which men have recklessly manipulated their monetary systems. As we have learned the different methods that were first experimented with and then ultimately perfected throughout history, emotions such as disbelief, anger, apathy, or thankfulness may have surfaced within you. We have been able to turn the pages of not only this book, but also those of history. Knowing that these monetary distortions were practiced long in the past, and after enough time, these insidious practices would become extinct. This process has become a repetitive theme throughout the last few chapters. We are now at the top of this recurring process, where a central bank is once again beginning to take shape. This time around, however, we cannot claim that valiant and honorable men, such as some of those that we have previously studied, will come charging up on a white horse to save the day. We will not get to the end of this chapter and give a sigh of relief, knowing that once again our nation came to its senses and abolished the despotic central bank. There are still plenty of details to sift through concerning our present day Federal Reserve System, but sadly, after nearly a hundred years this creature is not only still at large, its power and influence is growing stronger each day.

So in Mr. Vanderlip's own words, they were congregating together for the sole purpose of creating a banking bill. This comes as no great surprise to us. After nearly twenty-five years, one of the men in attendance came clean with the true purpose of this get-together, which come to find out, was clearly not to hunt ducks. He also admitted that if the public came to the realization that these men were meeting together, their chances of passing this bill through Congress were nil. We know that these bankers wanted to increase their already vast amounts of wealth and intended to do so not through entrepreneurial spirit or plain old hard work but through charging interest on loans extended to the public, financed by mere sheets of paper injected with green ink.

This was their goal, but how would they accomplish it? What scrutiny must be overcome? Who if anyone would they need to appease? What would be the main points of interest within their plan? What was their plan of attack? Although modern-day bankers dress in silk suits and ties, armed with leather briefcases, the destruction that they wield is no less vicious than if they suited up in body armor and charged with sword and shield. Make no mistake, we are currently in a battle against those who would rob us of our purchasing power. Although their war is staged from Main Street USA instead of on a battlefield in a far-off land, their precision and tactics are no less intimidating. However, theft is theft and a fight is a fight regardless of how calm, cool, and collected the perpetrators may be. Assaulting you with inflation is their modus operandi; dressing in suits and having the government in their pockets helps mask their true intent. Turning to President Benson again, we find that inflation:

> Is a hidden tax which is a deceitful and immoral method of collecting revenue, it is an unfair tax which shifts the heaviest burden of payment on to the shoulders of the thrifty who are attempting to save for the future, and upon the retired who are living on fixed incomes, and it is an irresponsible act which saddles future generations with the payments of our own fantastic debts.[13]

President Benson has continually proved throughout this book his keen insights and complete understanding of the immoral mechanisms involved in distorting and manipulating a monetary system. He has no trouble calling a spade a spade and has definitely taken his own advice by standing up for all things truthful, no matter what the cost.

A central bank must possess certain characteristics and traits. Powers and functions must also be granted to this entity in order to rule and preside with absolute authority. If any of these favorable conditions are missing, private bankers no longer look upon the potential new bank as a coveted cash cow. These men knew exactly what the ultimate benefits would be once a central bank was up and running; however, they had a few objectives that they still needed to hammer out.

These private bankers owned or represented the owners of the largest financial institutions in the country, they were seen by all as the "big dogs," and as such they were very territorial. Like any self-serving king of the hill, they did not like competitors and sought for the power to limit the number of private banks that were springing up all over the country. They wanted to be a banker's banker; lending to the people at large was not enough, they needed to hold the purse strings of all banks. Any bank that needed to borrow money would have to borrow from them, with interest of course. Senator Aldrich, in the July 1914 issue of a magazine that he owned called *The Independent*, was not afraid to say, "Before the passage of this act, the New York bankers could only dominate the reserves of New York. Now we are able to dominate the bank reserves of the entire country."

They thought the money supply in general was inadequate. Convincing Congress that the supply needed to be more elastic would be a major selling point because it would help reduce unnecessary bank runs, which ironically are always a result of unethical banking procedures. Murray Rothbard puts their true complaint in layman's terms,

> Big bankers couched their complaint in terms of "inelasticity." The money supply, they grumbled, wasn't "elastic" enough. In plain English, it couldn't be *increased* fast enough to suit the banks.[14]

If, despite all of their scheming, the wheels did begin to come off, they would need a backup plan in order to save their own assets. This particular part of their plan was every bit as insidious, if not more so, than the method of taxation by inflation. If these bankers ever had to stare at the possibility of this banking concept blowing up in their face, how would they be reimbursed for all of the outstanding interest, which in their distorted view, they were owed? They came up with the novel idea of sticking it to the taxpayer should the bank ever be confronted with a financial meltdown. Up to this point, our country did not have a Federal Income Tax; interestingly, or perhaps coincidentally, this unprecedented tax was passed into law the same year as the Federal Reserve System.

These were some of the sticking points discussed and addressed during their well-deserved hunting retreat. These concerns, if resolved and implemented successfully, would ensure a well-oiled mechanism in which they could indefinitely obtain something for nothing. They felt confident that the plan they had concocted would produce their sought-after results, needless to say they still needed the government's and the people's support in order to pass this charade. These bankers felt reasonably comfortable that they could find the support in Congress to ultimately push this bill through. The people in general had become very agitated with the banks, and who could blame them after experiencing directly or indirectly all of the bankruptcies that had taken place throughout the banking industry?

Cartels

These men were no doubt aware of public opinion toward high-powered Wall Street bankers. To counter this pending obstacle, they implemented a cunning plan of attack. This attack would be carried out with two separate advances. The first, and by far the most powerful and destructive, was to assemble a cartel. What is a cartel? The word conjures up various meanings for people. A typical response for many would be to describe the immoral practices found within a drug cartel. Others who are familiar with OPEC, a group of countries scattered around the world that export large quantities of crude oil, know that this group is also considered a cartel. So is belonging to a cartel necessarily a bad thing? That obviously would depend on a number of different factors. The dictionary defines the word cartel as a combination of independent business organizations formed to regulate production, pricing, and marketing of goods.

The objective of a cartel is primarily to reduce competition within a certain industry, which thereby increases profitability. When a certain trade or industry holds a monopoly over the goods or services that they provide, they are left in a powerful position enabling them to charge higher prices than they normally could, if they operated within a free market. We know without doubt that the bankers and those men representing them wanted to regulate production and would do so by controlling the amount of paper that was printed. Proving our assumption correct, we just read Senator Aldrich's quote that the Federal Reserve could now "dominate the bank reserves of the entire country."[15] With this power there would be no question that they could also control "pricing," which they do by adjusting, in either direction, interest rates—the cost of borrowing money.

But who is the Federal Reserve forming an organization with? There must be at least two parties involved to form any kind of a partnership. Their partner was none other than the United States government. Our government would certainly not throw their hat into this ring unless they stood to benefit in one form or another. Government does not borrow money from itself because it has none to lend. President Benson knew this, and stated so almost forty years ago, "As a nation, we must stop giving away money to foreign nations as though we had it."[16]

What they can do is promise to pay the interest due on the funds that they borrow, indefinitely if necessary. And they have graciously recruited the citizens of our country in helping them repay this interest, never mind the principle, by using their muscle in persuading us to keep current with our taxes. I'll scratch your back if you scratch mine is surely one of their many mottoes. We won't go into detail on how this cartel method works at the moment; we will, however, dig into the relationship that exists between these two completely separate entities.

"The bankers, however, faced a big public-relations problem," says Murray Rothbard in his book, *The Case Against the Fed*. He continues by saying:

> What they wanted was the federal government creating and enforcing a banking cartel by means of a Central Bank. Yet they faced the political climate that was hostile to monopoly and centralization, and favored free competition. They also faced a public opinion hostile to Wall Street and to what they perceptively but inchoately saw as the "money power." The bankers also confronted a nation with a long tradition of opposing Central Banking. How then could they put the Central Bank across?[17]

Again this process has been described as a monopoly. When a central bank receives authorization from Congress to be the only entity that can print money for a country, few scenarios better describe the concept of a monopoly.

The Central Bank is Given a Name

The second advance in this two-pronged attack was to devise a name for this central bank. Naming it "The Hydra headed monster" (as

President Jackson referred to it) or "the creature," as others have called it, would understandably not go over well with the public. We have already discussed the opinions and attitudes of the citizens concerning banking in general, and their negative attitudes toward a centralized banking power. These bankers were walking a fine line; they needed the majority of Congress to support their new plan, which wasn't all that difficult considering what these bankers had to offer them in return. They also had to appease the people, because it was they who sustained those political representatives that they voted into office. If enough voters were able to navigate through all of the smoke and mirrors, they would be in a position to crush this initiative before it ever got started. It was for this primary purpose that these bankers tried to blind the people by creating a name that would not set off alarm bells, thus displaying another prime example of "the craftiness of men" in action.

Read again, the words of Frank Vanderlip who sat in on this secret week-long meeting: "If it were to be exposed publicly that our particular group had got together and written a banking bill, that bill would have no chance whatever of passage by Congress."[18]

What simpler way to disguise a banking bill than to not attach the word "bank" at all? This was an unprecedented approach, for the first three central banks within our country all included the word bank. Decades have passed and men have been tempted once again to obtain something for nothing, achieving such by manipulating the currency and implementing a central bank. This time around, these men deemed it necessary to use deceit to bring about the establishment of a central bank. If there were nothing to hide, why would these bankers not include the word "bank" in its name or title? Their reasoning was that they knew the people would be set against what the bankers considered such a novel and grand idea.

In John Galbraith's book, *Money: Whence it came, where it went,* he relates Senator Aldrich's ideas on this topic, "It was his thought to outflank the opposition by having not one central bank but many. And the word bank would itself be avoided."[19]

It was agreed by those in attendance that this mechanism that would decrease the purchasing power of the money held by the people, but simultaneously increase their own net worth, would not be called the Third Bank of the United States or anything else with the word bank attached to it. It did, however, have to be referred to as some sort of institution. "Mechanism" or " The Great Inflator" were two more options we can be safe in assuming were never considered. The best name for a future central bank would be one in which a name could be used that would instill confidence and appear as though the federal government itself was at the helm. There are no public quotes or notes available in which to shed light on the assumed runners up. In the end, the name that was presented and accepted was "The Federal Reserve System."

These bankers are certainly guilty of many things. By conceiving this name for the new central bank they had once again exercised their subtle craftiness by implementing a title that would deceive the people. They were guilty of the sin of omission because they did not boisterously harp that this bill was being federally sponsored, neither did they proclaim that our very own government was the sole keeper and provider of the Federal Reserve, nor did they specifically say that the federal government and the Federal Reserve were not exactly one and the same. In hindsight, we find irony in the title of our nation's fourth central bank. It is not federally owned or run, nor does it have any reserves as we would define them. In fairness, to say that it has no reserves at all would not be totally true. The dictionary defines the meaning of the word *reserve* as "keeping secure, set aside, kept back for a future use." In the beginning, the Federal Reserve did have some reserves. Unfortunately even at its commencement they were already practicing fractional banking. So yes, they had reserves and originally even promised to redeem their notes for gold. We will discover later how this promise was eventually reneged upon. However, if all of the note holders in the country came knocking at once, there would not be enough gold or "reserves" to back all of the paper money. Appropriately this mechanism is referred to as "fractional reserve banking." So although the word "reserve" implied financial soundness and, to many, may have invoked pictures of a monetary well that would never run dry, in reality it was only a charade.

Another aspect in which these bankers were able to blur the lines of ownership between the privately held central bank and our federal government was the way in which the President of the Federal Reserve Board and the seven governors that sit on this board are chosen.

One of the reasons that people automatically assume that our government and the Federal Reserve, not counting the name itself, are one and the same is from the fact that the U.S. president appoints the president of the Federal Reserve. This power to appoint was granted to him through the Federal Reserve Act. The Federal Reserve was allowed to look like just another department of the government. At any time our government can also dissolve the Federal Reserve, making the government the dominant player in this cartel. After the U.S. president has made his selection, the candidate then addresses Congress before he is finally approved and given the nod to head the Federal Reserve. Twice each year the president of the Federal Reserve board delivers a report to Congress on our country's financial condition and answers specific questions that senators may have. And every now and then he will fire a verbal warning shot whenever financial conditions get out of alignment. Some use the fact that because the president of our country chooses the president of the Federal Reserve System, it therefore implies that they must be part of our government, just like the IRS is. Congress certainly has the power to relieve the president of the Federal Reserve of his duties at any time. Nothing stands in the way of abolishing their central bank either. However, that would be like biting the hand that feeds you; where then would the government go to cover their monetary shortfall each year?

Adding Legitimacy

The final word used in the title for this well thought-out institution is "System." Its neighbors "Federal" and "Reserve" provide illusions of Federal involvement and significant backing of financial assets. The role of the word "System" was to calm people's fears of an all-powerful, centralized banking monopoly, which, from the very beginning, had radiated from the financial districts of New York City. They stated to the public that this new financial institution would disperse its presence throughout the country through various locations, there would be no need to fear a regionally dominant power. The fact that this machine would have branches all over the country was not a hindrance to the bank, for unbeknownst to the public, in the end, all major protocols stemmed from the Federal Reserve Bank of New York anyway.

In order to be taken seriously as a system, this entity needed to have participants. The Banking Act that was passed stipulated that there could be no fewer than eight Federal Reserve banks and the maximum number would be capped at twelve. The cities that made the final cut were New York City, Richmond, Boston, Philadelphia, Cleveland, Chicago, St. Louis, Atlanta, Dallas, Kansas City, San Francisco, and Minneapolis. These cities held the 12 original and present Federal Reserve Banks. Each Federal Reserve Bank became a franchised corporation with shareholders and operates with a board of directors, very similar to how all large corporations conduct business today.

All national and state banks at that time were allowed and encouraged to become members of the Federal Reserve System. These bankers could purchase shares entitling them to future profits that the Federal Reserve would certainly make. Interestingly, there was a clause implemented that also allowed the public to purchase shares. However, there were more than enough bankers willing to invest in the new venture, thus public money was never accepted and never has been to this day.

Before the Federal Reserve Act was passed, the American Bankers Association held their annual meeting in late August of 1913. A. Barton Hepburn called the soon-to-be Federal Reserve System what it really was—a central bank—and predicted that the private bankers in attendance would soon become partners.

> The measure recognizes and adopts the principles of a central bank. Indeed, if it works out as the sponsors of the law hope, it will make all incorporated banks together joint owners of a central dominating power.[20]

We have previously discussed who these insidious "sponsors" are and what measures they are desperately trying to pass. There is no denying that although the three previous central banks in our country's history failed the people miserably, sadly this is what these men wanted to reinstate. We have read many quotes from certain men that have had no problem in referring to this institution as a central bank, yet in public and on paper they were afraid to label it as such, hence the terminology of "federal," "reserve," and "system."

Our Prosperity Will Now Be Free

There are mountains of information concerning the who, why, what, and when pertaining to the Federal Reserve System. Many topics and events encircling the FRS are in some groups considered a form of folklore. There are volumes of books written pertaining to some of the myths and other things that cannot be proven beyond a shadow of a doubt. Many of these other subjects are quite interesting and can easily cause one to raise an eyebrow when trying to determine if the presented information is fact or fiction. However, it is not the purpose of this book to speculate regarding all of the behind the scenes attitudes, thoughts, and motives that brought about the Federal Reserve. We are merely studying our country's financial history in order that we might understand where we were, and where we are now, in order that we may properly prepare for the future.

We have skimmed over the three previous central banks that were erected within our country. These banks always administer the same toxin—taxation through inflation—which President Benson described as "deceitful and immoral."[21] We have now come full circle, and once again our country's financial matters are tended to and overseen by a central bank. In this chapter we have discussed why these private bankers were panting to re-establish a mechanism in which to create something for nothing. We also know how and where their plan came together, who they formed a partnership with, and how they planned to put the people at ease by creating a non-threatening name for the bank.

The overall theme of this book has been whether or not our fellow men have honored the principle of just weights and measures, the consequence of those actions when they have not, and most importantly, how can we protect ourselves from future currency manipulations.

This chapter has undoubtedly left out many details concerning this enormous facet of our financial system. Very little attention was given to the fact that it took over three years from the time of that first meeting on Jekyll Island before the Federal Reserve Act was finally signed in December of 1913. As a matter of fact, this act did not materialize the first time it was presented to Congress and was incidentally named after the senator who owned that posh rail car that whisked those seven men away that November night in 1910. These facts, although interesting, won't alter the course we must take in order to preserve our current financial holdings. In 1913 it was reintroduced under the name of Glass-Owens Bill and almost a year later, on November 16, 1914, the Federal Reserve opened its doors for business.

On a Christmas Eve that will long be remembered, *The New York Times* in 1913 carried the following front-page headline: "WILSON SIGNS THE CURRENCY BILL!" Below this were two more headlines in bold print, "PROSPERITY TO BE FREE" along with "WILL HELP EVERY CLASS." The *Times* also went on to describe how the atmosphere swirling around Wilson as he signed this infamous Bill into law was full of holiday cheer. President Wilson's family and friends, along with members of Congress, stood around him with smiles on their faces, "The Christmas spirit pervaded the gathering," wrote the *The New York Times*.[22]

There was certainly a spirit present at this grandiose occasion—but it was not the Spirit of the Lord. And how could it be? He was witnessing once again that His pearls of wisdom, freely and generously given for the benefit of men, were being cast before swine.

Perhaps President Woodrow Wilson was only putting on a façade when he signed his name on that historic day, using an expensive pen and smiling for the cameras. When he reminisced about the manipulations stemming from the Federal Reserve only three years later in 1916, he somberly said:

> I am a most unhappy man. I have unwittingly ruined my country. A great industrial nation is controlled by its system of credit. Our system of credit is concentrated. The growth of the nation, therefore, and all our activities are in the hands of a few men. We have come to be one of the worst ruled, one of the most completely controlled and dominated governments in the civilized world. No longer a government by free opinion, no longer a government by conviction and a vote of the majority, but a government by the opinion and duress of a small group of dominant men.[23]

We can only imagine what President Wilson would have to say today, some 89 years later, concerning this group of dominant men.

NOTES

1. Abraham Lincoln, June 16, 1858; *Collected Works* 2:461.

2. Ezra Taft Benson, *An Enemy Hath Done This* (Salt Lake City: Bookcraft, 1992), 213.

3. Benson, *An Enemy Hath Done This,* 213–14. See Daniel Webster, March 15, 1837; *Works* 1:362.

4. Henry Ford, Online, *Wikiquote,* available from http://en.wikiquote.org/wiki/Henry_Ford.

5. *The New York Times,* May 3, 1931.

6. G. Edward Griffin, *The Creature from Jekyll Island: A Second Look at the Federal Reserve* (Westlake Village, CA: American Media, 1998), 8.

7. "Men Who Are Makng America," by B.C. Forbes, *Leslie's Weekly,* October 19, 1916, 423.

8. Nathaniel Wright Stephenson, *Nelson W. Aldrich in American Politics* (New York: Scibners, 1930; rpt. New York: Kennikat Press, 1971), 373.

9. Paul Warburg, *The Federal Reserve System: Its Origin and Growth,* vol. 1, (New York: Macmillan, 1930), 58.

10. Paul Warburg, *The Federal Reserve System: Its Origin and Growth,* vol. 1, (New York: Macmillan, 1930), 58.

11. Frank A. Vanderlip, "From Farm Boy to Financier," *The Saturday Evening Post,* Feb. 9, 1933, 25, 70. The identical story was told two years later in Vanderlip's book bearing the same title as the article (New York: D. Appleton-Century Company, 1935), 210–219.

12. Frank A. Vanderlip, *Farm Boy to Financier* (New York: D. Appleton-Century Company, 1935), 210–219.

13. Ezra Taft Benson, *An Enemy Hath Done This* (Salt Lake City: Bookcraft, 1992), 211.

14. Murray N. Rothbard, *The Case Against the Fed* (Auburn, AL: Ludwig von Mises Institute, 1994), 79.

15. Murray N. Rothbard, *The Case Against the Fed* (Auburn, AL: Ludwig von Mises Institute, 1994), 84.

16. Ezra Taft Benson, *An Enemy Hath Done This* (Salt Lake City: Bookcraft, 1992), 219.

17. Murray N. Rothbard, *The Case Against the Fed* (Auburn, AL: Ludwig von Mises Institute, 1994), 84.

18. Frank A. Vanderlip, *Farm Boy to Financier* (New York: D. Appleton-Century Company, 1935), 25, 70.

19. John Galbraith, *Money: Whence It Came, Where It Went* (Boston: Houghton Mifflin, 2001), 122.

20. Kolko, *The Triumph of Conservatism: A Reinterpretation of American History, 1900-1916* (New York: Free Press, 1977), 186.

21. Ezra Taft Benson, *An Enemy Hath Done This* (Salt Lake City: Bookcraft, 1992), 211.

22. *The New York Times,* December 24, 1913.

23. Woodrow Wilson, Online, *Liberty-tree.ca,* available from http://quotes.liberty-tree.ca/quote/woodrow_wilson_quote_51ce.

Chapter Nine

A FINANCIAL STORM BLOWS ASHORE

Truth will ultimately prevail, where there are pains taken to bring it to light.

—George Washington

When hurricane Katrina blew ashore, it inflicted unimaginable heartache and financial despair for thousands of people. We have been told by insurance companies and our government that it will take $100 billion and possibly more to rebuild the many cities that were ravaged by this storm. Even with unlimited funds it will take years before this part of our country is completely put back together again. Hopefully it will be many long years before these cities ever face this kind of destruction again.

About two weeks after this unprecedented storm attacked the states of Mississippi and Louisiana, I was in need of some help with my bank statement. Calling the 800 number on the back of my card, I was put in touch with an overly-friendly woman named Roxanne. After she had professionally taken care of the business at hand, the subject led to that of the hurricane. She relayed to me in great detail how her employer was organizing some of her fellow employees to go down and volunteer their time throughout the gulf region. Roxanne asked me if I would care to make a small donation and related that their company had recently donated a million dollars toward rebuilding efforts. I normally do not chat with customer service representatives over the phone; however, my inquisitive nature concerning financial matters got the best of me when she started to sling around provocative phrases like "one million dollars."

I commended their collective efforts in rolling up their sleeves and pitching in and donating their time and labor. She reminded me that they were one of the nation's largest banks after I commented that donating a million dollars was a pretty hefty contribution. I could sense that she was in no hurry to end our conversation.

Roxanne continued to discuss a few more details that were of no great significance but I found myself actually enjoying the conversation concerning national events. She worked for a prominent commercial bank and just might be one of the few who truly understood money and the significant contributions that her employer brings to our monetary system, I reasoned.

Roxanne and I agreed that between watching the news coverage and listening to leaders from our government the financial implications were going to be absolutely monstrous. Roxanne related a dollar amount to me for the overall reconstruction and contributions for those who were relocated to other parts of the country that was even higher than the $100 billion that I had recently heard. Claiming ignorance, I asked her where in heaven's name would all of the billions of dollars required to rebuild come from? Without missing a beat, she told me that a few days previous, President Bush proclaimed that the government would spend whatever it took to restore the Gulf region to its prior state. I asked her where our government would get its hands on the billions of dollars that would be needed to fulfill that particular promise. I reminded her that we were fighting an expensive war that was also costing billions of dollars each month. Before she could answer, I threw her a leading question and asked if the leaders of our country had unlimited access to a printing press. She kept the conversation light by laughing out loud for a few seconds but then I turned a bit more somber and said, "seriously, Roxanne, where will this money come from?" After about three seconds of silence she informed me that the government has always set aside large amounts of money in special accounts in case emergencies like this one should arise. She did not detect my sarcasm when I said, "it was certainly prudent that our government had the foresight to stash money away for such an unfortunate event."

Pretending not to know the answers, I asked her a couple of more questions concerning banking and money. When I asked "who does the actual printing of paper dollars when the banks need to replenish their supplies?" Roxanne replied that it was the Federal Reserve. I responded that I was pretty sure it was the Bureau of Engraving. She concurred and went on to say that both departments had the authority to print. I did not tell her that her answer was incorrect. Again pretending to be naïve, I told her I was unclear as to why printed on the top of all our currency were the words "Federal Reserve Note" and what exactly is a note? Roxanne was patient with me and explained that since the Federal Reserve literally did the printing, by law their name must be on all of our currency. She added that the word "note" is just another name for dollar. Not wanting to end this conversation on a negative tone, I did not bother to tell her that her explanations would have earned her a failing grade had this been a formal test. Roxanne told me to keep in touch, a send off I'm sure she extends to all of her call-in customers.

There were many other questions that I could've asked Roxanne that night. It was all too obvious that her knowledge concerning the Federal Reserve and who actually creates the money within our economy was very limited. Needless to say, she would be clueless if I had asked her what mechanism has enabled our purchasing power to decline over the last nine decades. Roxanne certainly wasn't to blame; this is a subject that gets very little attention, if any at all, through the media or in our public schools. She may or may not have had the opportunity to expand her knowledge by attending college. Inside most of our schools, studying the intricate details of the Federal Reserve is usually the exception and not the rule. To say that studying the Federal Reserve on college campuses is not done would be a fallacy, because it is no doubt discussed even in the entry-level economics classes. Obviously some professors go into greater detail than others by focusing on the behind the scenes shenanigans, trying to enlighten their students by lifting the fog that surrounds this entity. Some are successful, while others treat the mechanism in which the Federal Reserve System distorts and manipulates our monetary system as a taboo subject. Regrettably, there are even a few that just plain stick their head in the sand. Worst of all are those that take the side of the Federal Reserve, agreeing that our monetary system must be "elastic" in order to be successful, regardless of the destructive consequences that this position always delivers.

Our Greatest Need

Although unfortunate, many of us today know little or nothing at all about the inner workings of banking.

President Benson stated that of all the needs that Americans have at this time, "Our greatest need in America today is to be alerted and informed."[1]

Some may argue that he is not referring to the fact that we need to be informed about the Federal Reserve, implying instead that it is important to stay on our toes and keep informed with government and political matters. Even if this argument is correct in interpreting the true context of his statement, it is obvious that he feels we are inadequately informed. Let's assume for the sake of argument, regardless of the fact that President Benson has been quoted earlier in this book on his feelings toward our monetary system, that he was indeed referring to the lack of our collective political knowledge. If we the people are not informed enough concerning political matters, what do you think the chances are that any of us are truly alerted and informed concerning the Federal Reserve System and how they orchestrate the hidden tax of inflation? Considering that this is never talked about in mainstream media, I would venture to bet that our collective knowledge is, for the most part, grossly inadequate. After finishing this book, conduct your own experiment with your family and friends. See how many of them can answer your questions concerning what we have previously discussed and also those matters of importance that we will shed light on in the pages ahead.

We have been admonished to be alerted and informed, and this topic of study is crucial to our temporal well-being in securing our liberties granted to us within the Constitution. How can any of us ever consider ourselves completely free if we are in perpetual debt to the group of men who stand behind the Federal Reserve? In my optimism, I hope there are many who read this book who can say to themselves that they have followed our prophets' advice and have gotten themselves and their families out of debt. Unfortunately, by simply conducting a straw poll with your family members and close friends, you will see that the majority have a long way to go before they can say that they indeed have little or no debt. A select few may be able to stand and say that they are totally debt-free. However, many of us have done things in reverse order. President Thomas S. Monson explains this reversal of priorities:

Many more people could ride out the storm-tossed waves in their economic lives if they had their year's supply of food and clothing and were debt-free. Today we find that many have followed this council in reverse; they have at least a year supply of debt, and are food-free.[2]

Recurring Formations

As stated in the introduction, we are studying the dusty pages of history in order to better learn our opponent's battle plan. If we had a bird's eye view of a certain battle, we would be in an advantageous position, for our opponent's strategy and advancements would be within our view. If after watching them we discovered that with each advancement, regardless of the outcome, they would regroup and continually attack from the north, we could then fortify and position ourselves accordingly.

What we have learned so far from our bird's eye view of history is that Satan has stubbornly executed the same play over and over throughout man's existence on the earth. The names and faces of his followers have differed throughout the ages, but Satan's generals and captains have carried out his same insidious and destructive orders again and again, consistently lining up with the same formation, slowly grinding out their advancement with continual persuasiveness.

Knowing the devastating effects that the love of money can bring to mankind, Satan does everything in his power to persuade his brothers and sisters to love money more than God—whether it be through a brazen attempt such as promising Cain that through murder, the wealth of his brother Abel's flocks could become instantly his, or by using more subtle forms of craftiness such as shaving the edges of gold coins to increase one's wealth. Theft, either directly or indirectly, is still theft, and both methods are accomplished by taking something that belongs to another.

Miserable Like Unto Himself

While it is true that the tender roots of evil grow aggressively upward, benefiting from the care that only the love of money can provide, our study has focused primarily on one financial debacle. The financial travesty of which we speak is the way in which the just weights and measures principle has been continually trampled by artificially increasing the monetary system, paving the way for inflation, whose alias is really taxation. This process causes differing levels of deprivation among men, which can cause some to commit regrettable acts of pure desperation. And by doing so, Satan hopes that this will lead to one's forfeiture of eternal salvation.

He dwells in a continually desperate and resentful state and will for the eternities because of the choices that he has made. This realization has become a breeding ground for all things unholy and impure, and although incapable of experiencing true happiness, he must achieve some form of twisted satisfaction by trying to ensnare some of us into his realm of misery. "And because he had fallen from heaven, and become miserable forever, he sought also the misery of all mankind . . . that all men might be miserable like unto himself" (2 Nephi 2:18, 27).

This is his only objective, and the prospect of pulling more of his brothers and sisters into that everlasting gulf of misery is his way of seeking long sought-after revenge. No one should even pretend that the only way that men can become miserable like our brother Satan is to become financially destitute. Assaulting us with financial tactics is only one form of combat that he and his soldiers have mastered over the ages. Many people throughout history have scarcely had enough food in which to sustain life for themselves and their families, yet they were able to remain faithful to the Lord by observing his teachings and commandments. However the lure of greed and the concept of something for nothing has a very powerful pull for not only the rich and those blessed with abundance, but also to those who scarcely have the necessities of life. Knowing this vice beforehand has enabled Satan to assemble his infantry and to march with a full speed advance, conquering all those men who proposed, implemented, or benefited once the principle of just weights and measures was abandoned. Thus, Satan was able to kill two birds with one stone. All men that were found guilty of abandoning this eternal principle of truth would be found unclean from violating one of the Lord's eternal laws and have no chance of exaltation unless they followed all of the steps required for repentance. Then there was the group of men who found themselves as innocent victims of taxation through inflation. This group was unable to keep up with the ever-increasing prices resulting from the diminishing purchasing power of their money. Some of these men would lay hold of the ideology that desperate men were allowed to do desperate things, giving them the justification to disregard the second commandment which states, "thou shall not steal." In this scenario, Satan used a tactic that was field ready and had been battle tested numerous times, and by doing so he has been able to enfold many men into his never-ending misery.

Make no mistake: the man who conducts and initiates all of the world's economic and financial turmoil, although hidden behind the curtain, is not, despite the many similarities, the Great Oz. Rather, he is our lost and fallen brother Satan. Knowing who we are fighting is every bit as important as how we fight. By realizing that we are indeed battling against Satan himself instead of the greedy bankers, pushy loan officers, or other powerful banking groups, the fight becomes much more personal, and the motivation in fighting for and restoring the just weights and measures principle is rapidly increased.

Notes

1. Ezra Taft Benson, *An Enemy Hath Done This* (Salt Lake City: Bookcraft, 1992), 90.

2. Thomas S. Monson, "That Noble Gift—Love at Home," *Church News*, 12 May 2001, 7.

Chapter Ten

A Banking Holiday

*Can the liberties of a nation be thought secure when we have removed
their only firm basis, a conviction in the minds of the people that
these liberties are of the gift of God? That they are not to be violated
but with his wrath?*

—Thomas Jefferson

The *New York Times* was certainly doing their part in perpetuating
the myth that prosperity was now inevitable, and not for a select
few but for all citizens. In large lettering their headline read, "WILL
HELP EVERY CLASS." Had they decided to run with something closer
to the truth they may have printed something such as "WILL HELP
ALL CLASSES OF BANKERS" or "BANKERS HIT HOME RUN
WITH BANKING BILL." Closer still would have been "CHRISTMAS
COMES EARLY FOR WALL STREET'S FINANCIAL ELITE." There
is no doubt that the Christmas spirit floated joyously around those present at the signing of this festive event. Christmas had indeed come early
to all who would benefit from this newly-signed bill. These fortunate few
would now be the recipients of a gift that never stopped giving. But what
about those who worked for an honest day's wage? The front-page headline had declared that this bill would help the people in all classes—could
this headline be an oxymoron considering what this bill represented and
stood for? Perhaps it was one more piece of propaganda used in order to
calm and reassure the average citizen that everything was fine and that

our government was at the helm trying to restore order to a chaotic and monopolistic industry.

But under the spotless white clothing of this hybrid wolf, all was not well. How could we assume the contrary when all that we have studied thus far has proven otherwise? Not even two years had transpired when the very man who had signed this bill into law, President Wilson, exclaimed that he had, "Unwittingly ruined [his] country."[1]

While visions of sugarplums danced in many of the people's heads that historic Christmas season, the men who had embarked on a fabricated duck hunt, along with all others who rode this bill's coattails, envisioned all the things that their newfound wealth would buy.

These powerful bankers had finally succeeded in reestablishing a central bank after a lengthy hiatus. Although it had taken nearly four years and a name change before being accepted and approved by Congress, they had set the wheels in motion to ultimately secure the monopoly of printing and issuing all paper currency within the United States. Our government was now obliged to use the Federal Reserve for all of its banking needs and did so from that point forward. Until the banking bill was passed, the government had deposited all of their revenue into the U.S. Treasury, paying its bills by writing checks without paying any bank fees or service charges.

What a marvelous opportunity it would have been to be in attendance at George Washington's farewell address. After many decades of selfless service to our country, he stepped down and retired. Many notable things were mentioned on that day in September of 1796 by this man known as the Father of our Country. In his parting words to his fellow Americans, he exhorted us to cherish public credit as it was pertinent in maintaining our strength and security. He went on to say, "One method of preserving it is, to use it as sparingly as possible . . . avoiding likewise the accumulation of debt . . . not ungenerously throwing upon posterity the burden which we ourselves ought to bear."[2]

Getting off Track

Unfortunately, if President Washington were here with us today he would witness the unimaginable amounts of debt that have indeed been thrown down upon ourselves and our posterity. With a national debt currently over $8 trillion and with obligations to pay Social Security, Medicaid, and so forth, how could he conclude anything different?

This raises a question: through what process did we get ourselves so far off track and so deeply into debt? We know that our government spends more money than they collect through their various forms of revenue. It is also a fact that our Federal Reserve System is more than happy to oblige in lending our government, with interest, all that they desire. However, this is an overly simplistic answer. Certainly there are more pieces to this puzzle, so we must first identify them and then see how they fit together. If we can accomplish this, we will be able to answer how and when the economic wheels of our economy first began to violently shake as it rolled toward its final destination of perpetual debt.

When the Federal Reserve first opened its doors for business in 1914, there were certainly some positive attributes contained in what many businesses today term as a mission statement. However, from day one, things were not as accurate as they first appeared. When the Federal Reserve began to print and issue currency, the words "redeemable in gold" and "payable to the bearer on demand" were found on all paper bills. These statements meant exactly that: the bearer of the paper bill could walk into the bank and exchange or redeem his or her paper money for the equivalent in gold. Did this make the citizens feel safe and secure, enabling them to place their trust with this new creature in disguise? Without question. And why should they not? At any time during business hours they could march in with paper and walk out holding gold.

To the casual observer, all was well once again within the banking sector. There was no longer a centralized and dominating power hub where bankers could congregate and rule with their all-encompassing eye, or so the people thought. True, there were now twelve regional system banks. But in reality nothing had changed at all. For all directional power and critical decision-making was still taken care of from within the Federal Reserve Bank of New York, unbeknownst to the common citizen.

Half-truths

Despite the good feelings that were present during these early years, there was something else that the common man was not privy to. Although they could exchange paper for gold at any time, there was a fly in the ointment. One of the statutes contained within the Federal Reserve Act, was the fact that they did not have to back their newly printed currency with 100 percent gold. This is an example of fractional banking or fractional money, which represents one of the four different kinds of money a society can use. There is only a fraction of gold that backs the outstanding amount of paper dollars that are issued, which sows the seeds for a future economic collapse. This information that the Federal Reserve and our government had was not paraded around with a blow horn informing all those who were willing to listen. Neither is there anywhere on record where these two entities outright lied by saying that all of the newly created dollars were in fact backed 100 percent by gold, thus allowing the people to come to their own conclusions that there was now enough gold to back every dollar. It was a half-truth that kept this house of cards from caving inward. It is true that one could redeem his money for hard gold coins; it even stated such in the black lettering across each bill. But a half-truth is still a lie, because what it did not say on each dollar bill was the fact that if all citizens wanted to retain paper for gold at the same time, the Federal Reserve Bank, similar to its predecessors, would be out of business overnight.

This half-truth gives us another small glimpse at the lack of integrity behind the Federal Reserve. Imagine this scenario: you walk into any bank in your neighborhood and tell the teller that you would like to exchange the $100 in your pocket for its equivalent in gold. You probably wouldn't even be laughed at as though the request were some kind of joke—instead you would see an expression of complete confusion on the teller's face. This state of confusion would not only be visible with bank employees but also in any other retail environment where one was asked to accept gold as a form of payment. Many people would be just as perplexed if you asked to pay in gold or silver as they would if you had asked to pay in copper or platinum; to many people these metals are every bit as foreign as gold and silver in regards to using them as money.

Has our collective knowledge concerning gold and silver as true money deliberately been allowed to become foggy over time? Was gold slowly phased out of our everyday transactions or was it cut out overnight? If indeed our perception of gold as money has become tarnished over the years, how was this feat accomplished? Today you and I give little thought if any as to why our dollars are no longer redeemable in gold or silver. As a matter of fact there are few people currently living today that can still remember the time when they did have the choice whether to use gold as money or to be able to exchange one for the other. I would be willing to venture that 90 percent of the people that will read this book have never even had the opportunity to hold a real gold or silver coin in their hand.

So why did this happen?—or more importantly—how did it happen? Are there any parallels between the position that we presently find ourselves in and that of the proverbial frog that slowly had the heat applied to the pot of water? If you asked friends and associates why you can no longer request gold from your local bank, would their response be similar to the response given by the chimpanzee at the beginning of this book? Probably.

If we are correct in assuming that the answer to the question presented above is correct, then it is imperative that we understand why and how this came to be. We know that the people in the early 1900s were fed up with the corruption and dishonesty that was practiced by the majority of the banks throughout our nation. Senator Aldrich and those other notorious men used people's sentiments at that time as their chance to present a plan that they claimed would bring back stability and integrity to the banking industry. In the early years, some sense of stability did return and people's fears from the past were finally put to rest as they were able to exchange their paper dollars for gold.

As mentioned, there are still a few people among us today that can remember these circumstances. We aren't studying civilizations that lived thousands of years ago or even two hundred years ago—we are now studying a time that is merely a stone's throw into the past. Some of our grandparents and those that are currently grandparents were once able to walk home from the bank with gold coins in their pockets. Until now we have only been able to learn about the past through studying various pages of history that our forefathers and others have described in great detail. We have been warned and given prudent counsel regarding the evils and the unnecessary aftermaths that follow when currency manipulation is present.

Perhaps we should talk to those still living among us who have lived in that part of history that we are now discussing. They would agree that they were able to redeem gold for paper dollars. This is an experience that would definitely leave an impression. But could they tell you when this right to use gold that is mandated in our Constitution was taken away? Or how it was taken away? Some certainly could, but how many of those people did not realize the heat was ever so slowly being increased until it was too late? We know that the heat must be increased in incremental amounts. If not, the frog would jump from the water without hesitation.

Sifting for Details

Let's fast-forward just a few years and hit a few of the high points that will shed some light on how and when the heat was applied. Once we have discovered a few of the major tipping points we can then dig a little deeper in search of the fine details.

Take a close look at the picture of this bill—study it carefully. Is there anything that instantly catches your eye? Does there appear to be anything out of place, or is this your typical five dollar bill?

At first glance it resembles the bills you may currently have in your wallet. This one was printed in 1928; other than being nearly eighty years old, do you notice any other significant differences?

Right below President Lincoln you can see the words, "WILL PAY TO THE BEARER ON DEMAND FIVE DOLLARS." This simply means that you as the "bearer" of this piece of paper can exchange this "note" for five dollars. Sound confusing? It shouldn't be. Remember, at this time in history "dollars" came in the form of gold and silver coins. This is not a picture of a 1928 five dollar bill; rather, it is a five dollar note. A note is a promise to pay a certain amount of money sometime in the future. In this case, it promises to pay the bearer five dollars.

There are additional assuring words on the upper left hand corner which read, "REDEEMABLE IN GOLD ON DEMAND AT THE UNITED STATES TREASURY, OR IN GOLD OR LAWFUL MONEY AT ANY FEDERAL RESERVE BANK." Do the dollars in your wallet have those words on them?

Residents of the roaring twenties had a few options at their disposal if they were the "bearer" of similar five dollar notes. First, they could take this note and spend it on goods or services. Second, they could march down to the United States Treasury and swap it for five dollars worth of gold. Lastly, they could take it to any Federal Reserve Bank and get five dollars worth of gold, or "lawful money." Bearers of these types of notes felt confident using them. At any time they could cash out and receive gold or silver coins. Unfortunately, they were already being set up to be swindled and the water was about to get warmer.

Lawful money was both gold and silver. With this new wording, the Federal Reserve Banks could dictate which of the two they would dole out in exchange for their notes. Within just a couple of years, the wording "redeemable in gold" was taken off the notes altogether, and, in fact, it even became illegal to own as we will discover later.

There is also significant wording that is not found on this five dollar note which we can easily find on our notes today. The words, "This note is legal tender for all debts, public and private" were added a few years later. Until these words were added, we the people had a choice as to what we would except as payments for debt. This right was taken away from the people. The government was telling the people that not only will they not be able to exchange paper for gold and silver any longer but also, by law, they have to accept paper notes for all debt, public and private.

Over the years the wording slowly changed. Certain phrases were deleted and others became permanent. There were numerous types of notes or dollars as well. We had gold and silver certificates, National Currency, and of course Federal Reserve Notes.

This next bill, which happens to be dated 1957, is a silver certificate. It spent just like other paper dollars but the option was there to cash this in for a real silver dollar. Read the wording below George Washington: "ONE DOLLAR PAYABLE IN SILVER TO THE BEARER ON DEMAND." Gold had been done away with for over thirty years by the time 1957 rolled around, but silver was still hanging on—although not for long.

Look at this bill from 1963.

Except for the decorative differences, this dollar is exactly the same as the ones we find in our wallets today. It is a Federal Reserve Note. Ironically, it is a note that pays you nothing. It can not be redeemed for anything—certainly not gold or silver. The promise to pay in "lawful money" has also been conveniently removed. It offers the bearer nothing in return. The changes in the wording did not come about overnight, as you can see, but over a course of nearly fifty years

Sadly, this is more proof that the heat was indisputably, slowly, and methodically applied. Could there be any other conclusion after discovering firsthand that by the subtle craftiness of men we as a people were ever so gradually being weaned from the expectation of redeeming our paper dollars for gold? We were being conditioned to operate and function within our economy without the use of gold, but why? Did those men who meticulously massaged the wording found on our currency during those years know and understand human nature enough to realize we would all jump or revolt if the heat was applied too rapidly? I think they must have. Perhaps they knew and fully understood that it was impossible to manipulate a monetary system when a society insisted upon using gold as their standard of wealth. Perhaps they realized that gold acts as a knight in shining armor, protecting the poor and the less fortunate from having their precious few dollars confiscated through inflation. Perhaps they understood all of this and more, just as our current president of the Federal Reserve system, Alan Greenspan did nearly forty years ago when he said:

> In the absence of the gold standard, there is no way to protect savings from confiscation through inflation. . . . This is the shabby secret of the welfare statists' tirades against gold. Deficit spending is simply a scheme for the "hidden" confiscation of wealth. Gold stands in the way of this insidious process. It stands as a protector of property rights.[3]

A powerful statement to be sure. If Greenspan happened to be a member of the Church, and if gaining acceptance into the apostleship was based solely on being a master of linguistics, there is no doubt that he would become a certified apostle. If you have listened to Greenspan speak, you will agree that there are few men who can rival this man's ability to summon up such unique terminology. When this man speaks the whole world hangs on his every word, and rightfully so—he represents the world's largest financial institution. Twice each year after he is finished expanding on his thoughts and ideas to Congress, the news outlets will spend the next few days debating, reading between the lines and trying to reach some kind of consensus as to what was actually said. Interestingly, his talents as a wordsmith have led certain groups of people throughout the financial world to label his style of speaking as Greenspanese and Greenspeak.

The Ultimate Form of Payment

There is, however, no need to summon a translator in order to comprehend what was meant in his above quote. His eloquent words have been repeated many times throughout the chapters of this book. He agrees that there is no way to protect our savings if inflation is present. He uses the word "secret" plenty of times, he calls deficit spending a scheme, he uses the phrase "insidious process" repeatedly, and then he explains that only through backing of gold can this process be abated. These are unquestionably words of wisdom. Greenspan is without doubt a truly brilliant man, one who could never be a slouch or ever hope to be appointed as the head of the Federal Reserve System. This statement was delivered in the sixties, two decades before Greenspan was appointed president of the Federal Reserve. The phrase "do what I say and not want I do" comes to the minds of many people who have a clear understanding of today's financial turmoil. Greenspan's quote makes complete sense to us and we have to remember that at the time he was a great advocate for gold. Now, however, we can only speculate on the reasons that this man who holds the power to initiate great changes—like to enact a gold policy—has not done so in the nearly twenty years that he has reigned at the Federal Reserve.

Is it possible that he changed his mind? Yes, but I don't think that he did. Perhaps, although unlikely, after leaving his post in the private banking world and being appointed as the leader of the Federal Reserve, he saw the true error of his ways? Maybe his eyes were opened. Maybe after he became the newest member of the cartel he was given inside information that would compel him to rescind his convictions on gold. I have my suspicions as to why Greenspan has not reinstated a gold standard as I am sure you do. Reasons and suspicions aside, the facts are that he has done nothing to get rid of this "insidious process" as he once called it, nor has he fostered gold ownership as being pertinent any longer. His actions and procedures have spoken louder than his words from decades ago. But the question has not been answered yet as to whether or not he still believes as he once did concerning gold. I think this next statement of his makes his position quite clear: "Gold still represents the ultimate form of payment in the world."[4]

Since we cannot directly ask him, we will assume from his statements that he did, and does, have gold on his mind. There is no need to decode this statement unlike so many other of his riddles given over the years. Of all forms of payment in the world known to man, according to him, gold is the ultimate.

Flip back a page or two and reread Alan Greenspan's first quote that he gave back in the sixties. One cannot read his remarks and not come away feeling with certainty that he was a true combatant for gold. When we fast-forward through time and recognize the good that he could have brought about, through the position and influence that he holds, we can only speculate as to why his once contagious enthusiasm has grown dormant. If we were to venture our best guess, it seems likely that like other men before him who understood pure and true principles, when tempted he chose to swim with the current rather than against it. History is full of similar examples. Looking no further than the Old Testament, one of the more readily remembered examples is King David. He too was a combatant who understood many pure and true principles and steadfastly put his trust in the Lord. Unfortunately, when the whisperings of temptation spoke to his heart, his actions, like so many others', spoke louder than his convictions.

Although not following a perfect chronological order, we are still discovering the pertinent points of how and when our present financial system decoupled itself from the gold standard. We have uncovered the process of how the words found on our currency have "subtly" been changed over the years in order that we might disassociate ourselves with what true money is and means. Learning that even today's president of the Federal Reserve System once did, and still does, consider gold as the ultimate form of payment in the world yet has done nothing to promote or instill confidence in this metal, should come as no surprise considering all that we have discovered thus far.

Soup Lines

The sights and sounds within our country back in October of 1929 could not be described as encouraging or optimistic. For many, feelings of destitution came from the unprecedented collapse of the great New

York Stock exchange. The financial losses which virtually transpired overnight totaled anywhere from seven to nine billion dollars, which in today's inflated system would be equivalent to almost ten times that amount. The financial dam had just been blown apart, but it would take many years before it reached all the residents downstream, drowning many of the American people in the process. The roaring twenties was so named for good reason. Like many of the past and present boom and bust cycles, easy credit and loose lending policies ran rampant. To say that the banks orchestrated this predicament by flooding the market with money through the mechanism of lending (with interest of course), to every Tom, Dick, and Harry would be a great understatement. All great boom cycles come to an end. Sooner or later one must pay the piper. There are untold numbers of books written on the Great Depression, and, like many of our previous points of study, we are only trying to snatch out the pertinent facts that coincide with our general review of financial manipulation.

There was a reason that men stood in food and soup lines. They were unemployed or not making enough money at their current job to sustain life for them and their families. There was a reason why many men lost their jobs. Their past employers were farmers and owners of small and large businesses with debt and could no longer service that debt, resulting in dissolved or repossessed business. There was a reason why many business owners could no longer continue to pay on their loans: the banks had begun to constrict the money supply.

For close to a dozen chapters now we have discussed the various and creative ways that man has been able to increase the money supply. However, that which goes up must someday come down, and every coin is known to have two sides. Make no mistake that what can be artificially inflated or expanded can certainly be deflated or decreased.

Banking in general back then and currently is nothing more than a Ponzi scheme. It is held together not with integrity nor by the practicing of sound and proven principles but rather by faith and faith alone. If there happens to be enough faith among the people, then the banks are able to stay solvent. However, when a lack of faith is present amongst even a small percentage of the population, bank runs are the end result. It is not necessary for all depositors to madly rush in and demand payment nor even the majority. Unbeknownst to many, and obviously not to the bank, it requires less than 1 percent over the amount that they hold in reserve to force them into insolvency. If a bank has issued a million dollars in paper currency with only 10 percent or $100,000 in gold backing, then $100,000 is all that they could feasibly return to angry and demanding customers. The first dollar requested after they have returned the reserve of $100,000 back to previous demanders, is when the doors are shut and locked and the bank is no longer in business, ultimately stiffing customers who were holding a collective sum of $900,000 worthless dollars.

Many who were now desperately in need of financial help went to those banks that had not yet closed their doors, seeking financial assistance in the form of new loans. When banks go out of business, and when others simply say no to the requests for lines of credit, second and third mortgages, and other forms of borrowing, liquidity begins to shrink and constrict. When business owners throughout the country, whether they employ ten people or ten thousand, are unable to obtain the credit that they have become accustomed to receiving and using within their operations of business, employees must be laid off. The restrictions of credit and easy money have far-reaching and negative implications that very few people truly understand. It may be safe to assume that the numbers of people that understand this concept are about the same as the number of people who do not comprehend the financial destruction of just the opposite—inflating and expanding the money supply.

If we fast-forward to the year 1933 and without going into the intricate details of the what, why, and when of the Great Depression, we can now see thousands of banks across our country with signs in their window indicating that they are no longer in business. In fact, nearly eleven thousand banks had closed their doors for good. In February of that same year, numerous governors throughout the states declared banking holidays in order to prevent mass crowds of people from bombarding bank teller lines and demanding their money back. In Michigan, circumstances were so close to imploding that the state designated an eight-day bank holiday in hopes of buying some time and, more importantly, intervention on behalf of our federal government.

This was the scenario being played out all across our nation. The banks were finding themselves in short supply of paper money and especially gold and had few options. They tried calling in outstanding loans to a small degree. However, most of their lending contracts did not provide them with a clause to call in loans early. For the most part, this effort bore very little fruit because few people could afford to repay the outstanding amount anyway. The bankers again needed a knight to gallop in on a white horse and save the day. The only one capable of conquering such a mighty feet was the cartel's silent partner—the federal government.

The Need for a Fireside Chat

On the fourth day of March, Franklin Delano Roosevelt gave his inaugural address to the nation. This understandably was not a time when many men would care to preside over our nation. There was a massive depression raging throughout our country—thanks to the dishonesty practiced by most of the banks—and it would take the start of a second world war before things were arguably any better.

President Roosevelt declared a national bank holiday on the sixth of March, two days after taking office. The possibility of continued and increased bank runs had come to a halt for no other reason other than the president of United States mandated that no bank, private or public, be open on that day.

In an amazing feat, the Emergency Banking Relief Act was presented, reviewed, and approved by Congress all in the same day. It is remarkable how quickly these two groups, the bankers (a.k.a the Federal Reserve) and Congress, were able to come together and bring about a plan that would benefit them both handsomely.

In 1933 almost 90 percent of American households were proud owners of some sort of radio. Citizens all across our country were able to keep up-to-date and informed on current news and entertainment events by tuning into their favorite station. Families got together and sat around in their kitchen or family room to listen to radio programs like we now sit together and watch television. On the night of March 12, the National Broadcasting System or NBC aired a special live radio address from inside the President's study at the White House. This address, and others given by the president, became commonly known throughout the years as "Fireside Chats." The president had decided to speak to the people in layman's terms to explain why a bank holiday was implemented and what their government was doing to stem future bank runs. We know the implications that arise when men and governments abandon the principle of just weights and measures. A speech from the president, like the one President Roosevelt gave that night, would not even be necessary if the money supply had not been distorted and manipulated by unethical banking practices. He went live at 10 PM Eastern time and began by saying:

My friends, I want to talk for a few minutes with the people of the United States about banking, with the comparatively few who understand the mechanics of banking but more particularly with the overwhelming majority who use banks for the making of deposits and a drawing of checks. I want to tell you what has been done in the last few days, why it was done, and what the next steps are going to be. I recognize that the many proclamations from state capitals and from Washington, the legislation, the treasury regulations, etc., couched for the most part in banking and legal terms should be explained for the benefit of the average citizen. . . . I know that when you understand what we in Washington have been about I shall continue to have your cooperation.[5]

These were the first words of the President's speech heard by millions across the nation as they huddled around their radios. It is interesting to note that in the second sentence he admitted that only a comparatively few people truly understand the mechanics of banking. By saying that statement, he bet that after his address was over, people would cooperate. He continued:

A comparatively small part of the money you put into the bank is kept in currency—an amount which in normal times is wholly sufficient to cover the cash needs of the average citizen. In other words the total amount of all the currency in the country is only a small fraction of the total deposits in all of the banks.[6]

Undermined Confidence

President Roosevelt didn't explain why the small part of money that we put into banks as currency is "wholly sufficient" in normal times. This is an example of another half-truth. The money we put in banks is only "wholly sufficient" when the faith of the people who use the banks is sufficient. When it is insufficient, bank runs are the result. President Roosevelt admits that all of the paper dollars in circulation are but a small fraction of the total deposits in our banks. In fact there is typically no more than three or four dollars of paper currency per $100 that have been artificially created through checks, credit cards, and so forth. Translated another way, this means that out of one hundred families in your neighborhood, only three or four could come home with the physical cash that the bank owed them. President Roosevelt then went on:

What, then, happened during the last few days of February and the first few days of March? Because of undermined confidence on the part of the public, there was a general rush by a large portion of our population to turn bank deposits into currency or gold—A rush so great that the soundest banks could not get enough currency to meet the demand. The reason for this was that on the spur of the moment it was, of course, impossible to sell perfectly sound assets of a bank and convert them into cash.[7]

President Roosevelt blames the banking collapse on undermined confidence, which we have referred to as a lack of faith. They are one and the same. People rushed to cash out their savings into gold and currency. The inflated dollars were certainly better than no dollars at all. Who among us could blame them? Believing that the early bird gets the worm, most of us would do nothing differently if we were faced with the same situation. President Roosevelt mentions that when a rush develops so quickly that even the soundest of banks cannot obtain currency quickly enough to satisfy demand. What he really means is that it is impossible for a bank to print money fast enough to cover 96 percent of its deposits. He claims that had there been more time, banks would have been in a position to sell some of their "perfectly sound assets" to help raise currency. This scenario would not even have to be mentioned if banks dealt honestly and with integrity. If so they would only issue paper dollars up to the amount of gold that they currently held within their vaults. Is "perfectly sound assets" another oxymoron when the reference of such is related to a bank? How were these assets retained? Were they bought originally with unbacked paper dollars or where they acquired as collateral from those that came to the bank and borrowed their unbacked printed money? One thing is for certain, you can bet that none of these perfectly sound assets were originally purchased or obtained by gold.

President Roosevelt continues with his message, telling the people that there was scarcely a bank in the country that was open for business as recently as a week ago. This was why he went had proclaimed a national banking holiday. He said that banks would gradually begin to reopen starting the following day, proceeding with caution until most, but not all, had reopened. He continues:

This bank holiday while resulting in many cases in great inconvenience is affording us the opportunity to supply the currency necessary to meet the situation. No sound bank is a dollar worse off than it was when it closed its doors last Monday. . . . The new law allows the twelve Federal Reserve banks to issue additional currency on good assets and thus the banks that reopen will be able to meet every legitimate call. . . . It is sound currency because it is backed by actual, good assets.[8]

How are they going to supply the necessary currency? Apparently the Federal Reserve has been given approval to issue additional currency. Imagine how you might feel had you been part of the majority of the people that did not come home with currency or gold before the banks closed. As you sat with your family, huddled around the radio listening to that calm and reassuring voice, you would be secretly praying that somehow this new president would be able to restore order and save the day. Like salve on an infected wound, hearing the words that the Federal Reserve would now issue additional currency would certainly cure some of your own financial ailments. However, if you happened to be one of the comparatively few who understood the mechanics of banking, then you would realize as you and others became the recipients of additional currency, that this was merely applying a Band-Aid to a cut that required stitches. Perhaps you should look on the bright side; the president reassured all those within the sound of his voice that the currency was sound, not because it was backed by gold but because it is backed by actual, good assets.

Hoarding is Unfashionable

Let us read some more words of wisdom from President Roosevelt:

It is possible that when the banks resume a very few people who have not recovered from their fear may again begin withdrawals. Let me make it clear that the banks will take care of all needs—and it is my belief that hoarding during the past week has become an exceedingly unfashionable pastime. . . . People will again be glad to have their money where it will be safely taken care of and where they can use it conveniently at any time. I can assure you that it is safer to keep your money in a reopened bank than under the mattress.[9]

The president let the people know that the Government anticipated that there would still be people who would withdraw all of their money as soon as the banks reopened. But never fear! he assured them for the second time as he again explained that the banks would take care of all their needs. Incredulously, he stated that those who believed the rumors that the banks would not have sufficient funds to cover their deposits and therefore ran to the bank demanding their money were "hoarders." Unbelievable! There will no doubt come a day when members of the Church who had the foresight and took counsel from previous Church leaders to lay up a year supply of food will also be called hoarders. President Roosevelt, after delivering this pompous statement, tried to guilt "hoarders" into believing that they were part of an exceedingly unfashionable pastime.

This next part of his speech is a bit puzzling. It is puzzling because, in the second sentence of his speech, he admitted that there are very few who understand banking, and yet he announced this:

> Remember that the essential accomplishment of the new legislation is that it makes it possible for banks more readily to convert their assets into cash than was the case before. More liberal provision has been made for banks to borrow on those assets at the Reserve Banks and more liberal provision has also been made for issuing currency on the security of those good assets. This currency is not fiat currency. It is issued only on adequate security—and every good bank has an abundance of such security.[10]

Ask ten people to describe what fiat currency is and see how many correct responses you are able to get. Your answers reflect a day and age where many people have had the opportunity to finish secondary education and continue on to college, unlike those who grew up in the early 1900s. Most people couldn't give you a correct answer today. How many do you think could do so nearly a hundred years ago? The reference to fiat currency is only the tip of the iceberg in the above quote. The president would have been lucky if 10 percent of his listeners could interpret the procedures he had just explained, which would be taking effect within the near future. Was this on purpose or innocently? These procedures and implications will be looked at not here but in the pages ahead.

The president then wound down his speech. He admitted that the banking situation was in bad shape. He confessed that some of the banks lent out money to speculators whose investments hadn't panned out. It was true that this was not the case for many banks throughout the nation, but true for enough of them that it caused panic and bank runs. President Roosevelt added, "It was the government's job to straighten out this situation and do it as quickly as possible—and the job is being performed."[11]

The president was misinformed; it is certainly not the job of the government to straighten out financial debacles. Nowhere is our government given any power or control from within the articles of our Constitution to sort out and untangle financial turmoil.

However, he was completely informed of the facts found in his last paragraph:

> After all there is an element in the readjustment of our financial system more important than currency, more important than gold, and that is the confidence of the people. Confidence and courage are the essentials of success in carrying out our plan. You people must have faith; you must not be stampeded by rumors or guesses. Let us unite in banishing fear. We have provided the machinery to restore our financial system; it is up to you to support and make it work.[12]

In the presence of 60 million Americans, he stated that the confidence of the people—which we have called faith—was more important in supporting the financial system than either currency or gold. Was the heat of that proverbial stove just increased by the delivery of that statement? Did the people realize it? For the most part, sadly, no. The president finally calls it what it really is by telling us that we need to have faith. The printing presses, I mean "machinery," are again referred to as standing ready to restore the financial system. In closing, he delivered the most accurate and truthful statement made that Sunday night by admitting that without our support it would not work.

Earlier we read two separate quotes, both from Alan Greenspan. Without labeling him good, bad, or indifferent, and though we can't clearly see the intent of his heart, he has either been silenced or chosen to become silent through his lack of words and actions. There is no better teacher than history itself. Many men can see the light penetrating through the darkness yet fail to embrace it. Others, such as King David, are born into this world with an abundance of truth and light, yet are not able to hold on to it. It is apparent that although President Roosevelt's words and actions did not concur with his previous convictions, he too undoubtedly held what we would consider truth and light in an earlier time in his life, because when he was governor of New York he stated:

> The Constitution of the United States gives Congress no power

to legislate in the matter of a great number of vital problems of government, such as the conduct of public utilities, of banks, of insurance, of business, of agriculture, of education, of social welfare and over a dozen other important features. Washington must never be permitted to interfere in these avenues of our affairs.[13]

So why did he, along with congress, interfere in this banking problem and implement a national banking holiday?

NOTES

1. Woodrow Wilson, "Quotes from Woodrow Wilson," Online, available from *Liberty-tree.ca.*

2. George Washington, Farewell Address, September 17, 1796.

3. Alan Greenspan, "Gold and Economic Freedom," in *Capitalism: The Unknown Ideal*, ed. Ayn Rand (New York: Signet Books, 1967), 101.

4. Alan Greenspan, "Quote from Alan Greenspan," Testimony before U.S. House Banking Committee, May 1999, Online, *Liberty-Tree.ca,* available from http://quotes.liberty-tree.ca/quote/alan_greenspan_ quote_1cb8.

5. Franklin D. Roosevelt, "Fireside Chat #1," Online, *University of San Diego,* available from http://history.sandiego.edu/gen/20th/fc/01.html.

6. Ibid.

7. Ibid.

8. Ibid.

9. Ibid.

10. Ibid.

11. Ibid.

12. Ibid.

Chapter Eleven

CONFISCATING PRECIOUS METALS

The Federal Reserve Banks are the most corrupt institutions the world has ever seen. There is not a man within the sound of my voice that does not know that this nation is run by the International Bankers.
—Louis McFadden, U.S. Congressman

In his book *An Enemy Hath Done This*, President Benson recounts how it was through the manipulation of our own government, that we were taken off of the gold standard.

> With practically no new gold moving into the treasury to keep pace with the expanding paper money supply, it was essential for the government manipulators to have the nation go off the gold standard, that is, to remove gold as a guaranteed backing.[1]

But there were two primary reasons that gold was not moving into government coffers at a quick enough pace. The first and foremost was that U.S. citizens were exchanging paper for gold at their local banks or just plain hoarding it, as President Roosevelt graciously termed it. This was done because of the ever-expanding paper money supply. The second reason for the slowing of gold into the treasury was simply the fact that not enough gold was being mined. After a short time President Roosevelt mandated that the price of gold per ounce would become fixed at $35. The people are not the only ones who suffer when their purchasing power begins to decline due to unjust weights and measures. Businesses also endure hardships, and as the cost of mining increased, it no longer became profitable for mining companies to produce an ounce of gold, as long as the price was capped at $35 per ounce. Unlike printing paper dollars, which can be produced with little expense, mining involves exploration, drilling, excavation, blasting, trucking, and refining to name just a few of the major expenses. As the costs to produce gold continued to increase, the profitability and motivation to mine gold decreased. How many new cars would be manufactured this year if our government stepped in and put price controls into effect? If, in their wisdom, our government decided that the price of a new Chevy truck could be no more than $15,000, yet the price of labor, steel, glass and other pertinent materials needed to assemble a new truck was costing GM $15,000 or more, it would be safe to assume that truck production would quickly come to a halt.

Supply and demand are not limited to goods such as corn, wheat, and oil. Gold, like all commodities, is produced, mined, or harvested in order to secure the largest profit possible. Miners are no different than farmers and will not exert the effort required if no one is willing to pay them for their toils. These two scenarios were collectively able to slow the flow of gold into our government's hand, and understandably, make both the population and the banks very uncomfortable.

In the previous chapter we discussed the underlying motive that caused people to run to the banks and demand their gold. This in turn caused many banks to close their doors, spurring President Roosevelt to declare a banking holiday. Although paper currency had become diluted and almost worthless, if one could not obtain gold coin from the bank, paper dollars were better than nothing. President Benson comments on this rush into gold:

> Sensing that American paper money was now literally "worthless," many people began to put their savings into gold itself. If allowed to continue, this might have led to a parallel monetary system dealing in the private exchange of gold or credits against gold instead of government paper money.[2]

This was a scenario that the cartel was desperately trying to avoid at all costs. Imagine the banks' horror as they began to witness the events unfolding around them. These bankers were some of the brightest men in business and could certainly see that a parallel or dual monetary system would become a fact of life if nothing were done to stem the private exchange of gold between people and businesses. If there were two monetary systems, one with paper currency not backed by precious metals and one that consisted of only precious metals, ultimately the good money would drive out the bad. The bankers, of course, were in charge of the fraudulent paper scheme. If free enterprise were allowed to run its natural course, all banks that did not uphold the principles of integrity and honesty would be forced to close their doors forever. If this were to happen, how would they be able to create and extend loans (with interest) by simply issuing unbacked and unsound currency? How would their partner, the government, be able to secure the desperately sought-after funding required to pay its monthly liabilities? The government's only option would be to raise taxes drastically, angering the people who would then vote out those in favor of such a plan. This was an avenue the government did not want to walk down, because outright taxation was not nearly as subtle as taxation through inflation. President Benson continues:

> So the next step for government manipulators was to make it illegal for Americans even to own gold. The people of other nations may demand and receive gold bullion from Fort Knox for whatever American money they hold, but our own citizens are not permitted even to own an ounce of gold . . . That's right, Americans were forced by their government to abandon any claim to gold behind their paper dollars but foreign holders of these dollars are still entitled to cash in for gold if they wish.[3]

We have jumped the gun a tad in our study of financial manipulation. President Benson made reference to a few points of interest that we will look into in greater detail. However, the facts speak for themselves when he states that we were forced by our own government to abandon the practice of redeeming paper dollars for gold. Incredulously, we as the inhabitants of this land choice above all others, were unable to cash in our dollars for gold, yet all other nations of the world that held our paper currency were entitled to do such. Something is terribly askew when this can transpire here in the promised land.

In order to avoid a dual monetary system within the United States, and reiterating what President Benson said above, government manipulation was needed in order to make it illegal for Americans to own gold. And that is precisely what happened.

Executive Order 6102

Previously, we went into great detail exploring the Constitution and how it was framed and delivered by noble men inspired and guided by the Lord. Within this sacred document are many truthful principles along with guidelines that, if heeded, will bring about prosperity and freedom to all of those who gratefully embrace it. Our primary focus has been the economic security that can come to us by following the monetary council found within the Constitution. Not only have we discovered that our founding fathers abhorred the idea of issuing fiat money but also that they specifically proclaimed that the state could use nothing but gold and silver coin as tender in payments of debts.

There is now a new twist in our study of history. Up to this point we have uncovered a repetitive process concerning financial distortion and manipulation. We have continually witnessed instances where men throughout the ages have tried to obtain something for nothing by diluting their present monetary system. Whether these men have chosen to file and shave down the sides of gold coins or simply print or create paper dollars greater than the amount that they held in gold, the results have been the same. Through the mechanism of inflation, the hidden tax, people's money has been stolen. We are now witnessing a new modus operandi, quoting again the words of Alan Greenspan, "In the absence of the gold standard, there is no way to protect savings from confiscation through inflation."[4]

Instead of bankers and government manipulating a monetary system, they were now going to completely remove the only form of self-defense that the people held in battling inflation—owning gold.

On April 5, 1933, Executive Order 6102, which required gold coin, gold bullion, and gold certificates to be delivered to the government, was put into effect.

> I, Franklin D. Roosevelt, president of the United States of America, to declare that said national emergency still continues to exist and pursuant to said section do hereby "prohibit" the hoarding of gold coin, gold bullion, and gold certificates within the continental United States by individuals, partnerships, associations and corporations and hereby prescribe the following regulations for carrying out the purpose of this order.

It had been only a few weeks since President Roosevelt gave his first fireside chat from his study in the White House. The banking holiday he had implemented was over, but the banking crisis unfortunately was not. Just as he had predicted that Sunday night in March, many people bombarded the banks, engaging in that exceedingly unfashionable pastime of hoarding by demanding that their savings be returned to them in the form of precious metals. There were also those who had felt reassured and confident after listening to their new president proclaim that with time the banking industry would soon be back on its feet. We know the only way these banks would ever stand again, and as Roosevelt earlier admitted, was if the people had enough confidence in them. Apparently there were still people that did not feel calm and reassured after the banking holiday was lifted, hence the continued hoarding. Who among us could blame the people for not trying to secure something that held intrinsic value as opposed to obtaining paper IOUs?

Words alone cannot describe the hypocrisy that was taking place during this time in our country's history. Gold and silver were literally used as forms of money during this time, and the vast majority of citizens stored their savings in precious metals in one form or another. There is no dispute that paper money was more convenient in conducting daily transactions and the people used this "folding money," as they also called it, for such purposes. Conversely, when it came to savings, people secured their money in the form of gold and silver coins. The cartel wanted to stockpile gold, which was needed to restore order and provide stability and to prevent further financial turmoil, or so they claimed. Those that wanted to engage in the unfashionable pastime of hoarding would be considered evil, wicked, and selfish because they put their own interests ahead of what was best for the nation. The American people had been bamboozled. For the first time in history, people would be forced to use and accept only paper dollars whether they wanted to or not. This was certainly the farthest thing from our founding fathers' minds when they presented our country with the Constitution. Imagine what they would think or if they were here today?

The means by which a monetary system is manipulated and the inflation that follows has been referred to by many as insidious. Agreeably, nobody likes to have their purchasing power diminish, but what about their freedom? It is one thing to have your money taken from you through this hidden tax, or if you prefer, confiscation through inflation. But now we are discovering that people's freedom to choose, a right that was highly sought after and fought for by many, was being taken away from them.

Defining Executive Order 6102

By looking a little closer at the executive order that President Roosevelt gave, in Section 1 we find the definition of "hoarding." It means, "The withdrawal and withholding of gold coin, gold bullion, or gold certificates from the recognized and customary channels of trade." The Executive order proclaimed:

> Congress is not accepting this gold nor is the president. None of the national or state banks are standing as recipients either. Section 2 states:
>
> All persons are hereby required to deliver on or before May 1, 1933, to a Federal Reserve Bank . . . all gold coin, gold bullion, and gold certificates now owned by them or coming into their ownership on or before April 28, 1933, except the following.

There were a few exceptions that allowed those who used gold as part of their profession, such as dentists, and those who worked in art or jewelry to keep sufficient amounts of gold in their possession. It went on to say:

> Until otherwise ordered any person becoming the owner of any gold coin, gold bullion, or gold certificates after April 28, 1933 shall, within three days after receipt thereof, delivered the same in the manner prescribed in Section 2.

The people didn't return home empty-handed after unloading their yellow metal to the Federal Reserve banks, they came home with freshly printed money in exchange for their gold coins. Of course nowhere found on these newly created dollars, were the words, "redeemable in gold." For each ounce of gold that the people turned over to the banks they received in return $20.67. Could it be said that our government outright stole the gold from the people? No. Each citizen was completely reimbursed for his gold in the form of newly created currency. This was a great deal for the cartel. Our government wanted to spend more money than it had and the banks wanted to loan out more money than *they* had. Together they could continue to inflate the dollar as long as gold wasn't used as backing for currency. With gold forcibly taken out of the equation, there was almost no limit as to how much money could be created and lent with interest. Although the limits were nearly boundless, the federal government still had a ceiling on how much currency they could produce compared to the amount of gold that they held in their vaults. The irony was in the fact that although the dollar was still backed by a small fraction of gold, the citizens were unable to exchange their paper for gold coin. President Benson refers to this small amount of gold backing and the inability of redeeming it with paper bills when he said:

> Americans are not permitted to cash in their dollars for even that token amount. And if gold cannot be obtained in exchange for paper bills, then it is not really "backed" by gold at all. To say that it is, is merely to deceive oneself. The 25 percent so-called backing of gold is merely a bookkeeping ledger account designed to sustain the people's psychological confidence in and acceptance of our money system.[5]

I hold great admiration for President Benson. Throughout his life he was notoriously known for standing up for principles that encompass freedom and was not afraid of telling anyone who would listen what needed to be done in order to secure those freedoms. Calling the shots as he sees them, he states nearly forty years after this executive order was put into place, that people would be deceiving themselves if they felt that the dollar was actually backed by gold; it is not by the belief in dollars backed by gold that we have come to accept this monetary system, but rather through psychological confidence.

The word "forcibly" implies that this new mandate was done against the people's will. So far President Roosevelt had batted 1000 percent when it came to predicting the population's actions. He sensed, and later implied in his fireside chat with the country, that there may be those that would continue to hoard once the banks reopened the following day. He was right. Was it possible that he and his colleagues knew that the gold supply would continue to drain unless the people were forced to abandon this practice? How could a government enforce such a dramatic and unprecedented proposal? They certainly couldn't perform physical inspections of every farmhouse, penthouse, and henhouse. They needed a plan, and the Executive Order is what they came up with:

> Whoever willfully violates any provision of this executive order or all of these regulations or of any rule, regulation or license issued thereunder may be fined not more than $10,000, or, a person may be imprisoned for not more than 10 years, or both, and any officer, director, or agent of any corporation who knowingly participates in

any such violation may be punished by a like fine, imprisonment, or both.

This regrettably was their plan—a plan of intimidation. There were those who held opinions and beliefs contrary to this new executive order issued by President Roosevelt. Some of these men filed suits against our government, professing that this Executive Order was completely against certain mandates and personal freedoms found within the Constitution. Who among us, after learning of this unfortunate but historically accurate account, could with a clear conscience stand with the government while they desecrated these citizens personal property rights? They had no more right to demand that the people turn in their gold then they would if they were asking each family to fork over their kitchen dinette sets. Predictably, none of these lawsuits against the government ever ended in the plaintiff's favor.

In less than a month, our fellow Americans who previously had the financial freedom to choose which commodity of exchange they would use were labeled as hoarders, cheats, and possibly felons if they refused to turn in their gold. This freedom should have been their right as recipients of the many blessings that come to those who live within this promised land. Suddenly, this freedom was no longer available.

Was all the gold turned in before that mandated deadline? No. How do we know? In rare coin shops all across this country you can find one ounce gold coins that are dated 1933 or earlier. Cold hard evidence that you can hold in your hand, proving that there were many citizens that were not going to fall prey to those who were trying to obtain something for nothing.

Perhaps we are being too critical or even judgmental. After all, this was a banking emergency, and the government always knows what's best for the people, right? Just like recently when the government decided that it was best for the security of the whole to trample our Second Amendment rights by going door-to-door with armed military demanding that the citizens hand over their firearms because of the emergency situation in New Orleans after hurricane Katrina.

Three Wise Men

It was Benjamin Franklin who said, "They that can give up essential liberty to obtain a little temporary safety deserve neither liberty nor safety."[6]

Alexander Hamilton, using his own words but echoing the warning given by Benjamin Franklin stated: "Nothing is more common than for a free people, in times of heat and violence, to gratify momentary passions by letting into the government principles and precedents which afterward prove fatal to themselves."[7]

Of course my favorite activist for all spectrums of freedom is President Benson; he says:

> It is even possible that some of the government manipulators who have brought us into this economic crisis are hoping that, in panic, we, the American people, literally will plead with them to take our liberties in exchange for the false promise of "security."[8]

Three noble men renowned for their insight and wisdom gave three very distinct and prudent warnings of how the liberties and freedoms that we enjoy can, at times of heightened anxiety and panic, be taken from us under the guise of promised *security*.

Unfortunately, this is what transpired for many citizens in 1933. People were giving up their freedom, in this case the freedom of choice, pertaining to financial decisions and transactions, in order to secure a little bit of *safety*. There was, as we know, a banking emergency that caused temporary uncertainty and fear of the unknown. President Roosevelt only fanned the flames when he declared that the national emergency still existed. It was through this fear of uncertainty that the Emergency Banking Act was pushed through Congress and signed into law by the president all in the same day. How else can we explain how this bill was able to flash through the House and then to the Senate with lightning speed? New legislation typically doesn't jump over all the hurdles this quickly, does it?

The 73rd Congress

The House of Representatives called together an emergency Congressional meeting to discuss and vote on the proposed Emergency Banking Act. House Minority Leader Bertrand H. Snell from New York is quoted below. Decide whether or not his remarks aroused panic and urgency and whose side he may have been leaning more toward: the people or the cartel.

> The house is burning down, and the president of the United States says this is the way to put out the fire. And to me at this time there

is only one answer to this question, and that is to give the president what he demands and says is necessary to meet the situation.[9]

Next we hear from Majority Leader Joseph W. Byrns representing Tennessee. He exhorted his fellow representatives to debate the bill quickly—only forty minutes between the two political parties—because our country was facing "serious circumstances."

> Under the serious circumstances which confront the country, we agreed to take this bill up now, pass it, and send it to the Senate so it may become a law this evening.[10]

Finally, Congressmen Lundeen, who shared the beliefs and convictions that were express by Hamilton, Franklin, and Benson, stood up and explained the serious consequences that could develop as a result of hastily voting the bill through in times of panic:

> Mr. Speaker, today the Chief Executive sent to this House of Representatives a banking bill for immediate enactment. The author of this bill seems to be unknown. No one has told us who drafted the bill. There appears to be a printed copy at the speaker's desk, but no printed copies are available for the House Members. The bill has been delivered through the House with cyclonic speed after forty minutes of debate, twenty minutes for the minority and twenty minutes for the majority.
>
> I have demanded a roll call but have been unable to get the attention of the Chair. Others have done the same, notably Congressman Sinclair of North Dakota, and Congressman Bill Lemke, of North Dakota, as well as some of our Farmer Labor Members. Fifteen men were standing, demanding a roll call, but that number is not sufficient; we therefore have the spectacle of the great House of Representatives of the United States of America passing, after a forty-minute debate, a bill its Members never read and never saw, a bill whose author is unknown. The great majority of the members have been unable to get a minute's time to discuss this bill; we have been refused a roll call; and we have been refused recognition by the chair. I do not mean to say that the Speaker of the House of Representatives intended to ignore us, but everything was in such a turmoil and there was so much excitement that we simply were not recognized.
>
> I want to put myself on record against procedure of this kind

and against the use of such methods in passing legislation affecting millions of lives and billions of dollars. It seems to me that under this bill thousands of small banks will be crushed and wiped out of existence, and that money and credit control will be still further concentrated in the hands of those who now hold the power.

It is safe to say that in normal times after careful study of a printed copy and after careful debate and consideration, this bill would never have passed this House or any other House [sic]. Its passage could be accomplished only by rapid procedure, hurried and hectic debate, and a general rush for voting without roll call. . . .

I am suspicious of this railroading of bills through our House of Representatives, and I refuse to vote for a measure unseen and unknown.

I want the record to show that I was, and am, against this bill and this method of procedure; and I believe no good will come out of it for America. We must not abdicate our power to exercise judgment. We must not allow ourselves to be swept off our feet by hysteria, and we must not let the power of the executive paralyze our legislation action. If we do, it would be better for us to resign and go home and save the people the salary they are paying us.[11]

Admittedly this quote is a bit lengthy, but if not quoted in its entirety, some may feel that parts of Congressmen Lundeen's speech may have been taken out of context. However after reading his complete address there is no mistake in deciphering what his beliefs and moral convictions were. He thought it an insult not only to himself and other congressmen that were present but also to the citizens being represented because of this bill being passed with cyclonic speed. He was miffed, and understandably so after being unsuccessful in grabbing the attention of the Speaker. Adding to his frustration was the fact that the small number of hands that held the monetary power would then become concentrated even further, affecting millions of lives and billions of dollars. It was Lundeen's opinion that if everyone involved were able to carefully debate and apply a careful study of all aspects contained within this bill, it would have no chance of passing. Standing up and being counted regardless of the outcome or costs, Congressmen Lundeen refused to vote for this measure under those conditions of hysteria and believed that no good would come out of the bill.

The legislation was whisked away and presented to the Senate, who met under the same cloud of urgency. It was approved and signed into law later that night by President Roosevelt, thus ending the seven hour whirlwind tour of presentation, argumentation, and ratification of the Emergency Banking Act.

Texas Straight Talk

A few chapters back we read a quote from Ron Paul, a current Congressman from the state of Texas. He stands in the ranks of those who fight for the truths and freedoms that we have previously read so much about. He posts a weekly column entitled "Texas Straight Talk," and that is exactly what you find as you read his column. To solidify why politicians and central bankers, collectively known as cartels, despise currency backed by gold, Congressman Paul explained it this way:

> Gold is history's oldest and most stable currency. Central bankers and politicians don't want a gold-backed currency system, because it denies them the power to create money out of thin air. Governments by their very nature want to expand, whether to finance military intervention abroad or a welfare state at home. Expansion costs money and politicians don't want spending limited to the amounts they can tax or borrow. This is precisely why central banks now manage all of the world's major currencies.[12]

It was mentioned earlier but bears repeating, that if Congress was full of men who held the financial aptitude and moral courage in calling for dramatic changes in fiscal policy as Congressman Paul does, manipulated monetary systems would become a thing of the past.

It would be difficult after reviewing the extensive information just covered, to form any conclusion other than the fact that the pot of water has now started to simmer. By ushering in the Emergency Banking Act, which was closely followed by Executive Order 6102, the people's gold along with their private property rights, which are protected under our Constitution, were both simultaneously snatched away from them. Law abiding citizens, after trying to secure and preserve their wealth in the form of precious metals doing so under the protection of the Constitution, became instant enemies of the state if they continued to hoard the very metal their forefathers had instructed and insisted they use.

We are now navigating through uncharted waters. For the first time in American history, the people no longer had the freedom to choose whether they would use gold or paper in their monetary transactions. We have recently read a few words of society's prominent men and discovered some of the dialogue that took place within the 73rd Congress. Whether one finds these bits of trivia fascinating or not is of little significance, because while these glimpses into history have been informative, they have not altered the undisputable facts. Not only did our government force its citizens into solely using and accepting bills of credit, but they also applied salt to open wounds by disallowing them to physically own or store gold in their perspective homes and businesses. The final blow to the people's inalienable rights came by allowing all foreign countries to continue the practice of exchanging our paper dollars for gold. If asked, how many people could give the correct answer to whether or not this discriminative action is still practiced by our government today?

Bretton Woods

Jumping forward a decade, we arrive at the year 1944. It is in the middle of an abnormally hot summer and World War II is nearly over. The name Bretton Woods could easily be mistaken for someone's first and last name or perhaps a prestigious gated community shielding million-dollar homes. We find that, embedded within the pages of financial history, this name represents something quite different.

On July 22, close to fifty of the industrialized nations of the world came together for an international monetary conference. This was a conference where they would form a consensus on how they would handle currency controls, lending requirements and other economic activities on an international level. This three week get-together was held in Bretton Woods, New Hampshire, and from that day forward it has simply been referred to as the "Bretton Woods Agreement." It should come as no surprise that those in attendance, who totaled well over 700, were various politicians and people that floated within the circles of the banking elite. Two very powerful organizations were created at this financial conference: the International Monetary Fund, otherwise known as the IMF, and the International Bank for Reconstruction, commonly known as the World Bank.

The original purpose of this meeting with the industrialized nations of the world was to formulate a plan to more easily stabilize the currencies of the world. By accomplishing this, they hoped that they would be in a position to help rebuild many of the war-ravaged nations. Of course few, if any, of the 700 delegates who attended this meeting were actually going to roll up their sleeves and begin sifting through rubble and debris or any other kind of "help" that required much work. Not surprisingly, these do-gooders wanted to extend their help in the form of loans—repayable with interest.

This topic, like numerous others that we have previously discussed, is covered in profound detail in a number of books. To get an in-depth look and feel of how the banking elite has lent a "helping hand" to not only war ravaged countries but to any and all who are willing to sign on the dotted line, I highly recommend the book *Confessions of an Economic Hit Man* by John Perkins. The title of this book is certainly appropriate. Found within its pages are numerous confessions of how one man regrettably describes his role in seeking out those countries who were standing on their last financial leg and the appalling destruction that follows once they are unable to repay the loan or the mountains of interest that are past due. On the surface, the IMF and the World Bank seem like knights on white horses, rushing aid to the undeveloped nations of the world, feeding all of those who can't feed themselves and in general providing a higher standard of living to all mankind. Does one man's story or so-called "confessions" certify that the World Bank is nothing more than another group in search of something for nothing? No. You may, however, agree with his conclusions after reading about his life-long saga with his unique line of work. Should we be surprised that a worldwide organization now exists, and that its sole function is to prey on weaker countries, conquering them with relentless interest? Not if we have learned anything from the pages of history.

Numerous problems arise when unsound monetary systems and lending with interest are entwined. Many of the so-called recipients of the generously lent money from the World Bank ironically never see a dime. The problem can very easily be identified. These government-sponsored organizations loan money directly to other various governments instead of to the people. These new benefactors then increase the size and scope of their perspective governments along with helping themselves to a few well-deserved shopping sprees rather than using the money to directly help their own people. Regrettably, it is the people that are forced to help repay these loans. How can a people who were already living in such destitute circumstances be expected to help contribute in a financial way? Their own governments steal the few precious dollars that they have left through the age-old mechanism of confiscation through inflation.

The Bretton Woods Agreement was of historical importance because it marked the first time in history that the international community came together and actually agreed upon monetary concerns and matters. Ironically, the men representing the dozens of countries present at that meeting realized the importance of adhering to a gold standard and the stability that it brings to the world's economic stage. It must be noted, however, that none of those countries backed their respective currencies with 100 percent gold. They, like the United States, held gold in reserve to back the paper dollars that they issued, but it was a far cry from being a one to one ratio. Still, they felt it prudent enough for at least the time being to have some gold in reserves in which to back their currencies. This was the main element that all of the countries agreed to adhere to. All parties present agreed that they would peg their currencies to gold. They knew that this would provide economic stability while still allowing them to issue more paper than they had gold. The point was, they reasoned, that if all of the industrialized countries agreed to inflate only to a certain point, then all currencies would remain somewhat stable—like preventing a rotten apple from spoiling the whole bushel. This mandate meant that none of these countries would be allowed to issue pure fiat money, at least not yet.

The Water Begins to Dance

If you have ever had the patience to stare at a pot of water before it comes to a boil you know that it first must go through a few different stages. Although not yet at a full boil, the frog in our analogy is now surrounded by increasingly hotter conditions and it appears as though the water is starting to dance as bubbles slowly rise to the surface and pop. What has brought this proverbial pot of water to a near boil? We will need to fast-forward to 1965 to find out.

In the first few chapters of this book we discovered that not only gold but silver also has been considered true money for thousands of years. It was the silver coin also referred to as "pieces of eight" that was considered America's first true "dollar." At this point in history, silver was still considered money, and although not redeemable in gold, many of the paper dollars could be exchanged for "lawful money"—in silver. Silver is money. Whether we have a hard time conceiving or believing such does not change the facts. Reality does not care how we feel about any subject, for our beliefs do not alter truth. Silver was used as money more so even than gold for hundreds of years here in America.

Although it has now been well over thirty years since Americans faced a banking emergency which forced them to fork over their personal property in the form of gold, our government granted them the privilege of hoarding their silver—and in fact our dimes, quarters, half dollars, and dollar coins were made out of Silver. They were made out the silver just as it had been done for hundreds of years—but this was about to change:

Swapping Silver for Slugs

> Distinguished members of Congress, ladies and gentlemen: We are gathered here today for a very rare and historic occasion in our nation's history. . . . When I have signed this bill before me, we will have made the first fundamental change in our coinage in 173 years.[13]

President Lyndon B. Johnson had just begun his opening remarks, which preceded his signing of the historic Coinage Act of 1965. He makes reference to the Coinage Act of 1792, which he undoubtedly had not read word for word. If he had, he would most certainly be in fear of losing his life once this act was signed into law.

> Since that time our coinage of dimes, and quarters, and half dollars, and dollars have contained 90 percent silver. Today, except for the silver dollar, we are establishing a new coinage to take its place beside the old. . . . The new dimes and the new quarters will contain no silver. They will be composites, with faces of the same alloy used in our 5-cent piece that is bonded to a core of pure copper. They will show a copper edge. . . . There is no change in the penny and the nickel. There is no change in the silver dollar, although we have no present plans for silver dollar production.[14]

What is about to begin cannot be expressed in more simplistic terms. Our coins are no longer to be made of silver. President Johnson reassures the people that the penny and the nickel are exempt from any changes. This is a given, copper has never been used as a form of money nor has nickel, but had they been, we could safely assume that those two coins would also become antiques. The fact that the silver dollar would remain unchanged was mentioned, but new production of these silver dollars would not continue. From that point forward, silver dollars were created primarily for commemorative purposes and certainly not for use as money. He continues:

> All these new coins will be the same size and will bear the same

designs as do their present counterparts. And they will fit all the parking meters and all the coin machines and will have the same monetary value as the present ones.[15]

Perhaps had President Johnson expressed it another way the people wouldn't have gone along with this new plan so easily. They undoubtedly would have jumped right out of the pot had they heard President Johnson instead say:

> We want your silver, we need your silver and I am pleased to announce that Congress and I have devised a plan where we will substitute all silver coins with slugs made out of lead. Never fear, we are mandating that everyone use and accept these slugs of lead to purchase goods and services, and of course all of your favorite vending machines will accept these new slugs because they are identical in size and appearance.

The above quote is hypothetical; nevertheless, it covers the same topics and leaves the ultimate outcome which President Johnson described unchanged. It is interesting to me how easily some of us will follow counsel given by people who claim that they are implementing something that will greatly benefit the whole, even when what they propose is contrary to not only truthful principles but also ordinary common sense. His next paragraph defies all logic:

> Now, all of you know these changes are necessary for a very simple reason—silver is a scarce material. Our uses of silver are growing as our population and our economy grows. The hard fact is that silver consumption is now more than double new silver production each year. So, in the face of this worldwide shortage of silver, and our rapidly growing need for coins, the only really prudent course was to reduce our dependence upon silver for making our coins.[16]

See if this next hypothetical quote sounds any more ridiculous than the one above just given by the President Johnson:

> Now, all of you know these changes are necessary for a very simple reason, paper is a scarce material. Our uses of paper are growing as our population and our economy grows. The hard fact is that paper consumption is now more than double new paper production each year. So, in the face of this worldwide shortage of paper, and our

rapidly growing need for paper dollars, the only really prudent course was to reduce our dependence upon paper for making our dollars. From this time henceforth all paper dollars will be replaced with plastic dollars, they will be equal in size and dimension and all present engravings will also be found on these new plastic dollars.

Although this last quote is hypothetical, my analogy is closer to the truth than most people realize. Many people have grown up using and accepting a dollar that is non redeemable for gold or silver and do so without any idea that these metals were not only used for thousands of years but also for the first few hundred years of our own country's existence. There is no difference in today's dollars than there would be if the government mandated that we began using seashells for our mediums of exchange, both public and private. Yet people would scream and holler if forced to begin using seashells because our notion today is that "money" is a paper dollar or better yet a digital credit in our respective checking accounts. Unfortunately, we have been slowly brought to this boil, or realization, through the subtle craftiness of men. President Johnson starts again by answering a question:

> Some have asked whether our silver coins will disappear. The answer is very definitely no. Our present silver coins won't disappear and they won't even become rarities. . . . If anybody has any idea of hoarding our silver coins, let me say this. There will be no profit in holding them out of circulation for the value of their silver content.[17]

How could President Johnson claim with a straight face that the silver coins would not begin to disappear? This exact scenario developed when gold was confiscated in 1933. Of course the same situation would repeat itself again. Thousands of people began to save their silver coins because they knew that these coins represented real money, unlike the lead slugs they began to acquire from banks and retail outlets.

For further proof, walk into any local coin shop throughout the United States and see if they have any pre-1965 silver coins in inventory. If not, they would not be in business. Then pull a quarter from your pocket and try to explain to the person behind the counter that you would like to exchange your quarter for a pre-1965 silver quarter. This person may laugh at you, call you ignorant or throw you a strange look. But one thing this employee certainly will not do is exchange your quarter for the one behind the counter. This is because contrary to President Johnson's claim that there would be no profit in holding on to silver coins, there was indeed a greater monetary value placed on a silver dime than a lead slug. He was either ignorant or lying when he proclaimed that people would gain no profit from hoarding their silver coins. Maybe someone should have raised his hand and asked the president why, if that last statement was indeed correct, banks would not be re-circulating all silver coins that came into their possession? The banks were not about to redistribute the silver coins that came into their coffers because silver is real money. As one hundred silver dimes came through their doors they would issue in exchange one hundred silver-looking slugs.

We Will Be Well Served

In conclusion, President Johnson did not mentioned that he, along with Congress, was guilty of counterfeiting, but he did say that by implementing this new act all would be "well."

So, we have come here this morning to this, the first house of the land and this beautiful Rose Garden, to congratulate all of those men and women that make up our fine Congress, who made this legislation possible—the committees of both Houses, the leadership in both Houses, both parties. . . . I commend the new coinage to the nation's banks and businesses and to the public. I think it will serve us well.[18]

Without question it will serve the *cartel* "well" but not the people. The president next assured the people that now that these changes were implanted—and the principle of honoring just weights and measures completely abandoned, he had no intention whatsoever of returning to that honest monetary system found within the Constitution of the United States.

Now, I will sign this bill to make the first change in our coinage system since the 18th century. And to those members of Congress, who are here on this very historic occasion, I want to assure you that in making this change from the 18th century we have no idea of returning to it.[19]

It was inarguably a historic day and one that would not be soon forgotten. Regrettably, it is a day that not many of us were around to witness, or we were too young to comprehend its significance.

Signing off as though some theatrical performer in a Broadway play,

President Johnson ended by saying, "We are going to keep our eyes on the stars and our feet on the ground."[20]

This closing remark needs no explanation. Perhaps, however, someone should have pulled the President aside and explained to him that by signing this act his life could and should, according to the following law, be in jeopardy.

The Coinage Act of April 2, 1792 stated in Statute I Section 19 that:

> And be it further enacted, that if any of the gold or silver coins which shall be struck or coined at the said mint shall be debased or made worse as to the proportion of the fine gold or fine silver therein contained, or shall be of less weight or value than the same out to be pursuant to the directions of this act . . . every such officer or person who shall commit any or either of the said offenses, shall be deemed guilty of felony, and shall suffer death.

Our inspired founding fathers were adamant about using gold and silver as our country's money, and were even more serious in regards to the swift punishment that would come to those who felt and acted to the contrary.

NOTES

1. Ezra Taft Benson, *An Enemy Hath Done This* (Salt Lake City: Bookcraft, 1992), 215.

2. Ibid.

3. Ibid.

4. Alan Greenspan, "Gold and Economic Freedom," in *Capitalism: The Unknown Ideal*, ed. Ayn Rand (New York: Signet Books, 1967), 101.

5. Benson, *An Enemy Hath Done This,* 215.

6. Benjamin Franklin, compiled by John Barlett, *Familiar Quotations,* 15th ed. (Boston: Little, Brown, 1989), 226.

7. *Alexander Hamilton and the Founding of the Nation,* Richard B. Morris, ed. (New York: The Dial Press, 1957), 21.

8. Benson, *An Enemy Hath Done This,* 221.

9. Bertrand H. Snell, 77 CONG. REC. 83 1933.

10. Henry Mark Holzer, "How Americans Lost Their Right To Own Gold And Became Criminals in the Process," *Brooklyn Law Review* (1973), 39

11. Earnest Lundeen, 77 CONG. REC. 83 1933.

12. Ron Paul, "What do Rising Gold Prices Mean?" *Texas Straight Talk* on Decemeber 5, 2005.

13. Lyndon B. Johnson, "Remarks at the Signing of the Coinage Act," July 23, 1965, Online, *The American Presidency Project*, available from http://www.presidency.ucsb.edu/ws/index.php?pid=27108&st=&st1= [americanpresidency.org]

14. Ibid.

15. Ibid.

16. Ibid.

17. Ibid.

18. Ibid.

19. Ibid.

20. Ibid.

Chapter Twelve

THE WATER IS NOW AT FULL BOIL

Gold is not necessary. I have no interest in gold. We will build a solid state, without an ounce of gold behind it. Anyone who sells above the set prices, let him be marched off to a concentration camp. That's the bastion of money.

—Adolf Hitler

Distorting a monetary system can be achieved through numerous different methods. However, the mechanism of choice is irrelevant once a financial system—whether based upon precious metals, paper dollars, or seashells—becomes artificially inflated. Although the mechanisms employed can differ slightly from one another, the end results are always the same. Not only does inflation rob all participants in an economy, but does so with a discriminate attack on those who have the most to lose. Chief among those are the poor, those on limited incomes, and people who have their savings in fixed financial investments.

We have been given prudent counsel from many of our Church leaders to live within our means. This is sound advice not only for us but also for all people and businesses including government. Many of us have firsthand experience or have witnessed others striving to cope with the consequences that spring forth as a result of taking on too much debt. Of course, as our government continually takes on higher amounts of debt through the form of loans, we the people become collectively poorer each year as we become the victims of confiscation through inflation.

Debt Begins to Swell

In the early 1930s, people became more curious about the monetary system and began questioning the soundness of their currency. When the music plays and people have plenty of money at their disposal, very few stop to question how much longer their prosperity will continue. Ignorantly, many people back then as well as today assume that the music and the financial good times will play indefinitely. People only began asking tough questions concerning the stability of their money because they were now forced to. The roaring twenties, where loose terms and easy credit were found in abundance had now been replaced by our nation's severest depression. When individuals and families have little or no work, it makes paying down debt virtually impossible, greatly increasing the odds of foreclosure on a home, business, or both. In these dismal circumstances, retaining one's wealth regardless its size becomes the number one objective. The need to hold on to one's wealth is the only incentive needed to cause one to run to their bank in a desperate attempt to recover all that was previously promised.

Most of this information has already been covered. The end result was that in order to fix this emergency, President Roosevelt calmly issued a banking holiday. When hoarding continued, he called in all gold. We did not discuss in the previous chapter the mounting financial obligations or debt that our government owed. In 1933 the federal government had borrowed a sum of $22 billion. They were clearly living beyond their means, yet it was we the people that were left dangling from this hook in order to pay back this public debt. Thomas Jefferson, who would quite possibly go into cardiac arrest if he could witness our monstrous public debt today, expressed these words of caution:

> There does not exist an engine so corrupt of the government and so demoralizing of the nation as a public debt. It will bring on us more ruin at home than all the enemies from abroad against whom this Army and Navy are to protect us.[1]

Considered one of our founding fathers, Thomas Jefferson unfortunately understood and witnessed firsthand the destruction and peril that foreign enemies could and did inflict throughout the Revolutionary War. Interestingly, it was the taskmaster of debt, or public debt, that he feared would bring about more destruction and ruin to the people.

Without question, $22 billion is an extravagant amount of money.

Sadly, this number began to grow exponentially as the years and decades passed along. It was the lesser of two evils—or so our government reasoned. With help from their partner, the Federal Reserve, they began borrowing obscene amounts of money rather than taxing the people outright. If the government had been represented by men that honored moral integrity like our founding fathers did, then the national debt would not be the huge issue that it is today.

The stage was set for a rapid expansion of the nation's money supply. The Federal Reserve and all of its member banks had been pardoned from the burden of relinquishing their gold. Unfortunately, the people were not granted the same relief. With help coming in the form of new legislation passed by their partner, the Federal Reserve could now rest easy knowing that their millions of previously issued dollars could no longer be redeemed for gold. To say that the Federal Reserve began to inflate at a torrent pace in order to lend the government all the money that they desired would be an extreme understatement. By 1944 the commencement of the Bretton Woods conference had begun, and in just over a decade the public debt had ballooned to over $200 billion, an astounding 2000 percent increase.

Who could stop this maddening clip of debt from continually reaching new heights year after year? The only power strong enough to correct this misguided course was our government, who ironically stood to benefit the most from this maddening addiction.

Europe Grows Uneasy

As the decades rolled along our nation's debt obviously did not decrease nor did it even plateau. Think for a moment about all the consumer goods that we could acquire and the financial assistance that we could generously give to friends and others in need if we had unobstructed access to a perennial money tree. This is precisely what the government has at its disposal—a hybrid tree that instantly produces perpetual financial fruit. These effortlessly obtained funds began to flood the world in the decades that followed the Bretton Woods Agreement. Billions of America's dollars were being stockpiled in foreign countries as our nation paid to rebuild war-torn cities and gave substantial amounts of money away in the form of foreign aid, loans, grants, and so forth.

The European countries in particular had accumulated vast amounts of U.S. paper dollars. Remember at this point the citizens of our nation would no longer have the right or the privilege to redeem paper for gold but that all foreign nations were still allowed to do so. It became apparent to these countries that the United States was no longer adhering to the agreement made in Bretton Woods, which was to back currency with a certain amount of gold. Honoring this agreement would prevent the currency of those countries that were present from infinitely inflating. Gold was the tether that held the world's currencies from rising any further than agreed upon.

Anxiety was mounting among foreign governments and their respective central banks. It appeared to them that the United States would soon be in the position where they could no longer honor the redemption of dollars for gold. Their assumption was not without merit. The United States was rapidly increasing the pace at which they were borrowing money. Living within their means was an option not even allowed on the table at that point. But what, if anything, could foreign countries do about it considering that the United States was the largest and most powerful economy in the world?

This was the dilemma that many countries faced during the late 1960s. It was apparent to them that our government was no longer playing by the rules, and they defied anyone in trying to stop them. Gratefully, these illegal maneuvers taking place on the world's financial field were not hidden from those here at home, one just needed to know where to look.

The pending economic crisis that now faces America is painfully obvious. If even a fraction of potential foreign claims against our gold supply were presented to the Treasury, we would have to renege on our promise. . . . If the government can renege on its international monetary promises, what is to prevent it from doing the same on its domestic promises? How really secure would be government guarantees behind FHA loans, Savings and Loan Insurance, government bonds, or even Social Security?[2]

This quote was given by President Benson and reiterates the concern that it may be necessary for the government to take some drastic steps. President Benson made this statement just as the panic of other nations was beginning to rise and right before our government resorted to drastic measures. He stated quite plainly that it would only take a small fraction of the many billions of dollars that were floating throughout the world to be exchanged for gold before we would be forced to cry uncle. He hinted that our government may have to renege on redeeming paper for gold. He also raised the interesting point that if our government can and does renege on their promises, how safe can government bonds, various federal loans, and Social Security be? Could these promises to pay—that so many people now desperately depend upon—be here today and gone tomorrow?

Another Emergency

The pending economic crisis was undoubtedly known not only to men such as President Benson and others like him but also to all those foreign nations who held our dollars. It was for this reason that history again repeated itself and runs on the Federal Reserve erupted. Foreigners, like the U.S. citizens some forty odd years before, came to the realization that if they didn't redeem their paper for gold in a hurry, they might be left holding the short end of the stick. Wasting precious little time, foreigners began to hoard gold just as the people did during Roosevelt's time in office. A question from an earlier chapter remains: who among us could blame them? The foreigners wanted off the bus before the wheels flew off, so they scampered to get out of U.S. dollars as fast as they could.

Confidence in the United States financial system began to erode. This erosion stemmed from the fact that our nation was creating far more dollars than our gold reserve ratios allowed. At the time, our laws dictated that for every $25 that the Federal Reserve held in gold, they could only create $100 in paper bills. That practice, of course, was still unethical and is the main reason that the practice has been referred to as an insidious scheme. If that law had been adhered to, then our public debt would never have been higher than a four to one ratio of the gold our nation holds. As our nation's gold reserves were being siphoned away by foreign countries, the amount that we could legally inflate was simultaneously being lowered. This was not good news for the cartel. With their backs to the wall, our government threw the Bretton Woods Agreement pompously to the wind. The Federal Reserve began printing and loaning any amount of money that they saw fit, regardless of how much gold they had to back it with.

France led the charge and was far and away the biggest benefactor in regards to redeeming U.S. dollars for the Federal Reserve's gold. The cartel was facing an inevitable emergency and something needed to be done immediately before their gold reserves were completely depleted.

President Richard Nixon came to the helm and inflation continued to grow unabated. Considering that the nation's debt had risen to just under $425 billion, it is miraculous that foreign nations didn't start years earlier in their redemption of gold for paper. If we believed the words of President Roosevelt, our financial system could last indefinitely as long we the people had enough confidence. Apparently that confidence had started to wane, and not just for those foreigners holding U.S. dollars. The people here at home were up in arms over inflation and the high costs of goods and services. President Nixon paid great lip service. He is on record saying that:

> Inflation robs every American, every one of you. The twenty million who are retired and living on fixed incomes, they are particularly hit hard. Homemakers find it harder than ever to balance the family budget . . . your paychecks were higher, but you were no better off.[3]

He concurs with everything that we have previously discussed, yet he fails to mention what is causing this inflation in such great abundance. President Nixon, along with Congress, implemented price and wage controls hoping "to stop the rise in the cost of living."[4]

We could take the next few pages and speculate as to how and why this oblivious statement was given as the cure-all for stopping runaway inflation. The definition and solution to what inflation is and how to combat it has been given and explained multiple times throughout this book. Needless to say, we have not once proven that telling someone they can only earn X amount of dollars per hour or cannot sell their goods for more than X amount of dollars has ever reversed inflation or its ravaging effects.

Another Great Plan

Nearly forty years have passed since that first fireside chat delivered by President Roosevelt over the radio. Alongside the many financial changes that we have discovered there have been great advancements in audio and video technology as well. It was again a Sunday night and the date was August 15, 1971. This historic night would not only be broadcast to the people via radio but also by live TV. An earlier chapter mentioned that something needed to be done in order to stem this pending emergency. That plan was unveiled on this Sunday evening. President Nixon began his address to the nation outlining a new economic policy entitled "The Challenge of Peace."

He began by stating that although the war was over, there were still a number of things threatening the country's peace and prosperity. We recently read a quote from President Nixon where he alluded to the fact that because of inflation, many families were struggling to keep their personal budgets balanced. Restoring our nation's prosperity required leaders that were ready to take bold action, along with the help of the great people of our nation, he claimed. This requires a three-pronged attack, which he then lists, "We must create more and better jobs, we must stop the rise in the cost-of-living, we must protect the dollar from the attacks of international money speculators."[5]

President Nixon soothed the people by saying that although the cost of living was rising out of control, through bold leadership, our government could do whatever it took to nip inflation in the bud. Understandably, he acknowledged that inflation was rampant; unfortunately, he did not explain to the people by what mechanism inflation had been able to increase. Perhaps he felt similar to former President Franklin Roosevelt when the latter stated that there were "comparatively few who understand the mechanics of banking."[6] International money speculators were attacking the dollar, but there was no explanation as to why the dollar was being attacked. Why must it be protected? What did the dollar do to provoke an attack in the first place? Does the word *attack* even correctly described the situation that was taking place? Who were these international money speculators? Aren't there international money speculators found in all financial arenas such as bond markets, stock markets, currency exchanges, and hedge funds? Would the people have been shaken and brought to attention as effectively if the words "foreign neighbors" were used in place of international money speculators? These were some of the questions not asked and therefore not answered. Did any of the people stop to think about what had not been said? Certainly. Did enough of these self-aware citizens exhort their elected representatives to stand up no matter what the cost and repeal this soon to be implemented legislation? Apparently not.

A Pillar of Stability

President Nixon continued by explaining what he and Congress were proposing in order to restore peace and prosperity. Effective immediately, a 7 percent excise tax on all automobiles was repealed. In addition, taxpayers could now deduct on extra $50 for each exemption one year earlier than planned. He was also ordering a $4.7 billion cut in overall Federal spending. There was a 10 percent cut in foreign economic aid and a 5 percent tax credit for investing in new equipment for all businesses.

Regrettably, this was nothing more than what the Romans commonly referred to as *panem et circensis,* meaning bread and circuses. True, the government was not handing out fresh loaves of French bread to the people nor were they giving out tickets to Barnum and Bailey in order to have them entertained. They were however, quite literally handing out financial treats that would distract the people from the underlining source of all the economy's problems, which was not higher prices, mundane jobs, or attacks on the dollar—it was inflation.

President Nixon went on to say that the dollar needed protecting in order to maintain stability throughout the world:

The third indispensable element in building the new prosperity is closely related to creating new jobs and halting inflation. We must protect the position of the American dollar as a pillar of monetary stability around the world.

Once again, no explanation was given as to why the dollar needed protecting. As he said, the American dollar had been a pillar of stability. When the dollar's stability began to falter, it spurred the nations of the world to cash out their U.S. dollars. He continued:

In recent weeks, the speculators have been waging an all out war on the American dollar. The strength of a nation's currency is based on the strength of that nation's economy and the American economy is by far the strongest in the world.[7]

Incredibly, there was still no reason given for the cause of war against the dollar! Would it ever come? What the people deserved to hear was the truth. They had witnessed the *effects* firsthand but what most people didn't comprehend was the *cause* for their lack of peace and prosperity. Perhaps the citizens would have forced their elected representatives into immediately restructuring our monetary system had this so-called *emergency* been explained to them in a more truthful way. President Nixon could have said that it was our foreign neighbors demanding our gold, instead of indirectly implying that they were the equivalent of some elusive offshore terrorist group. Had he spoken the truth that Sunday night, he would also have told the people that the government was living well beyond its means and to fund such a lifestyle required them to create more money than the laws allowed. The president would have also mentioned that as a result of breaking the agreement made in Bretton Woods, the government had broken the trust of all those countries in attendance. He confessed in his conclusion that many foreign countries no longer had faith in our monetary system, which was causing them to cash in their chips and go home. Unfortunately, although he confessed this situation, he shamelessly spun it in the opposite direction.

In his conclusion, President Nixon tried to reassure the people that our nation's strong economy is indicative of tomorrow's. He accurately stated that America's economy was by far the strongest in the world. His realization was skewered, however, when he stated that a sound currency gets its strength from a robust economy. By now we have a good understanding of what is required in order to have and maintain a stable currency. We know that when currency is not backed 100 percent by precious metals, the only thing that keeps this Ponzi scheme afloat is the *faith* that citizens put into it.

President Nixon was infamous for a variety of well-documented reasons. The reason most pertinent to us in regards to our study of financial history is about to be delivered. He relayed to the people that he had directed the Secretary of Treasury to take the appropriate actions necessary in defending the dollar from would-be attackers and all other foreign hooligans. With that, the pin had been pulled, making it too late for foreign countries to scramble for financial cover. A live grenade has just been tossed in their direction that would completely destroy their hopes of ever obtaining gold from the U.S. again. President Nixon concluded:

> I have directed Secretary Connally to suspend temporarily the convertibility of the dollar into gold or other reserve assets, except in amounts and conditions determined to be in the interest of monetary stability and in the best interests of the United States.[8]

With the utterance of these words, which were later followed by the stroke of a pen, President Nixon was able to officially slam shut the teller window of gold redemption to any potential recipients. I can assure you that this measure was not temporary. Keeping their gold—not allowing it to be given away—was in the best interests of the United States. This was President Nixon's counterattack to those foreign governments who were supposedly assaulting the United States gold supply. Through this unethical maneuver President Nixon essentially told the rest of the free world to go fly a kite. Their options were few, so many of these foreign countries wound up holding the short end of the stick after all. A few years previous to this unprecedented procedure, President Benson had predicted this type of outcome. He said that foreigners, "would be left holding the bag with American dollars"[9] if our government were to renege on its promise to redeem paper for gold. Unfortunately for those foreign nations, that is exactly how it played out.

Putting the Bugaboo to Rest

It was indeed a historic night. The damage had been done but President Nixon wasn't finished. Assuming (and possibly correctly) that many of the citizens within earshot were a bit perplexed as to the interpretation of his recently announced resolution, he stated the following: "Now, what is this action, which is very technical, what does that mean for you? Let me lay to rest the bugaboo of what is called devaluation."[10]

The president stated that his counterattack against international speculators was quite technical. I would respond to President Nixon by stating that it's not that complex. In simplistic terms, the government printed lots and lots of money that found its way into foreign hands over time. Our government promised to redeem paper dollars for gold. Many foreigners decided to do just that. This scared our government because they knew there were not enough gold coins to cover all of the paper dollars that they had printed. Word spread quickly and a run on our central bank ensued. With gold draining fast our government decided to change the rules. They told all the foreign nations that were "attacking" our dollar to take a hike and if they didn't like the new rules, too bad. Did this explanation seem very technical to you?

President Nixon next tried giving a financial lesson to the people by explaining his idea of devaluation. He wanted to assure the people that this new policy would not cause their decreased purchasing power to continue, or in other words, inflation would no longer strangle family budgets. Here, in his own words, he explains how it works:

> If you want to buy a foreign car or take a trip abroad, market conditions may cause your dollar to buy slightly less. But if you are among the overwhelming majority of Americans who buy American-made products in America, your dollar will be worth just as much tomorrow as it is today.[11]

On that Sunday night I was not old enough to grasp the significance of the events that had just unfolded on live TV. I can only speculate how those old enough to comprehend the very technical procedures that our president was taking must have been feeling that night. Surely there was some solace in knowing that if they purchased only American automobiles, Nike tennis shoes and Levi's jeans they would not feel the drastic effects of inflation. According to the president, as long as Americans didn't purchase any of the other 50,000 consumer goods that were produced overseas, the people had a good chance of keeping their family's budget in line. Yes as long as the overwhelming majority of Americans follow these guidelines their dollars would be worth just as much tomorrow as they were today, the president promised. This was a truthful statement. Too bad no one could have asked him that night what their dollars would be worth in a year or two or ten down the road, because they will undoubtedly have lost significant purchasing power.

President Nixon closed his address exhorting the American people to collectively proclaim that, "Our best days lie ahead."[12]

We must determine for ourselves in the pages ahead whether we find this motto to be fact or fiction.

It Is Now Too Late for the Frog

The United States has now in theory and application abandoned all attachment to gold and silver. It did not happen overnight, nor *could* it happen overnight. History has shown that people would revolt if this shameless ploy were implemented over a short span of time, just as surely as a frog would jump out of boiling water.

Our founding fathers presented us with a game plan that, if followed, would bring our nation the peace and prosperity that our ancestors fought for. They did not promise us bread and circuses in the forms of tax cuts, credits, exemptions, budget cuts, or promises to cut back on financial aid. No, these God-fearing, noble men believed that we should adhere to a monetary system that had been proven in providing financial stability for thousands of years.

It took nearly 184 years for those men in power to break free from the gold chains that bound them from creating unlimited amounts of money. There is no doubt that these men tried repeatedly to break those restraints throughout the years and they unquestionably had some successes along the way. They secretly triumphed when no alarms were sounded as they began to change the wording on our currency over the years. There was a festive atmosphere when the Federal Reserve Act was announced on the front pages of numerous newspapers on Christmas Eve. Undoubtedly many high fives were exchanged amongst cartel members when gold was confiscated as a result of the banking emergency. Chances are that if one listened carefully enough, they could hear the bankers snicker as citizens made their deposits with real silver coins, yet in return were given slugs that only looked like the real ones. Little imagination is needed to envision the numerous hallelujahs expressed by bankers and government alike once President Nixon closed the gold window, signaling an all-systems-go for inflating the currency.

The forerunners to the above subtle events were the first two central banks which helped condition the people into thinking that unbacked paper money was okay as long as you could spend it the same way as gold and silver.

The way in which these men have sought after the ability to obtain something for nothing over the years is eerily similar to the way in which Satan tempts us to doing his bidding. Getting us to commit just a little sin, rather than a whopper, is his modus operandi. For the most part, these objectives above were accomplished by small incremental changes and through the subtle craftiness of men. By recognizing this pattern it becomes easier to identify the true leader who stands in the shadows directing this attack, eagerly anticipating the financial destitution and despair that will no doubt soon follow.

All of these minute alterations to our monetary system over the years have unleashed financial misery on many unsuspecting people. Although at first they seemed small and insignificant, each time a new modification was first proposed and then implemented the heat was unquestionably kicked up another notch. This was done repeatedly and as the temperature continually increased, the water also began the process of going through its different stages. Regrettably, it is now too late, not only for our proverbial frog but also for the people of this country. As a result of gold and silver no longer being used as currency backing, or for that matter, in any other way, shape, or form, the water has finally reached a full boil.

N o t e s

1. Thomas Jefferson, To Nathaniel Macon, August 19, 1821.

2. Ezra Taft Benson, *An Enemy Hath Done This* (Salt Lake City: Bookcraft, 1992), 216–17.

Chapter Thirteen

THE FEDERAL RESERVE

This is a staggering thought. We are completely dependent on the commercial banks. Someone has to borrow every dollar we have in circulation, cash or credit. If the banks create ample synthetic money we are prosperous; if not, we starve. We are absolutely without a permanent money system. When one gets a complete grasp of the picture, the tragic absurdity of our hopeless situation is almost incredible, but there it is. It is the most important subject intelligent persons can investigate and reflect upon. It is so important that our present civilization may collapse unless it becomes widely understood and the defects remedied very soon.

—Robert Hemphill, Credit Manager of
Federal Reserve Bank, Atlanta, Georgia.

The quote above comes from a man who once worked behind the curtain. His comments are indeed staggering, and they certainly solidify all that we have discovered so far.

When a government adheres to the protocol of a gold standard, it is legally bound as to how much paper money it can print. Prior to President Nixon's decision to rid our nation of its obligation to redeem paper for gold, the Federal Reserve could only print paper dollars that equaled four times the value of the country's gold reserves. The promise to redeem gold to citizens had been extinct for nearly forty years. By disallowing foreign nations of this privilege as well, the final thorn embedded within the cartel's side had finally been removed. It was a process that spanned many lives and nearly two hundred years, but our nation was finally able to disassociate itself from the truthful financial principles found within our Constitution.

The green light had flashed and the Federal Reserve was pushing the pedal to the metal. This partially describes the explosive acceleration in which the two participants, the Federal Reserve and our government, were seeking to inflate the money supply. And inflate it did. In the ten years leading up to when President Nixon decided to cut all gold ties from the dollar, the national debt had gone from just under 300 billion to just over 400 billion, an increase of roughly 30 percent. Moving forward a decade to the year 1981, the dollar amount the government has put us on the hook for is a whopping one trillion dollars—an incredible, and one would think unsustainable, increase of over 150 percent. The sky truly was the limit, for no longer was a stipulation in place mandating that our government hold a certain percentage of gold, albeit small, to back our currency. From this point forward, our currency was purely fiat, sustainable only through the faith and confidence of the people who were forced to use it.

FIAT Fait-money has been argued over since the days of our founding fathers. Bankers and economists alike were finally satisfied because their gripe had always been that the quantities of gold were insufficient to promote economic expansion and stability within an economy. Before President Johnson handed over the reins to President Nixon he made the following statement indicating which school of thought he agreed with:

> The world supply of gold is insufficient to make the present system workable, particularly as the use of the dollar as a reserve currency is essential to create the required international liquidity to sustain world trade and growth.

I am not sure which statement makes less sense, the one above or the one he made after telling the American people that silver coins were now going to be replaced by silver-looking slugs.

We have seen through various examples and from reading the words of inspired men, that the only way to accomplish a sound monetary system is to honor the Lord's counsel by following and honoring the principle of just weights and measures. It is a fallacy to say or believe that a given medium of exchange is not beneficial to an economy because it is limited in supply. In our hypothetical village that used golf balls as the medium of exchange, it was apparent that there was neither additional stability nor other financial gains that could be attributed to the fact that their supply had doubled over night. This skewed way of thinking that a money supply needs to be flexible and have the ability to be increased is continually perpetuated by men who are striving to obtain something for nothing.

The Barbaric Metal

Gold in many ways was placed on an endangered species list for nearly forty years. However, once President Nixon relinquished gold's honorable duty as a minute backer of paper dollars, it did not become extinct but instead merely put out to pasture. What did become extinct though was the Executive Order of 6102, which required gold coin, gold bullion, and gold certificates to be delivered to the government. This, along with all the penalties and fear of imprisonment for being found in the possession of gold, had now been revoked.

In 1974 Gerald Ford was the president of the United States. It was on his watch that all Americans were allowed the opportunity to once again own gold in all of its various forms. This feat was accomplished when Ford signed Executive Order 11825 on December 31 of that same year. Interestingly, the occasion was not marked with a fireside chat or the modern day equivalent. There were neither newspapers running headlines on the front page describing this occasion as being festive nor any other front-page acknowledgments for that matter. Strangely, this executive order was presented and signed into law just as similarly as dozens of other Executive Orders signed during a president's term.

Since gold no longer acted as a restraint against runaway inflating of the currency and could not be used as true money, our government graciously allowed us to own the yellow metal again. But it was too late; the damage had been done. To most Americans, gold was became nothing more than something to be used in creating jewelry.

Change can be difficult. For some, breaking life-long habits can be next to impossible. People become comfortable with ideas and concepts they have grown up with. Many of us put a great deal of stock into what others who hold authoritative positions over us have to say and offer. When listening to such leaders, it can become difficult to differentiate between fact and folklore. There are many who fall into the trap of complacency. They feel that as recipients of the blessings given to those who dwell within this promised land, all is well and collectively we are immune from political mischief and turmoil. However, the Lord has been very specific about this exact possibility.

President Lincoln noted that if we the people were given the truth we could then weather any storm: "I am a firm believer in the people. If given the truth, they can be depended upon to meet any national crisis. The great point is to bring them the real facts."[1]

The people were not given the real truth as to why President Roosevelt mandated a banking holiday. President Johnson uttered a half-truth when he said that the reason for substituting slugs for silver was due to scarcity. President Nixon omitted the truth when he did not explain why our dollar was supposedly under attack by foreign nations. Although Ford, who without ceremony or fanfare, reinstated gold ownership after a decades long hiatus, the people were misguided into believing that it was now nothing more than a relic.

Seeking for and comprehending the truth and the unfortunate financial events that follow, has been one of our primary topics. It has also been mentioned that knowledge is power. We are studying the pages of history from past to present in order to obtain certain knowledge. We cannot become empowered in the future if we sit and do nothing with this newly acquired information. If we vacillate after being presented with knowledge that could be instrumental in providing for ourselves and our families, we do so at our own peril. "But if any provide not for his own, and especially for those in his own house, he hath denied the faith, and is worse than an infidel" (1 Timothy 5:8).

The Money Tree Takes Root

Without exception every chapter up to this point has focused on history. Whether it be in the time of Moses, our founding fathers, or as recently as 30 years ago, those events and circumstances have now come and gone. Numerous ideas, concepts, mechanisms, manipulations, and confiscations have transpired over the centuries. Just as we have assuredly learned many valuable things from studying the pages of the past, there must certainly be things that we could add to our arsenal of knowledge that can be found in our day. From this point forward we will try to decipher the truth and the facts pertaining to the corruption of the currency, as President Benson encouraged.

The topics that this book has covered are artificially inflated monetary systems, negative effects of inflation, the sound reasoning behind using precious metals, and the involvement of the Federal Reserve and our government surrounding such. Throughout the chapters of this book I have used an accusing tone directed at the cartel. It is assumed that this partnership between the Federal Reserve and our government has represented the financial albatross that helplessly hangs from our nation's neck. Are we justified in branding them as the scapegoat every time our financial economy finds itself in various upheavals? If history is an accurate indicator, then we will soon be able to answer this question.

In today's financial realm there are no monetary systems left that back their currencies with precious metals. We now use paper dollars in our currency system; this unique form of money is called fiat, and through enforced legal tender laws, the freedom to choose whether or not to accept this funny money is no longer available to our population. This type of money is the sole cause of inflation, which by now we know is nothing more than a hidden tax or a subtle way of confiscating wealth. Once gold was removed as the protector of stability, the government's prized hybrid money tree began to shoot skyward.

Many of us have heard the old adage about our government creating money out of thin air. Firing up the printing press is another frequently expressed analogy that refers to the government's ability to create money from nothing. Is it really that easy? Does money magically appear any time our president and Congress decide that their immediate funds are not sufficient? Who oversees the highly coveted printing presses and does our government even use paper money any longer? Although it may seem that money is indeed created out a thin air, there is certainly a better explanation than this. Consider the following words from James Madison as we begin an in-depth look at how and where all fiat money is created:

> History records that the money changers have used every form of abuse, intrigue, deceit, and violent means possible to maintain their control over governments by controlling the money and its issuance.[2]

The mechanism in which money is created does not involve violence, but it is assuredly full of intrigue and deceit and it will soon be obvious how the moneychangers are able to control our government.

Acquiring Money through Taxation

Our government is able to derive the financial funds that it thinks it needs through two different procedures. The most familiar—and the one that we all begrudgingly contribute to—is taxation. This form of wealth accumulation is continually a hot topic. President Ronald Reagan was widely known for his sense of humor. He once explained that the way in which government views the economy could be summed up briefly in the words: "If it moves, tax it. If it keeps moving, regulate it. And if it stops moving, subsidize it."[3]

On a different occasion and in a more somber mood, President Reagan also said the following: "The federal government has taken too much tax money from the people, too much authority from the states, and too much liberty with the Constitution."[4]

Congressmen J.C. Watts, Jr. from Oklahoma would wholeheartedly agree with President Reagan that our government has taken more than its fair share from the people through taxation. He lists just a few of the areas where our government has taken a generous piece of our financial pie:

> The government taxes you when you bring home a paycheck. It taxes you when you make a phone call. It taxes you when you turn on a light. It taxes you when you sell a stock. It taxes you when you fill your car with gas. It taxes you when you ride a plane. It taxes you when you get married. Then it taxes you when you die. This is insanity and it must end.[5]

It is not the intent, nor is there space enough in this book, to dive into all of the pros and cons—mostly cons—of taxation by our government. This vast topic that is so critical in maintaining our inalienable rights of independence will have to be discussed elsewhere. For now, we will suffice in saying that through the means of taxation, the government is able to secure a part of the revenue they need in order to fund its monstrous budget.

When you or I find ourselves a little short of cash in covering our monthly expenditures, we unfortunately do not have the benefit or leisure of taxing our neighbors, coworkers, or friends. Therefore, the only option left to us in which to cover our deficit is to borrow. When we the people solicit lending institutions, we are scrutinized very carefully through background checks, credit scores, and verification of financial net worth. Once approved, we are then allowed to sign our life away for an amount of money that does not even exist until it is digitally credited into our account by the bank.

Fortunately for our government, they are not required to go through the strenuous and intimidating hoop-jumping that is required by the rest of us in order to obtain funding. If their credit history were pulled and magnified as intensely as ours is, the government would simply receive an apologetic letter explaining that the bank had decided to pass on their request for a loan (and an address where they can send off for a free credit report).

The government is able to extract enormous amounts of money not only through income taxes but also from the dozens of other taxes that Congressmen Watts described earlier. When the government casts its net over everything that moves, it is able to haul in over $2 trillion each year. Remarkably, this amount of money still falls short of funding the government's yearly liabilities. This is the time when our government is in need of tapping their bottomless line of credit the most. With the season drawing to a close, it is now time for them to harvest the financial fruit that their hybrid money tree has graciously provided.

Issuing Bonds or Promises to Pay

In reality, when the need arises for our government to borrow money it does so in a unique and unorthodox way. In simplistic terms, the government sells bonds, but before these bonds can be redeemed for paper dollars a game of follow the leader, or in this case follow the money, must first ensue.

A bond is an impressive and distinctive looking piece of paper adorned with fancy borders and stately looking signatures. In actuality it has no more intrinsic value than an elementary school reading certificate, which in many ways is similar in appearance. A bond is nothing more than a promise to pay. If you have ever borrowed money from a close friend or relative, they may have had you sign a promissory note. Found within this note would be the amount you borrowed plus any interest that the two of you had previously agreed upon, along with the date that this money was to be returned and your signature promising to honor this agreement. A bond is essentially the same thing. The government promises to repay the bearer the original amount plus interest on a specified future date.

Our government is able to sell these bonds or treasury notes as they are also referred as, to numerous different lenders. They borrow money by selling these bonds to large corporations, municipalities and foreign governments, which are substantial buyers and we the people buy many of these bonds also. This avenue of providing additional income to supplement the already vast amount collected by taxes, helps cover the financial shortfall of the government's yearly budget.

The government taxes everything that it can possibly imagine along with issuing bonds to any and all willing participants, in hopes of amassing still more money. Incredibly, this Mount Everest sized pile of revenue is still not sufficient to retire the government's annual debts! So now what do they do? Is this where the old motto kicks in about money being created out of thin air? Do they give their hypothetical money tree another good shake? The game follow the leader was mentioned previously. Perhaps a more appropriate synonym would be, follow the money trail. There is without question a trail, or a particular process, that must be followed in order for the government to obtain its desperately needed cash. We must follow it from start to finish to fully comprehend the mechanism in which our government obtains something for nothing.

Following the Trail

Our government has two distinct methods in which it can accumulate revenue. We briefly discussed one of the ways this is brought about, and, although certainly not popular, taxation is very effective. The second process involves issuing bonds, which enables our government to borrow the money directly from its citizens. The government still comes up short, so they begin to sell additional bonds, but this time around there is a twist in the plot: they only sell bonds to those registered on an exclusive list. In fact, this list is so short and the prerequisites so demanding that in reality there is only one group that could pass such rigorous requirements. This elite group is none other than our government's partner, the Federal Reserve System.

For a simplistic and easy to comprehend example, let's assume that our government, after taxing and selling bonds to foreign countries, corporations, and us common folk, still finds itself needing a million dollars in order to pay all of its bills. To solve this dilemma our government grabs a piece of paper, writes a few inspiring words across it, stamps a formal looking border around the edges and slaps on an indistinguishable signature or two. The government, with virtually no effort and very little expense, has now just created a million-dollar bond. But a bond cannot pay their bills. They need hard cash or its equivalent such as checkbook money, or better still, digital credits that represent paper dollars. Either one will work fine as long as they can redeem this bond for some type of money.

So our government rings up the Federal Reserve and asks them if they would be interested in purchasing some of their debt. This is legal jargon; in reality, a government representative would pick up the phone and say something more to the effect of:

> Hey guys, how you doing over there today? Good, good. Say listen, we're a little bit behind the eight ball today and we were hoping that you could spot us a quick million dollars? Super! We'll send Paul over with the bond sometime after lunch. Thanks for your help, I'll talk to you tomorrow.

The Federal Reserve is more than willing to help their partner; in fact, they are eager to do so. They welcome this opportunity to serve, albeit their service is based on alternative and selfish motives. Every time they extend a helping hand in the form of lending, they will be paid back not only in principle, but with interest as well.

So an agreement has been made. The Federal Reserve has committed to lend the government a million dollars, and to keep it legal, our government gives them an IOU, or bond, which states that they will repay the loan with interest, due within a predetermined number of years. A bond, although only a piece of paper, acts as a unique form of collateral. The way that the Federal Reserve holds a bond is similar in terms of how a commercial bank retains the title to one's car until the loan has been completely repaid. Once the bond is in the possession of the Federal Reserve it is labeled a "Security Asset." It is referred to as an asset because the issuer, our government, is the largest and most powerful organization on the planet. The Federal Reserve is not worried about the government defaulting on this loan because they know that the government has the power to tax the people in order to obtain the necessary money needed to repay the loan. Could it still just be a coincidence that the Federal Income Tax Act was passed in the same year as was the Federal Reserve Act?

So in a very literal sense our government does indeed have access to a perpetual money tree—us. This wealth is obtained by harvesting the fruit of *our* labors. Because of this, the Federal Reserve sees little chance that our government will default on this million-dollar loan. This reassurance is how the Federal Reserve is able to comfortably reclassify this bond as a Security Asset.

Before the year 1933 there was a different type of security asset used—gold. In theory, if there were $10 million in gold sitting in a bank vault somewhere, then legally the bank could issue $10 million in paper currency. The assets that stood behind that paper currency was, of course, gold. In sheer amazement the Federal Reserve System today defines assets as official looking pieces of paper signed by our government and backed by the taxpayers.

With asset in hand, the Federal Reserve is now ready to issue money just as it did decades ago when their assets were held in gold. Now it is the Federal Reserve's turn to grab a piece of paper and scribble an official signature across the bottom righthand corner. This paper document is known as a "Federal Reserve check." It is used in the same manner that you or I would issue a personal check. The only difference is that we would not write a check if we knew there was no money in our account—but that is precisely what they do. They take out their checkbook and write a check to our government for the promised one million dollars. It is a paper check written off the account of the Federal Reserve, hence the name Federal Reserve check. This is the truest form of creating purely fiat money. Yes, there are so-called assets backing these checks, but they are nothing more than our government's promise to pay, issued in the form of bonds.

The money trail makes a U-turn and the Federal Reserve check is now headed back to our government. They treat this check just as any of us would by flipping it over and endorsing it with their signature. The government is now in possession of a million-dollar check with their name on it. Although not paper dollars, checkbook money as we know spends just as easily as cash. There are many areas of the government that will wind up being the recipients of this million-dollar loan. Without a doubt the government has some legitimate areas and programs where this money is desperately needed. Conversely, many of these so-called needs are nothing more than wants. President Reagan seems to agree when he said, "Government always finds a need for the money it gets."[6]

This million-dollar check is then taken by the government and deposited into its account located within one of the Federal Reserve's banks. The government has now successfully swapped one piece of paper for another and is a million dollars richer by doing so.

What happens next is not complicated, nor is there any difficult banking jargon that needs to be defined. Once the government deposits their check, they now have sufficient funds to begin writing their own checks in order to pay their outstanding liabilities. Tens of thousands of these checks are written every month: they have thousands of federal employees to pay. There are also hundreds of various organizations that routinely approach our government with their hand out, fully expecting to be compensated in one form or another. This something-for-nothing attitude from these numerous groups is one of the main contributing forces that drive up our nation's overall debt. Nowhere in our Constitution does it dictate that our government should finance special interest groups, nor see to it that every American has a roof over their heads and plenty of food in their cupboards. It was President Grover Cleveland who said, "Though the people support the government the government should not support the people."[7]

President Benson also admonishes us not to solicit handouts from our government:

> Avoid looking to government for handouts or future security. Again, this is not only good practice in normal times, but especially important today. A government which is unable to pay its own bills can hardly be depended upon to pay yours.[8]

Unfortunately, there are many organizations that represent vast amounts of individuals seeking for nothing more than a free lunch. This is where much of the recently borrowed million dollars will end up. Financing a war, along with operating and maintaining military bases throughout the world, will also grab its piece of the financial pie. Park rangers, mail carriers, armed servicemen, correctional officers, elected representatives, criminal justice employees, and all of the other federal employees that it takes to manage, enforce, protect, and enlarge a bureaucracy, expect to be financially compensated as well.

It is now the federal employees' turns to endorse and deposit their checks into their respective personal bank accounts. This process is known as a commercial deposit because banks such as Bank of America, Wells Fargo, Chase, and Citibank, along with countless others, are considered commercial banks.

Without any toil on our government's part, they were able to instantly create a million dollars. Some will say that the word "create" is inappropriate. They will argue that our government borrowed the million dollars. In reality, this mechanism of obtaining money, whether defined as creating or borrowing is nothing more than a Ponzi scheme. Sure, issuing a bond is the equivalent of promising to pay, but our government has lived far beyond its means for decades now. The only ability they have in which to repay this loan is through forced taxation.

The regrettable effect of this government-initiated cause is that our monetary system has now been artificially inflated by one million dollars. There is now floating throughout the collective commercial banks a million dollars that did not exist a few days before. Where did this million dollars originate? Did our government borrow a million dollars in gold or silver coin that had previously been stored away for safekeeping deep inside the Federal Reserve's vault? No, it had long ago abandoned the policy of honoring the principle of just weights and measures. The government was instead given a check, which is only a piece of paper that represents money, in exchange for another piece of paper, a bond, that our government originally gave the Federal Reserve. This procedure is not too far removed from the game of hot potato. Would the money supply still become artificially inflated if the government had borrowed one million dollars in gold versus fiat money? No. If the Federal Reserve had an extra million dollars in gold and if they decided to lend it to our government, the money supply or gold would only be stored or located in a different location. However the *amount* of gold would not change, it would only change hands. Changing the location of a pre-existing amount of money does not increase the overall supply. This can only happen when money is created by decree.

The commercial banks of our nation have collectively just assumed guardianship of the recently deposited million dollars. Through coercion by our government our mediums of exchange have changed over the decades but banking terms and jargon have not. What you and I would commonly call bank deposits is referred to as "bank reserves" in the world of commercial banking. Of course in the old days it was the gold and silver that sat inside a bank's vault that was considered bank reserves. Today, it is paper checks and paper money that hold this title.

I'm Starting a Bank

Several years ago I had the opportunity to meet and associate with a certain highly successful businessman. He was at least twenty years older than myself and I thoroughly enjoyed picking his brain and exchanging various business ideas with him. Jack had employed my company to do a significant amount of work for him and because of this I was able to meet with him frequently over the course of a few months.

I would often meet Jack at his house when he wanted to go over certain aspects of his project or make additions or deletions to it. He lived in an upscale neighborhood that could easily be the equivalent of

Beverly Hills if it weren't located in the desert. His neighborhood was like a mirage. Pristine lakes and mature landscaping surrounded it as far as the eye could see. On one occasion Jack gave me a rundown of the numerous marquee neighbors that called this area home such as media personalities, star athletes, and intermixed were a few very interesting rags to riches stories.

By putting in his time, Jack had made his millions by working in the field of banking and finance. It certainly wasn't the most flashy or exciting day job. However, there was no doubt that Jack had been very successful. He had then retired and seemed to be living the good life.

He counseled me with sound advice after I relayed to him some of the details surrounding a few business deals that did not turn out as I had hoped they would. We discussed the amazing returns from the stock market at the time. We related some of the better trades that we had made, but of course his transactions were on a much larger financial scale than mine.

I obtained priceless information from a man who not only worked in finance but also had many years of experience with the business world in general. It wasn't until our time of working together was nearly completed that he shared with me some of his plans for the future. He explained to me how he and his partner had been out looking around town to purchase a commercial building. As soon as he had uttered these words, commercial real estate investing immediately came to my mind. I had known two other individuals who did nothing else except invest in commercial properties—both of whom were extremely successful.

But Jack had no intention of becoming a real estate investor. He was starting a new bank and was looking for an appropriate place to house his new business. Jack did not offer many more details nor did I pursue any. I had worked at a bank for two years while I attended college, and although there was plenty of money in the bank, I was not convinced that a bank could ever earn substantial amounts of money. Yes, there are monthly charges for checking accounts, ATM fees were outrageous for non-members, and one would pay dearly if they were ever to bounce a check, but I was still not convinced that banking could be a lucrative business.

Of course, the enterprise that Jack was about to start would require him to invest a small portion of his own money. However, the greatest thing about starting and owning a bank is that you can earn substantial amounts of money simply by loaning that which you do not have. This mechanism is made possible through the assistance of the Federal Reserve System. At the time I had no knowledge of what fiat money was or how a monetary system could be artificially expanded. In my mind's eye, Jack was a brilliant man, but for the life of me I couldn't figure out why he would want a business that would require thousands of customers and their measly transaction fees to keep him financially afloat. Uncharacteristically, he left me with no further details concerning this business topic and I left scratching my head. Today I not only know why Jack wanted to start his own bank, but how he and most other banks large and small have been able to arrive at their success.

Excess Reserves

The commercial banks now erroneously refer to their newly collected million dollars as reserves. The fact that these reserves are nothing more than pieces of paper promising to pay is irrelevant to the banks. As far as they are concerned, these newly deposited checks that came from the thousands of our government's employees will now be classified as reserves.

This next step is where things begin to get interesting for the bankers and like Pavlov's dog, they start to salivate at the mere sight of these newly arrived reserves. These commercial banks are not considered Federal Reserve banks, but they are, however, members of the Federal Reserve System. As members they are entitled to all the same incentives and benefits.

When deposits are placed into the commercial banks, the Federal Reserve mandates that these banks retain 10 percent of each new deposit as reserves. Let's simplify our ongoing example of how a monetary system becomes artificially inflated. Let us assume that the million dollars that has been deposited into numerous commercial banks was instead deposited into just one bank. This will not change the outcome in terms of the number of dollars that will soon be created, but it will make it slightly easier for us to follow the money trail. Once one of the numerous commercial banks, we will call it Comm Bank, receives the million-dollar deposit, it is then required to hold 10 percent, or $100,000, of it in reserves. This now leaves Comm Bank with $900,000 more than the Federal Reserve requires them to hold in reserve. Since the bank only has to hold $100,000; the remaining $900,000 now in Comm Bank's possession is, unbelievably, looked upon as "extra." This of course is a layman's definition. Within the banking industry this phenomenon is properly referred to as "excess reserves."

In reality there are no excess reserves. If one million dollars had been deposited in the form of gold coin, then that million dollars, not 10 percent, would need to be kept in reserve in order satisfy all withdrawals once they were presented. Since precious metals have been conveniently taken out, all of our monetary system withdrawals are funded with paper money backed by nothing more than the faith or confidence of the people. The rationale behind saving 10 percent of deposits and thereby labeling the remaining 90 percent as *excess reserves* makes about as much sense as people who, after paying the minimum amount on their credit cards, feel that they now have *extra money* since they did not pay off the entire balance.

Putting Excess Reserves to a Good Use

Comm Bank now has $900,000 that they can legally loan out. As long as they hold the stipulated amount of 10 percent in reserve, the bank can lend out the full $900,000 that remains. At first glance this process may seem like a wash. Sure, the bank is now charging interest on the newly issued loans, but at the same time, they must pay interest to the original customer who deposited the million dollars. Typically a bank charges its customers a few percentage points higher for borrowing money than it pays other customers for depositing their money. This is understandable we reason, because after all a bank, like any other business, is entitled to make a profit for itself and its shareholders. But does this spread between the interest rate that the bank charges for its loans and the interest rate that it pays depositors to keep their money in the bank create enough stimulus to cause a banker to salivate at the mere sight of excess reserves? Not at all; but what follows next most certainly will.

Money is notorious for burning holes in people's pockets. Many of us find a good use for our money as soon as we discover that we have any extra lying around. Banks are certainly no different. They too want to put their excess reserves to good use, and no one has perfected this philosophy more than banks.

With the 10 percent set aside as reserves, Comm Bank is now legally ready to loan out the $900,000. There are many different ways in which the bank can lend out its money. Some applicants may be trying to secure a second mortgage. Others simply may want to borrow money and have the convenience of paying it back rapidly, which is what a line of credit can provide. Loans that require the applicant to sign a personal guarantee but no collateral are only available to people with perfect credit. There are numerous loans extended for automobiles, boats, and recreational vehicles and typically the bank will hold the title to these assets until the loan has been fully satisfied. Credit cards are another vehicle that the bank uses to lend money. It is one of their favorites because of the high rates of interest that they are able to charge. These are some of the more popular, but by no means all of the methods in which a bank can lend money. Once this $900,000 has been lent out to various people with different backgrounds, educations, and occupations, people start doing what most of us do best—they spend it.

These people from all walks of life now venture out into their community and purchase the goods and services that they have had their eye on. This $900,000 now begins to exchange hands as various financial transactions are completed. Hundreds of individuals and business owners now become the recipients of the same dollar amount that was originally borrowed from Comm Bank. However, before these people and shopkeepers can spend the money that they have just received in exchange for the goods and services that they provided, they must collectively deposit the $900,000.

Like carrier pigeons that ultimately return home after a long flight, every one of these dollars that left the bank in the form of a loan is now returning from its financial journey in the form of a deposit. Since the vendors that sold these goods and services were not paid in precious metals, they cannot use the cashier's checks, personal checks and credit cards that they accepted as payments as a medium of exchange. These forms of payment must first be converted into checkbook money so that they can pay their own suppliers, employees, and overhead. This is why the $900,000 must once again be deposited.

With open arms Comm Bank now welcomes back their $900,000. It is a joyous reunion. There is, no doubt, a festive atmosphere lingering about. This return of their original investment is far superior to even a repossession or foreclosure. Not only do they have their seed money safely back again, but they are also still collecting interest on the $900,000 that they had previously lent out.

What happens next is one of the primary reasons that this whole mechanism of inflating a monetary system has been frequently described as insidious. This process painfully illustrates how man has unapologetically shown total disrespect to the counsel that was given concerning the principles of just weights and measures. This immoral and unethical maneuver would not have to be brought to light if, through the years, man would have honored our founding fathers' wishes and believed in a monetary system as President Benson most assuredly did:

> I believe in honest money, the gold and silver coinage of the Constitution, and circulating medium convertible into such money without loss. I regard it as a flagrant violation of the explicit provisions of the Constitution for the federal government to make it a criminal offense to use gold or silver as legal tender or to issue a irredeemable paper money.[9]

This quote is more than worthy of a second read and should be highlighted, making it easily accessible for future reference. It reiterates everything that we have discovered and concurs with the truths that were given to us by our inspired forefathers. Being able to paraphrase, if not memorize this quote, will provide prudent strength to those who seek to come off victors in this economic battle we are all facing. His remarks are straightforward and to the point, which is why President Benson is one of my favorites. Nothing within this quote could be interpreted as obscure or ambiguous.

Multiplying Excess Reserves

The $900,000 has come home to roost in the form of deposits. Incredulously, the 10 percent reserve requirements that applied to the first million originally deposited within the bank is now repeated with the $900,000. The Federal Reserve's rule, which is seldom if ever enforced, mandates that 10 percent of all deposits be held in reserve. Comm Bank now has bank reserves of $900,000. After pulling aside the mandatory 10 percent or $90,000, Comm Bank is now left with $810,000 in excess reserves. Now it is time once again to find a good use for their extra money. The best way in which to make more money from their money is of course to lend it out with interest. Remarkably, the lending process starts all over again and this time around the amount that the bank has available for lending is $810,000.

Once the $810,000 is lent out the process begins to repeat itself. Individuals and businesses spend money on goods and services and those that provided the goods and services send the collected dollars back to the bank in the form of deposits. These returning dollars are given a soldier's welcome for they have performed their duty well. Among these dollar reserves $81,000 will have to sit out the next tour of duty. However, $729,000 are already lining up and readying for deployment.

This third advancement of dollar reserves that are deployed by issuing loans and credit now comes to a total of $2,439,000. The first wave of loans sent out $900,000. The second wave sent out $810,000. The most recent wave is sending out $729,000, bringing the total amount that has flooded the economy to just over $2.4 million. Did the banks originally start with $2.4 million to lend? Did the bank have $2.4 million in precious metals backing this checkbook money and digital credits? No. Are banks able to create money out of thin air? This certainly appears to be the case.

Like a bad habit, this procedure of turning deposits into loans that later return in the form of deposits only to be sent out the door again as loans, is repeated continuously. Once Comm Bank receives the $729,000 back in the form of new deposits, it will set aside 10 percent to be held as reserves and will then have $656,100 ready to loan again. This unscrupulous mechanism will continue, and when each deposit comes in they will keep 90 percent to issue for new loans. Since the law dictates that the bank keep 10 percent of each new deposit on hand, not that anyone believes that this Ponzi scheme is ever enforced, each new wave of lending must be reduced by 10 percent. If we reduce 10 percent from each new wave of deposits starting with the $656,100 that will shortly be coming back to Comm Bank, the totals that they would be able to lend in each proceeding wave would look like this:

5th wave of lending would be $531,441
6th wave of lending would be $478,297
7th wave of lending would be $430,467
8th wave of lending would be $387,420
9th wave of lending would be $348,678
14th wave of lending would be $205,891
22nd wave of lending would be $88,629
27th wave of lending would be $52,374

So how much money has Comm Bank been able to lend out through the course of these numerous and repetitive waves of lending? The question would be irrelevant if they were lending out gold and silver, for this action would not increase the overall money supply which always leads to inflation. It would merely be spreading the money supply around, which is vastly different. Unfortunately, this bank did not lend out precious metals. Instead they issued pure fiat money, which negatively affects all people within a community, regardless of whether or not they were the recipients of the banks' financial generosity.

The maximum amount of fiat money that can be created by a commercial bank is approximately 9 times the original amount of any deposit. In our example, Comm Bank started with deposits that collectively totaled one million dollars. Therefore, if this bank were able to find enough borrowers it could quite possibly loan out $9 million from this one deposit alone. The bank's potential profits are gargantuan while their overhead consists primarily of the paper and postage it requires to send and maintain their customers' monthly statements and cash their checks.

For the sake of simplicity, we used Comm Bank as a hypothetical example in order to explain and follow the money trail of where deposits become loans and vice versa. We took the liberty of stating that thousands of government employees took their paychecks and deposited them solely into Comm Bank. In reality there are numerous commercial banks where one can make their deposit. Although tracking the one million dollars through only one bank made it easier to visualize the financial process involved, the results would be the same if the original one million dollars had been deposited amongst six commercial banks. Whether through a group working together or a bank going solo, once one million dollars is deposited into the banking system, it has the potential to increase nine fold.

Incredibly, this mechanism is able to flood our economy with millions of dollars that were neither earned nor previously in existence until the banks issued this money as loans. It is a hard concept to grasp when one considers that millions of dollars can be created from something as simple as an IOU or government bond. In reality, today's money is backed by nothing more than debt. We now know that ever since President Nixon closed the gold window, the restrictions of a 25 percent backing of gold for every dollar no longer applies. So for over thirty-five years there have been no precious metals backing even 1 percent of our currency. It is the confidence and faith among we the people that propels and sustains this financial charade. But what really backs our nation's currency? It is not thin air or the strength of our national government—it is debt. The more bonds that our government can sell to the Federal Reserve, the more reserves commercial banks can accumulate. The reserves that a bank accumulates determines their ultimate pile of excess reserves. These excess reserves are the basis for all loans. This is the scheme from which our government is able to discreetly confiscate our wealth without directly taxing us. It is worse than taxation—it is stealing. It is done without our consent and unfortunately carried out unbeknownst to the masses. This heinous process robs us all of our purchasing power and hits those who need it the most the hardest. Some people may argue that there is nothing wrong with a little inflation. Just as assuredly there are those who argue that a little sin is nothing to fret over. However, once Pandora's box has been opened, it is seldom ever resealed as tightly as before. President Benson again weighs in with his thoughts on this sinister process.

> It is true that a little inflation is not as harmful as a great deal of inflation. But, in *principle*, there is no difference. I am opposed to *all* inflation—and that means *all* deficit spending—because (1) it is a hidden tax which is a deceitful and immoral method of collecting revenue; (2) it is an unfair tax which shifts the heaviest burden of payment onto the shoulders of the thrifty who are attempting to save for the future, and upon the retired who are living on fixed incomes; and (3) it is an irresponsible act which saddles future generations with the payments of our own fantastic debts.[10]

NOTES

1. Abraham Lincoln, compiled by John M. Barry, *The Great Quotations,* 338.

2. James Madison, "Quote from James Madison," Online, *Liberty-Tree. ca,* available from http://quotes.liberty-tree.ca/quote/james_madison_quote_b37f.

3. Ronald Reagan, "Quote from Ronald Reagan," Online, *Liberty-Tree. ca,* available from http://quotes.liberty-tree.ca/quote/ronald_reagan_quote_d79f.

4. Ibid.

5. J.C. Watts, Jr., "Quote from J.C. Watts, Jr.," Online, *Liberty-Tree.ca,* available from http://quotes.liberty-tree.ca/quote/j._c._watts_quote_b6e8.

6. Ronald Reagan, *Liberty-Tree.ca.*

7. Grover Cleveland, quoted in *An Enemy Hath Done This*, 135.

8. Benson, *An Enemy Hath Done This*, 220.

9. Ibid.

10. Ibid., 211.

Nelson W. Aldrich
Jekyll Island Museum

Henry P. Davison (L) and Charles D. Norton (R)
UPI/Bettmann

Abraham Piatt Andrew
Jekyll Island Museum

The seven men who attended the secret meeting on Jekyll Island, where the Federal Reserve System was conceived, represented an estimated one-fourth of the total wealth of the entire world. They were:

1. Nelson W. Aldrich, Republican "whip" in the Senate, Chairman of the National Monetary Commission, father-in-law to John D. Rockefeller, Jr.;
2. Henry P. Davison, Sr. Partner of J.P. Morgan Company;
3. Charles D. Norton, Pres. of 1st National Bank of New York.
4. A. Piatt Andrew, Assistant Secretary of the Treasury;
5. Frank A. Vanderlip, President of the National City Bank of New York, representing William Rockefeller.
6. Benjamin Strong, head of J.P. Morgan's Bankers Trust Company, later to become head of the System;
7. Paul M. Warburg, a partner in Kuhn, Loeb & Company, representing the Rothschilds and Warburgs in Europe.

Frank A. Vanderlip
Jekyll Island Museum

Benjamin Strong
UPI/Bettmann

Paul M. Warburg
Jekyll Island Museum

Courtesy of *The Creature from Jekyll Island*

Andrew Jackson was our 7th president, and a staunch supporter of the principle of "just weights and measures." His campaign motto for his second term was, "Jackson and no bank, or Bank and no Jackson." He let the people know that the central bank would be abolished if he were re-elected president. He ended up winning a second term.

Courtesy of http://www.vintage-movie-poster.com

Some claim Alan Greenspan was the epitome of economics. Decades ago he said, "In the absence of the gold standard, there is no way to protect savings from confiscation through inflation. . . . Deficit spending is simply a scheme for the confiscation of wealth. Gold stands in the way of this insidious process." After 18 years as president of the Federal Reserve System, he will retire in January 2006. During those 18 long years of service, he never once reiterated his convictions of gold being a protector of wealth. Why not?

Courtesy of http://home.millsaps.edu

The Glass Owens Bill was signed on Christmas Eve 1913 by President Woodrow Wilson. This banking Bill blew the breath of life into the creature of fiat money, commonly called the Federal Reserve System. In just three short years he expressed remorse for allowing such a bill to reach maturity. In reflection he mused "I am a most unhappy man. I have unwittingly ruined my country."

Courtesy of http://www.etsu.edu

The founding fathers implement "wise and holy principles" within the Constitution and sign it on September 17, 1787.

Courtesy of http://teachpol.tcnj.edu

Here is Ezra Taft Benson as Secretary of Agriculture on the cover of Time magazine 1953. He is on record stating, "The root of all evil is money, some say. But the root of our money evil is government." He also stressed that, "Few tasks, if any, are more important for the preservation of freedom than the preservation of a sound monetary system."

Courtesy of http://img.timeinc.net

This was the clubhouse for the private resort on Jekyll Island. It was the birthplace of the Federal Reserve System and where Senator Nelson W. Aldrich, father-in-law to John D. Rockereller Jr., pledged all participants to secrecy.

Courtesy of Jekyll Island Museum

Once banks decide to abandon the sound monetary principles found within the Constitution, the practice of fractional reserve banking will shortly follow. Today all banks are engaged in this dubious practice. For every $100 a bank has on deposit, it will have $3–$5 on average in actual green paper dollars to hand back to customers.

The rest is held in the form of digital credits. With averages like these, possibly 5 people in this above photo of another bank run would be paid back in full.

Courtesy of http://img.slate.com

Citizens standing in line hoping to withdraw their hard earned money. This somber scene was captured in Detroit. This was just one of many bank runs that occurred in the early thirties.

Courtesy of http://www.authentichistory.com

Franklin D. Roosevelt was our nations 32nd president. He played a major role in debasing our country's monetary system. In his first presidential radio broadcast, he claimed that those Americans who were hoarding their own money were engaging in an "exceedingly unfashionable pastime."

Courtesy of http://www.jolaf.com

The Coinage Act was passed in 1792. Our country then went nearly 173 years without any fundamental changes to our coinage; that is until this man, Lyndon B. Johnson, took over as president in 1964. He subtly applied more heat to the impending boiling water.

Courtesy of http://countrystudies.us

In 1971 President Nixon said, " Inflation robs every American, every one of you." To help deaden the pain, he offered them, "panem et circenses"—bread and circuses.

Courtesy of http://www.hrc.utexas.edu

Chapter Fourteen

TRUTH IS ETERNAL

The rich ruleth over the poor and the borrower is servant to the lender.

—Proverbs 22:7

How many of us could be referred to as *servants*? Is the promised land really the home of the free? Are any of us are currently borrowing from a *lender*? If you are, do you consider yourself a servant? If one is a servant to an individual or group, how can they truly be considered free? Certainly most of us have played the role of servant at one point or another throughout our lives. Is all borrowing to be frowned upon? Some of these questions are rhetorical in nature. Others need to be answered sooner rather than later. Our current president of the Church, Gordon B. Hinckley, makes no bones about the repercussions of debt and claims that freedom is beyond our reach when it looms over us.

> Self-reliance cannot be obtained when there is serious debt hanging over a household. One has neither independence nor freedom from bondage when he is obligated to others.[1]

Thirty years earlier, President Spencer W. Kimball also warned us of overextending ourselves.

> The Lord has blessed us as a people with a prosperity unequaled in times past. . . . But I am afraid that many of us have been surfeited

with flocks and herds and acres and barns and wealth and have begun to worship them as false gods, and they have power over us. . . . Many people spend most of their time working in the service of a self-image that includes sufficient money, stocks, bonds, investment portfolios, property, credit cards, furnishings, automobiles, and the like to guarantee carnal security throughout, it is hoped, a long and happy life. Forgotten is the fact that our assignment is to use these many resources in our families and quorums to build up the kingdom of God.[2]

Going back even further into history we see that our prophets have warned us for quite some time about the dangers of debt. Although President Heber J. Grant did not claim that our personal sovereignty would be at risk from excessive debt, he instead promised our families certain blessings if we would live more frugally. "If there is any one thing that would bring peace and contentment into the human heart, and into the family, it is to live within our means."[3]

From the above quotes we are warned that our freedom is out of reach and bondage will be our fate, if we allow ourselves to become perpetual servants of financial lenders. Conversely, promises of peace and contentment can be ours if we as live within our means. Are we to believe then that all forms of borrowing are to be frowned upon? Absolutely not. There are many instances where borrowing, when done in moderation, is not only appropriate but also can be beneficial. President Benson lists a few areas in our lives where acquiring financial assistance may be appropriate: "Sound business debt and a reasonable debt for education are elements of growth. Sound mortgage credit is a real help to a family that must borrow for a home."[4]

However, he also says that if we must borrow money in order to obtain homes and other items, that we should do so wisely. He continues by saying, "I implore you to value your solvency and happiness, buy within your means."[5]

Hyper Inflation

Although these four prophets led our church at different times over a hundred-year span, their messages agreed with one another providing prudent counsel not only for individuals and families but corporations and nations as well. If our nation, as well as many of us, would have followed their sound advice by living within our means, our country, along with the rest of the world, would not now be suffering the consequences that debt and inflation always deliver.

In the previous chapter we were able to blow the smoke aside, enabling us to clearly see how the Federal Reserve System commercial banks are able to multiply their excess reserves. The Federal Reserve has set some forms of restraint by mandating that all commercial banks keep a reserve of 10 percent from all incoming deposits. This act in and of itself is highly inflationary, but what if all reserve requirements were completely abandoned? So far our government and the Federal Reserve have not yet reached that point. Our government is still able to borrow money by selling bonds to individuals, corporations, and many foreign countries—Asian countries in particular. This scenario cannot last forever. We the people are not the only ones who have found that it takes more dollars to purchase goods and services than it used to. These foreign central banks who hold vast amounts of our government's bonds will soon begin slowing their purchases and ultimately stop buying bonds altogether. Until then, our government will continue to borrow from whomever it can, and when it comes up with no prospects, it will turn again to the Federal Reserve as their lender of last resort. So what would happen if foreigners no longer generously lent us their money and the Federal Reserve withdrew the insignificant sum of the 10 percent reserve requirement? The presses would start to run night and day and we would begin to experience hyperinflation.

There has not been a civilization throughout history that has ever sustained a purely fiat monetary system. If this was exclusively a history book, we could take a chapter reviewing all of man's past attempts at initiating and ultimately failing in his quest for implementing paper money, backed only by faith and confidence. Suffice it to say that any and all attempts throughout history have completely failed. Some people feel that history will not repeat itself, believing that because we are the most powerful and financially well-off, not to mention that our land is choice above all others, our present day fiat monetary system will continue indefinitely.

Not long ago countries such as Brazil and Argentina experienced firsthand the menacing effects of hyperinflation. The financial turmoil that followed was undoubtedly brought about by their respective governments printing fiat money day and night. Their money, like ours, was backed by nothing other than monstrous piles of IOUs.

The epitome of hyperinflation in this last century belongs to Germany. What follows are a few of the high points. Soon after World War I broke out, the Reichsbank, the equivalent of our Federal Reserve, suspended its practice of redeeming paper money for gold. This meant that there was now no legal limit as to how many paper dollars it could print. Germany was at war, and like all governments during war, it borrowed heavily in order to pay for the enormous expenses of war. Once the war was over, our nation and those other countries that were on our side imposed reparation payments on Germany. These payments made by Germany were used toward rebuilding many of the war-torn countries that had suffered from the physical destruction of the war. Although the war had ended, Germany's habit of printing money with no gold backing had not. They continued printing at a furious pace in order to pay off their financial share that was owed to the international community. When money is simply created by decree, it is never long before inflation arrives on the scene.

By 1922, prices for goods and services had risen by nearly 700 percent. It was in the middle of this year that all confidence in Germany's money started to vanish. One year later many employees were being paid twice each day because the value of money, or the purchasing power, was declining at such a rapid pace. Thousands of people who were previously on fixed incomes were now destitute. Their savings had been confiscated through inflation. They began selling furniture, watches, kitchen appliances and anything else they could get their hands on in order to secure enough money to buy the necessities of life. Farmers would not bring their produce to town because they were tired of receiving worthless paper money in exchange. This in turn caused mobs of men to forage in search of food.

There are stories of women taking piles of paper money and burning it in their wood stoves, not only for heat but for cooking as well. Apparently, the paper money that was needed to purchase a small bundle of wood in town could burn longer than the actual wood itself. President Benson experienced Germany's runaway inflation when he visited this country for the first time. Many years later on a return visit he mentioned how outrageous prices had become back then: "I came here first in December 1923. On that visit, my first German breakfast cost me six billion marks— then about fifteen cents in American money."[6]

Six billion of anything, whether it be pennies, marks, or kernels of corn, is a staggering amount. Interestingly, when was the last time any of us could purchase breakfast from a restaurant, bakery, or school cafeteria for fifteen cents?

There are other distressing details we could use to describe the dire conditions that many went through once hyperinflation commenced its financial stranglehold on the ill prepared. However, with no pun intended, there was a silver lining for a select few. Those who had stored their wealth in silver and gold coins were able to come away virtually unscathed from the financial ruckus which was inflicted upon thousands of others. As the purchasing power of the German mark became less and less, gold and silver coins began their ascent upwards in terms of purchasing power. Surely this phenomenon played out because governments, businesses, and a few individuals knew that at the end of the day, real money is not paper promises, it is gold and silver.

Will Hyperinflation Repeat?

Most people reading this book were not yet born or were too young to remember the devastation caused by the Great Depression that started in the late twenties. President Benson said that if our nation's current economic crisis is not resolved, our country will enter a depression that makes the one in the twenties and thirties look like prosperity. Regrettably, our nation's currency is traveling down the road toward extinction. As it runs out of gas it will slowly roll to a stop—never to start up again. It is then that it will find itself in that same graveyard where all currencies throughout history have been laid to rest. President Benson again paints a visual picture of what will play out before paper dollars become worthless and warns that those whose savings are dominated primarily in dollars will become financially ruined.

> Even though American citizens would still be forced by law to honor the same pieces of paper as though they were real money, instinctively they would rush and convert their paper currency into tangible material goods which could be used as barter. As in Germany and other nations that have previously traveled this road, the rush to get rid of dollars and acquire tangibles would rapidly accelerate the visible effects of inflation to where it might cost $100 or more for a single loaf of bread. Hoarded silver coins would begin to reappear as a separate monetary system which, since they have *intrinsic value* it would remain firm, while printed paper money finally would become

worth exactly its proper value—the paper it's printed on! Everyone's savings would be wiped out totally. No one could escape.[7]

Gold and silver played a major difference between our country's Great Depression and the hyperinflation that Germany painfully endured. There is no doubt that the depression inflicted untold amounts of sorrow and financial pain for thousands of people in our country. However, the vast amount of the population still held some of their wealth in various forms of gold and silver coins. The people who lived during the Great Depression could at any time take their paper money and exchange it for gold or silver at their local banks. This monumental fact is what prevented many people from becoming wiped out financially. This was a sharp contrast to the dismal options that the Germans faced. Unfortunately, their sole monetary system after 1914 was based upon the dishonest principles of fiat money.

Contemplating whether or not hyperinflation could possibly occur in our own country, spurring a devastating depression, is certainly not a favorable pastime. There should be no doubt however, that if our government continues the current torrent pace of obtaining something for nothing, it will not be a matter of if but of when. Just as unsettling as the above thoughts, consider the ramifications of not having enough food for the family after the numerous warnings from prophets exhorting us to obtain a year's supply of food. Although thinking about the unpleasantness associated with starving is not on the top of most people's list, it is nevertheless frequently brought to our attention in the hopes that we will properly prepare ourselves and our families before it is too late. The information presented in this book has been given in order to show how we can prepare ourselves financially and do so before it becomes too late to escape the ravaging effects of a depreciating dollar.

Defining a Trillion Dollars

All of the quotes by President Benson, which have shed light upon and solidified many of the important concepts that we have been reading about, were given before the year 1969. No one can accuse him of using ambiguous terms in the way he described our nation's financial problems—he has plainly told us what must be done in order to avert further monetary chaos. We haven't the room here to review all of his outstanding remarks, but this one bears repeating:

Spending more than is in the treasury and then merely printing extra money to make up the difference. Technically this is called "deficit spending." *Ethically, it is counterfeiting. Morally it is wrong.*[8]

When President Benson gave this address, our nation's debt was roughly $400 billion. A staggering amount to be sure, yet it was still under half of a trillion dollars. It took over a decade for the debt that we are all collectively on the hook to repay crossed the one trillion dollar mark. It sounds quite impressive when you roll the words "trillion dollars" off the tip of your tongue, and indeed it is no small sum. Very few of us conduct business transactions that involve millions of dollars with any regularity. I would speculate that most of us do not, nor do we socialize with, those that spend or earn billions of dollars. That being the case, it should be safe to assume that none of us have had any experience with the enormous purchases that a trillion dollars can make.

To fully understand the magnitude of debt that hangs around our nation's neck we need to be able to fully comprehend how large these numbers really are. Another way of expressing a trillion dollars is to say that we have 1000 billion dollars. Although they do not make billion dollar bills, if they did it would take 1000 of them to equal a trillion.

Recently, my family and some friends took a week-long cruise through the Caribbean. At the time, the ship that we sailed on was the second largest vessel in the world. The ship's overall length was over 1000 feet and it stood fifteen stories high. Once in open water we were told that the ship burned through nearly 2900 gallons of diesel per hour. It weighed in at an impressive 138,000 tons and was able to carry just over 5000 people. This brand new solid steel edifice met every criteria needed to properly be labeled a true behemoth. A ship like this one could be built for you and some of your closest friends for a mere 650 million dollars. This is a respectable amount even for those few who are considered billionaires. For a more solid-footed example, if you were to double the ships asking price, you would then have the same amount of money that it took to build the Bellagio, a monster mega-resort in Las Vegas. So what could we purchase with one trillion dollars? Well hopefully we would receive a wholesalers discount, but if not, we could purchase 1500 of these colossal cruise ships for $650 million apiece. If we anchored them one behind another as we began to take delivery of them, they would soon disappear over the horizon, for they would stretch out over 284 miles in one direction. This, my friends, is one example of how staggering the amount of one trillion dollars actually is.

Is the Promised Land Bankrupt?

If we use the true definition of the word bankruptcy, then there is little doubt that our nation is completely bankrupt. The dictionary defines bankruptcy as having one's funds "totally depleted" along with being "insolvent." As we again flip through the pages and find the word insolvent, the dictionary defines it as being unable to meet debts or liabilities. Unfortunately, these definitions describe the financial state that our nation is currently facing and has been for quite some time.

In the prior chapter the mechanism used by governments and banks to create money was explored in great detail. Quickly summarizing, we found that our government can sell a piece of paper, or bond, to the Federal Reserve and in exchange receive more paper, or dollars, which are then used to pay their liabilities. So, are the government's funds totally depleted? Are they able to pay their outstanding liabilities? No and yes. If we adhere to the definitions of the word bankruptcy, then in theory we must conclude that they are not. There is a vast difference though between theories and reality—and the reality is that our government has been bankrupt for generations.

It goes without saying that there is an immense difference between what we the people and our government can do if we find ourselves short of cash. Although our options differ greatly, there are a few things that we can do. We could immediately begin to cut back on all unnecessary goods and services. Many of us have assets that we could sell in order to help raise cash, whether that be small appliances, electronics, boats, RVs, or vacation homes. These areas should be vigorously pursued first and foremost. However, if our revenue is still not sufficient to meet our needs, then there is always the option of borrowing the needed money. This is a route that almost all of us have taken at one point or another throughout our lives. However, it is an avenue that begins atop a slippery slope and one that we have been warned about repeatedly. President Hinckley, in just one of his many addresses on debt says:

> What a wonderful feeling it is to be free of debt, to have a little money against a day of emergency put away. . . . If you have paid your debts, if you have a reserve, even though it be small, then should storms howl about your head, you will have shelter and peace in your hearts.[9]

The financial storm clouds have been howling over our nation's head for generations now. Speaking of storms, Allan Sloan's article published on September 26, 2005 in *Newsweek* entitled "No Money? No Problem!" talks about the monetary mess that hurricane Katrina left in its wake, and in closing he mentions that, "Instead of a 'perfect storm' of the physical variety, we'll have one of the financial variety. And like Katrina, it's going to be devastating."[10]

Unfortunately, in the last two decades financial storms have rolled in more frequently and at much higher levels of intensity. We can trace the biggest of these storms to date, which ushered in our nation's insolvency, back to the year 1933. This is when President Roosevelt accused the citizens of participating in an unfashionable pastime: protecting themselves by hoarding their gold. It was during this year that the president declared a national banking holiday and our government suspended the practice of backing currency with gold. The government's gold supply was draining rapidly because they were spending way beyond their means. They thought that if they discontinued redeeming gold for paper dollars then they could do away with the restraints imposed upon a monetary system when the principles of just weights and measures are honored.

Sadly, this is exactly what they did. The truthful principles found within the Constitution were thrown into the back seat and greed along with something for nothing took over the wheel. Together they have driven nonstop for nearly three quarters of a century and have no intentions of ever stopping. However, one day in the near future the lack of faith and confidence will together act as a giant spike strip, blowing out the tires and causing unrecoverable financial mayhem.

Fiscal Hurricane

Storm analogies have been used to describe the state of excess debt and our country's worsening financial condition. Keeping within that theme seems to be pretty easy. In the business section of *USA Today*'s November 15, 2005 edition, a bold headline reads, "A Fiscal Hurricane on the Horizon." In this article reporter Richard Wolf recaps many of the candid high points that were given to a group of reporters over a breakfast meeting by David Walker, the Comptroller General of the United States. Walker, who is the nation's top auditor, says that the government's finances are in dire straits. More specifically Walker says that, "We face a demographic tsunami!"

It is hard to forget the catastrophic events that resulted from the 2004 tsunami as it slammed ashore in southeast Asia. After this life-shattering event, the waves ultimately returned to the sea and hopefully will not return. However, according to Walker this financial tsunami "will never recede."

Walker was pulling no punches. He laid all his cards on the table and without any nudging said that the financial dilemma facing our government today is, "worse than advertised."

These kinds of statements and accusations could be considered routine if they came from a member of some political party that was trying to undermine the current administration. Perpetual finger-pointing and playing the blame game are longtime favorites in the Washington crowd. Interestingly, Walker's position is not one that can be negotiated for. Heading the Government Accountability Office is a fifteen-year appointment. This being the case, one could reasonably assume that he was not notoriously known for projecting hyperbole in public. A reporter once asked Walker, "Aren't you depressed in the morning?"

Twelve Thousand Stately Ships

It was mentioned a few pages back that the quotes from President Benson were given before 1969 and that our nation's debt was less than $400 million at that time. What would he think if he were with us today after we told him that the interest alone on the nation's debt for 2005 was an incredulous $352 billion! This is the amount of interest due from all of the thousands of bonds that the government issued. So in a few short decades, what was once the government's total outstanding debt is now nearly the amount needed to pay only the yearly interest!

As our government continued to live beyond its means and the Federal Reserve kept its partnership alive by creating the necessary funds to lend back to them, the nation's deficit went into overdrive. It was around Halloween of 2005 when our country hit a memorable milestone. There were no treats for the American public, only a recurring vicious trick that most of us have become immune to. Unfortunately this event in particular had been preceded by seven similar ones, for it was during this week that our nation's outstanding debt inched past $8 trillion.

When you look at a map of the United States it can be difficult to truly appreciate the size and scope of our country. To help you appreciate the immensity of our nation, let us take a hypothetical drive across the country. San Diego, located a few miles north of the Mexican border and right on California's coastline, makes a great starting point for a hypothetical trip. First we would head north and hop on the eastbound Interstate 40. We would cross through the barren desert and pine country of Arizona. Once over the state line we would hit New Mexico before cruising through the Panhandle of Texas where we might see some armadillos. Texas, the biggest of the continental states, is by itself bigger than many other countries. Pressing eastbound we would pass through Oklahoma and Arkansas. Still heading east, Interstate 40 would bring us to Memphis, Tennessee, and then Nashville, the home of country music. Our journey would finally come to and end as we crossed the state line and entered North Carolina on the east coast.

Earlier we determined that a trillion dollars could purchase 1500 colossal cruise ships. So with our nation's current debt of $8 trillion, we can now place an order for 12,000 of these cruise ships. Our 1500 cruise ships stretched over 284 miles. With 12,000 of these stately ships we could line them up single file from San Diego to past the North Carolina state line—a 2272-mile string of gigantic, luxury cruise ships. Imagine the untold man-hours and it would take to manufacture these 12,000 iron vessels. Obscene amounts of natural resources would be consumed to fulfill this order. The labor would be exhaustive and it would take tens of thousands of employees working together to pull off this monumental feat. Unfortunately, the same work ethic has not been instilled in our government. All they "manufacture" is bonds when they find themselves short of money.

Eight trillion dollars is a monstrous sum of money. And that was in 2005—imagine what our nation's debt will be in a year or ten or twenty. We could not properly discuss government budgets without including all long-term liabilities. When these future payments come due, our government will be on the hook for an additional 40–60 trillion dollars, depending on whose yearly report you give more credence to. These future liabilities will begin coming due within the next decade. The money will be paid to the recipients of programs such as Social Security, Medicaid and Medicare. Can anyone seriously think that this colossal amount combined with today's $8 trillion in debt will ever be paid back? By now you have a pretty good idea of what your future purchasing power is going to amount to.

A Picture Paints a Thousand Words

We have just used mental images in order to help us fully comprehend how massive an amount $8 trillion actually is. The following graph tracks our government's debt for about the last seventy-five years. This information was calculated through the end of the fiscal year ending on

September 30, 2005. It is not difficult to see how the total debt began to launch progressively higher starting in the early 80s and then commenced an almost vertical climb over the last five years. If this rate continues unabated, we would most certainly see the government's deficit climb upward to $11 or $12 trillion over the next five or so years.

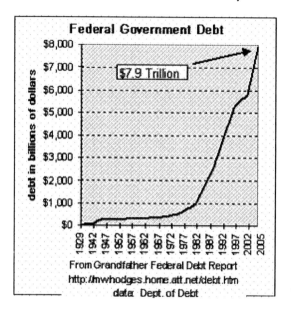

Some people have become misguided, thinking that since we the people originally gave power to and set up our current government, we should be able to stop paying the billions of dollars each year in interest and perhaps even cancel the debt altogether. President Benson weighs in against this fallacy.

> Often we are admonished not to worry about deficit spending and the national debt since, after all, we only owe it to ourselves. What utter nonsense! If that were the case, why don't we just cancel the debt to ourselves and stop paying all that interest?[11]

The fact is that we owe nearly $2 trillion to foreigners; the bulk of that is due to the governments of Japan and China. There will come a day when these countries, along with many others, will begin to say no thank you to the bonds that our government will desperately try to sell them. They are no different than any of us when it comes to financial matters. Watching your purchasing power slowly diminish is not a favorable pastime for anyone. You can bet that these countries are witnessing the uncontrollable debt that our government continues to bury itself under and are not thrilled that it takes more dollars today to purchase the same goods and services than it did just a handful of years ago.

This next chart is also very telling. It paints a humbling picture of what every individual within the United States would need to come up with in order to pay off the national debt. By the end of the fiscal year (September 30, 2005), we know that the nation's debt stood at $7.9 trillion. If we divide this amount among every man woman and child living within the United States, it requires each to pay the staggering sum of $26,750.

This dollar amount is not chump change. To make matters worse, if you had four children and thus a total family unit of six, your household would owe over $150,000.

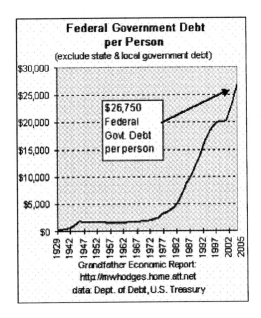

The final chart also paints a gloomy picture. It is an economic snapshot of the last forty plus years up to 2004. The steepest line represents all outstanding debt in America. This includes our government's debt, both federal and state, along with all public and private businesses and personal households. The chart shows that from 1957 to the mid-seventies that debt and our nation's income were growing at close to the same rate. However, beginning in the late seventies, the concept of living beyond our means went into overdrive. As we can see, it is not just our government that is fiscally out-of-control but also businesses, families, and individuals as a whole. This chart shows collectively how much we have spent compared to how much money we have earned. Our piece of the financial pie has now grown much larger. If we only use the figures from 2004, and I can assure you that today's total debt in America is higher than the 40.1 trillion found in 2004, our share would be $136,479 per person. Continuing our example of a six-member family, their share would be a staggering $818,874.

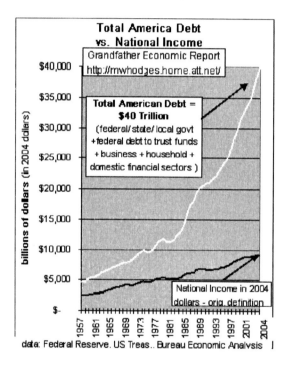

All of these graphs have shown a dramatic rise in debt, whether it be solely the federal government's or the collective debt of all Americans and businesses. The end result is the same. Our country has been inundated with bills of credit. In the introduction, reference was made to this four letter word *debt* and its partner in crime, *debt-based money*. We previously discovered how the Federal Reserve System is able to create debt-based money. The money that we borrow from banks or other lending institutions, whether it be in the form of mortgages, lines of credit, credit cards, or personal loans, is not true money. True money is gold and silver as described in our inspired Constitution. The medium of exchange lent to us by banks is nothing more than digital credits and pieces of paper, backed by debt or excess reserves.

Conversely, this debt-based money could never be brought into existence, if there were not millions of us desperately trying to borrow all that we possibly could. Borrowing money for a worthwhile cause is one thing. Borrowing to live above our means is quite another.

In the previous chapter Robert Hemphill, the credit manager of the Federal Reserve Bank in Atlanta, Georgia, gave a profound statement. He mentioned that every dollar that is currently in circulation was originally borrowed from a bank. How could anyone dispute this, knowing that we no longer use precious metals to back our nation's currency? He stated that if the banks create enough synthetic money, then collectively we will be fine, if not, we starve. This man, who knows better than most about how the game is played, solidifies the fact that today's money is nothing but debt. It is no doubt a hard concept to visualize. Even more mind numbing is the fact that if all dollars in our economy, which were originally issued as loans, were paid back, there would not be one dollar left in our economy. This is only possible because our money system is backed by debts. It goes without saying that if gold and silver were used to back all of our currency, the above fact would not be possible. This is one of the largest ramifications of dishonoring the principle of just weights and measures.

On September 30, 1941 there was a hearing held before the House Committee on Banking and Currency. The chairman of that committee was Congressman Wright Patman. He was seeking information pertaining to the Federal Reserve and the conditions that led to the Great Depression. One of those questioned was Mariner Eccles, Governor of the Federal Reserve system. He was asked how the Federal Reserve came up with $2 billion in order to purchase government bonds in 1933. Here is their brief exchange:

Eccles: We created it.
Patman: Out of what?
Eccles: Out of the right to issue credit money.
Patman: And there is nothing behind it, is there, except our government's credit?
Eccles: That is what our money system is. If there were no debts in our money system, there wouldn't be any money.[12]

This testimony is admittedly not very comforting. It brings to mind the old adage that sometimes the truth hurts. Many of the quotes in this book have been less than soothing. However, these quotes have been very informative and have helped shed light and understanding on what we must do in order to prepare ourselves from being financially conquered by others. With all of the debt that our nation holds, as individuals and collectively, the land of the free is certainly years away, if ever, from being financially free. And, as President Benson said, "Few tasks, if any, are more important for the preservation of freedom than the preservation of a sound monetary system."[13]

Artificial Sense of Prosperity

Most of us at one point or another have played the grade school game of musical chairs. Because this game is fun and easy to understand it has been a favorite among kids. While the music is playing everyone is in a great mood. They know that as long as the music continues to play there is no fear of being eliminated from the game. Once the music stops, however, it is every man for himself. If you have ever played with a group of adults you know that this simple children's game can become quite competitive as elbows fly and smaller or less nimble players are knocked out of the way by bigger and more aggressive ones.

When the dust finally settles and the chairs have been stacked and put away, congratulations are typically given to the victor and many of those who had been eliminated make boastful claims of wearing the crown next time around.

Today's economy rotates like a game of musical chairs. In that game, as long as the music continues to play, people are happy, content, and will continue joking around with each other. In life's financial game as long as we have enough money to keep cash registers continually ringing, we are content. Perpetual spending keeps the music playing, so some people feel that there is little need to worry about becoming financially *eliminated*. Ironically, nothing could be further from the truth. But where do we get the money to keep the cash registers humming? Do we extract money from our savings in order to finance our wants and needs? Could many of our needs be more correctly classified as wants? At what consistency and at what tone would the cash registers ring if we could only spend what we truly had?

Look around your neighborhood and the street you live on. Chances are, almost everything around you has been purchased with credit.

How many new cars would be in the driveway, and how many boats, motorcycles, wave runners and other toys would be in your neighbors' garages if they had to pay cash for these items? As a group, how many new pools, landscapes, additions and kitchen remodels would be installed if we could not borrow to do such? Would there be as many vacations, lavish furnishings, and speculative investments in our lives if we did not seek out, and grab a hold of easy credit? Yes, it appears as though we are living in a time of unprecedented prosperity, but at what price? Collectively, we wear big hats, but have no cattle.

On Monday, January 30, 2006, the Commerce Department reported that Americans' savings rates for the year 2005 was actually in the red. The official rate was a −0.5 percent. Martin Crutsinger of the Associated Press reported that, "Americans not only spent all of their after-tax income last year but also had to dip into previous savings or increase borrowing."

He then continues by saying that although this event is not unprecedented, it has been decades since our collective savings rate was this dismal.

> The savings rate has been negative for an entire year only twice before, in 1932 and 1933, two years when the country was struggling to cope with the Great Depression, a time of massive business failures and job layoffs.

This is a sobering statistic. How can we expect to prevail against the many financial battles we face when, as a whole, most of us did not even save a measly one percent of our incomes last year? But it gets worse. Not only did we not save, we did just the opposite.

David Rosenberg, who is employed by Merrill Lynch, stated that through refinancing their homes last year, Americans, "Produced over $700 billion in increased consumer spending."

This colossal amount of money does not even include lines of credit, personal loans, or credit cards. This is irrefutable evidence that the music is indeed near the end. When we are being robbed of our purchasing power through the scheme of inflation on top of spending beyond our means, can we really believe that cash registers will continue to ring at a supercharged hum indefinitely?

Changing of the Guard

January 31st, 2006 was the end of an infamous saga. Alan Greenspan relinquished his eighteen-year rein as the president of the Federal Reserve

System. Many years before this title was bestowed upon him, he was not afraid to say many noble and great things pertaining to gold. As a matter of fact he was a great advocate for its cause. It was Greenspan who said in 1966, "In the absence of the gold standard, there is no way to protect savings from confiscation through inflation. . . . Gold stands in the way of this insidious process."[14]

Unfortunately, at least in public, it has been many long years since he sang that tune.

Tomorrow is a new day. Tomorrow, there will be a changing of the guard. Ben Bernanke, or Helicopter Ben as he is affectionately referred to within the financial world, will become the new president of the Federal Reserve System. Regrettably, there is little chance or hope that things will be any different on his watch than they were on Greenspan's. However, there may be some small glimmer of hope while our economy is under his control. Bernanke is known for his truthfulness—but sometimes the truth can hurt. As one of the governors of the Federal Reserve in 2002, Bernanke told reporters that "The U.S. government has a technology, called a printing press, that allows it to produce as many U.S. dollars as it wishes at essentially no cost."[15]

Unlike his predecessor, Greenspan, there is no need in deciphering or reading between the lines of this quote. It is very direct and to the point. If the government needs money, there is an easy way to obtain it. It will be interesting to see if Bernanke will continue to be so open and truthful in the coming years.

Counter Attack

One of the more difficult challenges in writing a book is to decide how much information should be included in the book and what percentage will be designated to the various different topics. Public and private debt covers a vast amount of information. Nowhere has it been construed that the information concerning our topic has been exhaustively covered from top to bottom nor from every possible angle. It would require a book with three times the amount of pages to do justice to all of the world's financial facets, and even then many things would slip through the cracks. This book has merely tried to hit the important points throughout history, explaining what man has used for thousands of years as a medium of exchange, and the consequences that follow when monetary systems are deceitfully distorted. A simplistic summary could be that when men seek to obtain something for nothing by desecrating the Lord's commandment of honoring just weights and measures, one's wealth will begin to disappear by the means of confiscation through inflation.

Knowledge is power but only if we act upon it. The best and only way to fortify ourselves in this late stage of the game is to acquire gold and silver. This request may seem unnatural to many, and for good reason. Most of us have no idea where to purchase precious metals even if we wanted to. Changing life-long habits or engaging in something that we are uncomfortable with is much easier said than done. However, if inflation continues at its current pace, something will ultimately have to give. President Benson said that if it is allowed to run its full destructive course, "The country may well have to start over with a brand new currency."

There are already thousands of others who have acted upon the same knowledge that we previously discussed throughout this book. One of the more notable is the world's second richest man—Warren Buffett. Buffett is the founder of Berkshire Hathaway, a publicly traded investing company, and if you have an extra $89,000 laying around, you could purchase one share in his company. He is notorious for seeking out overlooked companies that are straightforward and valuable but can also be purchased at a discount. That is the premise of all great investors —buy low and sell high. Cutting to the chase, this Sage of Omaha as he is frequently referred to, recently acquired a large amount of silver bullion. The word bullion refers to actual metal in the form of bars or coins, not paper silver contracts or tradable silver futures. Buffett is an advocate for sound and honest currency and is a holder of both gold and silver. Interestingly, his purchase of silver alone was close to 130 million ounces in 1997. The weight of this mammoth pile of silver would be over eight million pounds. Should we be surprised that the world's second richest man has taken the necessary steps to protect himself and his family financially by eliminating some of his risk against a continually depreciating dollar?

Another well-known and savvy investor is Robert Kiyosaki. If his name does not sound familiar perhaps the title of his best selling book titled, *Rich Dad Poor Dad*, will help ring a bell. This book on investing has been on the *New York Times* number one best-selling list for five consecutive years now. Since then, he has added many more titles dealing with such topics as debt, real estate, and a handful of other financially related subjects. In the book *Rich Dad Poor Dad*, Robert describes the differences between his two dads. One dad was quite brilliant and held a

Ph.D.; this was his poor dad. The other dad, the rich one, never finished the eighth grade. However, it was this dad who taught him everything he now knows about money—how to manage it, and how to make it grow. It was this dad that wound up being one of the richest men in Hawaii. It is quite eye-opening and I highly recommend reading this book if you have not already. Kiyosaki put a large emphasis on real estate and how it can play a major role in securing financial stability. I first read this book nearly five years ago and was curious what he might think of today's extremely over-heated real estate market. I wondered if his feelings would parallel mine in believing that the housing market is on the cusp of imploding. I looked up his web page and admittedly was a bit taken back at what I read. Under the subtitle "Savers are Losers" I found his article called "All Booms Bust" in which he stated:

> I am getting rid of my U.S. dollars. As you may know, the U.S. dollar has lost nearly 40 percent of its value against other currencies in the last four years. That means if you have $10,000 in savings in the year 2000, it is worth about $6000 in purchasing power. Rather than holding cash in the bank, Kim and I have been holding our excess cash in gold and silver bars.[16]

Initially I was a bit taken aback by his statement. I half expected to hear him say that real estate investing always ran in cycles and although things were presently in a frenzy he was going to continue his real estate purchases unabated. He is obviously aware that our dollar is losing its purchasing power and went on to say that as a result of this process, gold and silver will continue to go higher.

Where can someone take their excess cash and exchange it for real money as expressed in the Constitution? Going to a bank to make this transaction has not been an option for over seventy years. Any coin shop in town will carry both gold and silver, and can usually be found in both bars and coins. If you are not sure where coin shops may be in your area just open your yellow pages and look them up under "coins." Just be sure to stay away from any "collector" coins. We are after regular gold and silver coins and bars only. If you want to collect something, start a stamp or antique collection instead. There are also many reputable coin dealers to be found through the Internet. Many have spotless reputations and have been in business for decades. I would suggest starting in your own neighborhood for your first few purchases and perhaps ordering through the mail after you become more comfortable with a purchase of this nature. In reality, this should not be looked upon as a purchase at all. We are merely exchanging bills of credit for honest money, which we have been exhorted to use by our founding fathers.

Look at the charts below and do the math with whatever savings you held in a bank over the last five years. Compare that same amount to what it would be worth today had you put it into gold or silver. Gold and silver will only continue to climb higher in terms of purchasing power in the coming years as the paper dollar continues its downward march.

The Coming Hangover

It would be next to impossible to accurately describe and answer all questions as it relates to financial history and the manipulation that is always present. If this book has done nothing but pique your curiosity, propelling you to investigate this vast subject more thoroughly, then it has accomplished its sole purpose. Three chapters into this book, a neighbor of mine caught wind that I was writing some sort of book. When I mentioned that it was about gold and the U.S. Dollar he asked, "What in the world do gold coins and dollar bills have to do with each other?" It is my hope that anyone who has read this book would feel comfortable answering my neighbor's question and any others that he may have.

We have spent a good deal of time discovering the ins and outs of inflation and the crucial roles that gold and silver have played in keeping it restrained. In our day and age it is now too late to ask, "What can we do to prevent this creature from awakening?" It awoke at the precise moment our proverbial frog fell into that eternal sleep. President Benson said, "How can we prevent this from happening? The honest answer is, we can't!"[17]

He is referring to all of the information we have previously discovered and discussed relating to gold and inflation. He sums it up quite simply by describing this phenomenon as the "Gold Problem." He continues by saying:

> Like the drunkard at the end of a weekend spree, there is no way in the world to avoid the inevitable "morning after." We have been feeling the exhilarating effects of inflation and have become numbed to the gradual dissipation of our gold reserves. In our economic stupor, when we manage to think ahead about the coming hangover, we have merely taken another swig from the bottle to reinforce the artificial sensation of prosperity. But each new drink at the cup of inflation, and each new drain on the gold supply of our body strength does not prevent the dreaded hangover, it merely postpones it a little longer and will make it that much worse when it finally comes.[18]

In his opinion, there is nothing that we can do to keep this from happening. This is a logical assumption considering that this process has been ongoing for decades. This being the case, he then asks us what we should do. And here is his answer: "We should get a hold of ourselves, come to our senses, stop adding to our intoxication and face the music!"[19]

President Benson went on to say that, unfortunately, there are no happy solutions to our financial problems. He threw in a disclaimer that if we the people used our initiative and drive, we might get through the trying readjustment period that lies ahead. If we can successfully adjust to these financial problems, he states that we could then go on "to higher levels of real prosperity and security than we have ever known."[20]

No church leader past or present has ever pounded the table with more firmness or frequency in support of an honest monetary system than President Benson. I will quote him one last time as he sums up his beliefs:

> I believe in honest money, the gold and silver coinage of the Constitution, and a circulating medium convertible into such money without loss. I regard it as a flagrant violation of the explicit provisions of the Constitution for the federal government to make it a criminal offense to use gold or silver as legal tender or to issue a irredeemable paper money.[21]

There is a day coming in the not so distant future when the music will finally stop. The question that gets very little attention today and seldom ever a response is who will get a chair and who will be left standing?

Satan is the master of deceit. He knows no shame and will stop at nothing to enslave all of us for eternity. He is a master storyteller, and notorious for spouting half-truths. He would gladly lead us to believe that indeed this is a "land choice above all others" if it ensured that many of us, after comfortably believing such, would let down our guard. Those that would casually lower their guard because of this premise would not feel it prudent to prepare for the impending financial battles. Those that were not prepared would one day stand an excellent chance of being wiped out financially as history has undoubtedly proven throughout the years. Devastation and misery for all mankind are the ultimate objectives that Satan set out to accomplish thousands of years ago. A distorted monetary system is without doubt one of the most successful weapons he can employ. It places all mankind not only into financial bondage but also psychological and emotional bondage.

The Lord, knowing all of this in advance, gave us our own weapon in which we might thwart Satan's ploy. Did he tell us that he thought it best to acquire and use precious metals as the perfect medium of exchange? No. He did, however, promise us that if we were to honor him and keep the commandments we would "prosper in the land." And what was this commandment that if kept would disrupt Satan's plan for our financial misery? It was a very simple one and completely effective if adhered to. The Lord exhorted us to use a monetary system that was fair and honest to all participants and mandated that a system of just weights and measures be used—anything less would be an abomination to the Lord. There is no question whatsoever that today's monetary system is neither fair nor honest and that our weights and measures have become terribly askew.

With few exceptions man has chosen to ignore this eternal truth in hopes of acquiring something for nothing. Sometime in the future these men of power and influence will receive "something" else and it will cost them "nothing." It will be their chance to stand in front of the Lord. They will desperately and pathetically try to explain to him why they initiated those practices that were completely contrary to his commandments. By then they will undoubtedly recognize, albeit too late, that they were pawns in Satan's plan to flood the earth with financial misery.

As a nation we mustn't think that we can collectively escape the impending economic crisis simply by ignoring the clues or by not openly discussing them. One should not let ignorance cloud their judgment by claiming that financial preparedness and talk of a falling dollar is nothing but doom and gloom. The facts have been presented without speculation. It should now be obvious to all that our founding fathers, who we agreed were led by the hand of the Lord, insisted that certain truthful principles be found within our Constitution. We have regrettably seen how kingdoms, governments, and elite groups of powerful men throughout history have mocked the principle of just weights and measures. However, the Lord will not be mocked indefinitely. Whether it be in two years or twenty, a day of financial reckoning will undoubtedly come. When that day arrives, will you have the peace of mind that comes from knowing your lamp is full, or will you be left in the dark, frantically scurrying about in search of oil?

NOTES

1. Gordon B. Hinckley, quoted by Lyle and Tracy Shamo, *Debt-Free on Any Income*, (Salt Lake City: Deseret Book, 2004) 17.

2. Spencer W. Kimball, "The False Gods We Worship," *Ensign*, June 1976, 4.

3. Heber J. Grant, quoted by Lyle and Tracy Shamo, *Debt-Free on Any Income*, (Salt Lake City: Deseret Book, 2004) 59.

4. Ezra Taft Benson, "The Dangerous Threat of Increasing Indebtedness," *The Instructor*, May 1962, 159, 162.

5. Ibid.

6. Ezra Taft Benson, *An Enemy Hath Done This* (Salt Lake City: Bookcraft, 1992), 14.

7. Ibid., 217.

8. Ibid., 210.

9. Gordan B. Hinckley, "To the Boys and to the Men," *Ensign*, October 1998.

10. Allan Sloan, *Newsweek*, "No Money? No Problem!" September 26, 2005

11. Ibid.

12. G. Edward Griffin, *The Creature from Jekyll Island: A Second Look at the Federal Reserve* (Westlake Village, CA: American Media, 1998), 188.

13. Benson, *An Enemy Hath Done This*, 211.

14. Alan Greenspan, "Gold and Economic Freedom," in *Capitalism: The Unknown Ideal*, ed. Ayn Rand (New York: Signet Books, 1967), 101.

15. Ben Bernanke, quoted in *Demise of the Dollar* by Addison Wiggin, 82.

16. Robert Kiyosaki, "All Booms Bust," Online, *Rich Dad,* available from http://www.richdad.com/pages/article_dollar_crisis.asp.

17. Benson, *An Enemy Hath Done This*, 218.

18. Ibid.

19. Ibid.

20. Ibid.

21. Ibid., 145.